A SHAGGY YAK STORY

A SHAGGY YAK STORY

by

PETER SOMERVILLE-LARGE

SINCLAIR-STEVENSON

First published in Great Britain by
Sinclair-Stevenson Limited
7/8 Kendrick Mews
London SW7 3HG, England

British Library Cataloguing in Publication Data

A CIP catalogue record for this book is available from the British Library.

ISBN: 1-85619-038-2

Photoset by Rowland Phototypesetting Limited
Bury St Edmunds, Suffolk
Printed and bound in Great Britain by
Clays Ltd, St Ives plc

In memory of H. Rahman Qul

1913–1990

'The mountains wear the soft bloom of a grape
The river glitters in a mist of rain,
The passes that we crossed are blocked with snow:
When shall I ever come this way again?'

from 'Autumn in the Hindu Kush'
by John Bowen

CONTENTS

PART ONE

PART TWO

PART THREE

PART
ONE

1

Nineteen Eighty-Two

Hⁱɢʜ summer in Hunza. The scent of pot hanging over the little group of foreigners.

'Have you had your stools examined?' the hollow-faced American with the red bandana asked a deadly-pale girl who had arrived that afternoon. 'Those apricots they offer you are lethal. Dynamite.' He spat out the word. 'Do what I say and keep off the fruit, even if they tell you it will make you live to a hundred.'

No one would eat the special omelette prepared by the Chitrali who owned the new Palace Hotel. It lay in a swamp of congealed ghee.

'There is something wrong with their eggs,' said a German with a blond brutal haircut. 'I have noticed so many sickly hens pecking in filth. Who is to say what enters their oviducts?'

At a far table on which a bottle of Vichy water stood like a flag, Frenchmen and Frenchwomen were tucking in like savages to a huge dish of croissants which had come out of a tin.

It was the year of the French. None of them seemed to get sick. They were everywhere. A French team was climbing in the majestic Concordia mountains, another had arrived on foot from Chitral, a lepidopterist had discovered a rare butterfly below the lonely Shandur Pass for the glory of France.

After stools, the second most popular subject of conversation was travel and the cheapest places to go. That year, 1982, Zanskar and Leh were in fashion, so were the Johnson route around Annapurna, the hippie trail around Sri Lanka which had not yet turned nasty and, of course, Goa.

'What about Kulu?'

'No bloody good. No bloody good at all.'

'I stayed with a hill tribe,' volunteered the German. 'Very cheap.'

The American with the terrible sunburn listened attentively.

'What do you mean, cheap? They take you in for nothing?'

'Why not?'

The talk returned to disease. 'Remember Harold, the Australian with the tattoos? Poor guy died of cholera down near Trivandrum.'

'The goddam insects will kill you in their own time.'

The majority had lost their traveller's cheques and money. The stories they told were hair-raising.

'My hotel door was locked, but they tore it off.'

'This guy took out his knife.'

An Englishman recalled how he had been drugged on the Delhi–Amritsar train and lost everything. The American girl who crouched at the end of the room began crying once again. 'Oh God, why has it happened to me? What am I to do?' Another American sat up in his sleeping bag reading aloud: 'Baltistan is rich in markhors, ibexes, snow leopards, chakors, ram chakors, partridges and duck.'

'Shit man . . . you can't be serious!'

'That's what it says.'

'Who do they think they are kidding?' This from the tall youth with acne so severe it was positively floral. He had spent the last two days curled up on the floor clutching his belly.

'Kailash women will allow you to take their photograph if you pay them something.'

'They shit in your mouth.'

'That's what the tourist blurb says.'

The French had not stopped eating, and the manager left them to coax pâté and foie gras out of tins while he retired to his small dark annexe where he could smoke his own supply of hash. I looked outside and saw a dozen dark figures squatting in a deep ravine under a grove of apricot trees. I was sick of hearing how Hunzacuts lived for ever on apricots and mulberries and Hunza water.

Hunza was situated at eight thousand feet above sea level, and the visitor might have expected a temperate climate to nurture all the apples, apricots, plums, cherries, peaches and grapes. Today the sun was as hot as fire; it was like sitting on the burning embers of a log, while all the time the snow was in sight. The great glaciers hanging around our heads were radiating heat. Like ovens the breathless valleys shut it in.

The five-hundred-mile-long all-weather Karakoram Highway, KH for short, ran through bare rocks and glittering shards connecting Pakistan and China. The Chinese completed it in ten years, in 1978; making it involved heroic labour, and for once, the word 'heroic', so frequently debased by patriotic propaganda, had full meaning. Just beyond Baltit on the road to China was a small obelisk 'erected to the memory of those martyrs of the Frontier Works Organization who laid down their lives constructing this highway through the mighty Karakorams'. There was a long list of dead Chinese, whose sacrifice was partly to encourage tourism. Others were still digging away, completing other stretches of road. I watched groups of soldiers slaving with pickaxes and shovels on a narrow track above the river where the heat and dust were terrible. High above the airless gorge birds of prey crossing and recrossing the deep blue sky induced vertigo.

A notice greeted the traveller. 'Welcome to Hunza. Hunza music and local dances arranged on request. Tent accommodation with modern toilet facilities.' Every tourist was obsessed by toilet facilities. Groups of middle-class Punjabis in cars and jeeps whose transistors were turned full on bounced to wailing music up and down the stretch of KH between Hunza and Gilgit.

I sought out Sheba, reputed to be the oldest man in Hunza. He had seen Mirs come and go, had feuded with countless Nagars and claimed to remember the siege of Nilt in 1876 when red-coated soldiers stormed the fort and Manners-Smith won his VC. Sheba, everyone said, was at least a hundred and thirty years old. I found him holding court with other village elders under yet another grove of apricot trees. His face was like a wrinkled apricot, and he sat up very straight watching the hippies.

'We don't like foreigners with long hair.'

He looked about my age. Not so long ago he had married again. I told him that a few years before I had met a man at the Chelsea Royal Hospital who had sounded the bugle for the Malakand Field Force. He had been a lot younger, only ninety-five or so. That made Sheba laugh, and he laughed again when I told him that in Europe his name was associated with Solomon's queen. He took off his woollen cap and showed me his hair which was dyed a brilliant red. With his light complexion he could have been taken for an Irishman. He was growing sleepy, and he nodded off, looking like a crocodile when his eyes were closed. Around him the other elders went to sleep.

While they were dozing, the young Mir was sitting in his office in his concrete palace. Built in the nineteen-fifties, it had long cool rooms and many superb views of Rakaposhi. I walked through the gateway past a pair of grinning stone leopards and an engraved sign saying 'WELCOME'. There was little fuss or protocol. I was shown into the Mir's private study crammed with old photographs and polo trophies. One photograph showed the boys of Gordon College which the Mir had attended; underneath in capitals were the words 'LEST WE FORGET'. In another rows of boys stood to attention at the Tyndale Briscoe Public School in Srinagar where the Mir's father had been educated. This was the famous establishment where manliness had been encouraged, boys were thrown into the river in order to learn to swim, and sodomites, after chastisement, were forced to walk hundreds of miles to Gilgit to expunge their sins.

The Mir was a small man with sharp green eyes who spoke six languages, including his own native dialect of Burshisky. His father, Mr Jamal Khan, after leaving Tyndale Briscoe, had become an old-fashioned feudal ruler; there had been no police in Hunza and no crime apart from the odd blood feud. The Mir had been the dispenser of all justice. In general the system worked well and the six thousand people in Hunza's mountains and valleys lived long and were quite satisfied with their lot. In 1974 Hunza, together with neighbouring principalities, was taken over by Pakistan, and the present Mir no longer had a say in running the state.

I had to wait to talk to him because he was speaking on the telephone in a mixture of Urdu and English.

'Put a lot of pressure on that bastard. Don't let him get away with it.'

The phone snapped down and the sun came out. Outside the window beyond the green lawn and the roses in bloom was a display of vast mountains where the snow twinkled like glass. The Mir lit up a cigarette and we talked. When the little kingdom was run on paternalistic lines there had been no shortages of food, and little or no poverty. Travelling by horseback to the outside world had taken many days, three days to Gilgit, about thirteen to the distant oasis of Kashgar in Chinese Turkestan.

I asked him about the effects of tourism, which had become more important than farming in Hunza's economy.

His face flinched. 'We have always regarded ourselves as a hospitable people.' He would say no more on the subject.

Later I was given a business card by one of the new breed of guides. 'D. A. Shah, BA. Punjab Guide to Travellers, Tour Operator, Organizer, Interpreter to Writers, Researchers, Climbers, Swimmers, expert Traveller in Chitral, Ghizer, Hunza and China.' On his advice I visited the ancient palace of the Mirs standing above Altit which had been turned into a tourist attraction, just like a stately home in England. An old man sold entrance tickets for five rupees and unlocked the creaking door. A cold wind from the Ulthoro glacier blew into the small dark rooms full of ghosts and a few dusty relics of past times. Here was a cupboard full of sodawater syphons and some old drums. I blundered among rusty swords, a Victorian cane chair which the rats had gnawed, and pieces of rusty chain armour. Holding up a wooden board I read 'Bayliss and Jones, London 1889' on an attached metal plate. The dusty walls were hung with photographs of worthies, the young Francis Younghusband, one of the first Englishmen to explore the Pamirs, Field-Marshal Lord Roberts, VC, the young Nathaniel Curzon, soon to be Viceroy, King George V, King George VI, Reza Shah and a good many Thums, Mirs, Walis and Rajas whose internecine feuds had kept the Empire busy.

The wind blew down the narrow valley from the glaciers tossing the flowers and brushing the little fields and terraces of barley. At this time of year the Hunzacut men decorated their flat woollen hats with bunches of wild flowers sticking out from behind their ears.

Outside the ramshackle little palace there was nothing above me but snow and rocks; it seemed that at any moment the old mud walls of the fort might topple from their crag and disintegrate in a pile of broken rubble. Soft grey powdery shadows were creeping up the mountain as I made my way down. The fading sun made each snowpeak shine like a star.

At the hotel the foreigners gathered again, sitting around in silent groups. Once again there was no food to be had. A servant, sent out to look for chickens, returned, eloquently shrugging his shoulders. They had run out of tea, Pepsi and Seven-Up. Once again the discussion centred on diarrhoea – mechanical diarrhoea, intestinal, amoebic dysentery, bacillary dysentery, mystery diarrhoea. . . .

Not every guest was a hippy. I talked to a Hunzacut lady who had left eighteen years before to go and live in England. When she was last here the Mir ruled properly and Hunza had been cut off from the rest of the world. She thought there was more freedom now. She was small and dumpy and wore the traditional Hunza knee-length shawl and baggy trousers whether she was in Hunza or Birmingham. Her children wore Western clothes and whined for television and chip shops. They far preferred a skyline of television antennae to these shining white mountains.

'I am a Hunzacut, not a Pakistani,' the manager was grumbling. 'Why do these people come here?' The last guest had written in the hotel register, under the heading of Nationality, 'Human Being', and under Occupation: 'Human Stud'.

The manager was looking at me intently. 'Do you wish anything more?' A large bloodshot eye closed in a wink. 'We can supply Hunza water . . . nice and fresh.'

'Hunza water?'

'Many foreigners find it good for all illnesses.' Another wink.

'Oh, all right.'

'One or two bottles, sahib?'

'One should be plenty.'

Hunza water was some sort of fermented millet which tasted like dubious poteen and was certainly not worth running the risk of forty lashes or whatever General Zia decreed. Sipping it and chewing apricots, I sat on the topmost of a curving set of terraces that fell with infinite grace towards the valley floor. Across the way were great mountains, among them, rising out of wisps of bronze cloud, the white spoke of Rakaposhi. The view was overwhelming. I watched the peaks like sharks' teeth vanish into darkness and thought of Hunza's cruel history, largely a story of feuding with neighbouring Nagar. In their hatred people would hurl carcasses of cats across the deep ravine that divided the principalities; at other times they killed each other for sport.

Next day I travelled with other tourists to Nagar where a number of brawny Frenchmen (bringing their own supplies as usual) had taken over the only accommodation near the Hopar glacier. More tourists flooded the little garden surrounding the Mir's pavilion, which was furnished with an English gun whose barrel was engraved with 'Honi soit qui mal y pense'. A party of Germans with hands stained blood-red from eating mulberries was quarrelling with a local man about prices. A Japanese was photographing some picturesque women wrapped in bright shawls, and across the ravine where the dead cats had flown I could hear the sound of blasting for the new Hispar road.

Back to Hunza and another night with the hippies. Once this small pasteboard state with its unrivalled opportunities for polo and shooting animals and birds had attracted European travellers and Empire builders in droves. I read an account of how young Lieutenant Etherton of the 39th Garwal Rifles visited Hunza on his way to Siberia. After inspecting the Mir's bodyguard at Baltit, 'a score of strapping cheery ruffians dressed in dark uniforms with red fezzes', which he photographed with the Mir and his young son, he was taken to the old palace for tea. The old ramshackle eyrie with its open court on top framing the same stupendous view was manifestly the same place that was now the highlight of Hunza tourism. Etherton described how rugs and carpets were spread on mud floors, and how many of the photographs were upside down, 'which did not seem to worry the Mir in the least'. In those days they included Edward VII, an old Aga Khan and the Russian generals Kurapakia and Limevitch. The young English officer sat on the terrace quaffing cups of tea and discussed with the Mir the new obsession for flying. 'When I informed him that flying was to become an established fact and that ships were now made to sail in the air, he was very keen on having one to explore the skies.'

Again I watched the sun's glorious descent behind Rakaposhi, and then in the darkness there was a celebration of the Silver Jubilee of the current Aga Khan. The majority of people round here belonged to the Ismaeli sect of Islam, and were in general more affluent and better educated than their neighbours. The Jubilee was marked with the opening of a new school and hospital and bonfires on the mountains. Teams of climbers ascended hilltops and crossed jagged ravines to light up; the more daring youths climbed peaks that seemed inaccessible and carried up rubber tyres which they lit and threw so that they rolled down the mountain in hoops of fire. Other bonfires shone on white peaks in darkness, candles on a great birthday cake.

This was a traditional method of celebration. In 1936 Peter Fleming saw similar bonfires at the end of his epic journey from China, when the hills were lit up for the Resident's visit. 'The flames twinkled tinnily thousands of feet up in the darkening sky, fitly enhancing the savage beauty of the scene. The display was perhaps not great pyrotechnics, but it represented formidable feats of mountaineering.'

In those days Hunza was a distant mysterious place, a remote outpost of the British Empire.

More apricots. There are at least fifty varieties, and every now and then, like a duck's egg, one will turn up that will poison you. I was sitting in the garden of the Deputy Commissioner in Gilgit toying with delicious food carried by barefoot servants across the lawn. The DC, an intelligent young man in charge of the mountain area bordering Chitral and Afghanistan, had inherited his post under the system devised by the old Indian Civil Service. His duties had not changed much, and the cases he dealt with seemed to echo past Imperial problems. Recently a woman was kidnapped by a soldier from Altit. A local cable station had been burnt down and scores of people were locked up.

In the library his predecessors and other colonial worthies were preserved in sepia. All over north-east Pakistan the old photographs stayed. Was it admiration, respect or nostalgia that kept this particular gallery in its place, Lieutenant-Colonel Biddulph, the first resident of Gilgit, beside Durand, Bruce, Robertson, Manners-Smith, the hero of Nilt, Lieutenant-Colonel Bacon, the last Resident, who departed in July 1947?

How they had all enjoyed themselves! They combined ruling a wild frontier with polo, hunting and even tennis. There were so many things to kill. 'In the nullahs around Bunji and Gilgit is found the fine goat, the markhor, whilst the ibex, urial and bear flourish in goodly numbers.'

There were other factors, hard to define by plain men, that induced satisfaction. In his old age Sir George Robertson wrote wistfully of the advantages of being posted to this region. 'The

Gilgit district has a strange and enduring charm, and the desire to return is almost inevitable.' One of the reasons was isolation which 'leads to enduring friendships and generous sympathies; plain food, if not particularly associated with high thinking, certainly induces simplicity of thought and clearness of mind.'

In the early nineteen-fifties I had briefly experienced Gilgit's isolation. Now the polo ground, the graveyard and the old straggling bazaar had been exchanged for concrete and dust, a new airport and all the new hotels.

It was pleasant that Biddulph's 'Agency House' survived as the old agents would have remembered it, 'a gabled house, snugly nestled among fruit trees and willows'. I sat with the DC in the English garden, drinking mint tea, once again indulging in the Himalayan pastime of watching the sun go down. The lower hills were rust-coloured with patches of speckled green, and here too Rakaposhi blotted out much of the sky. As it grew dark, yellow jabs of flame flickered high over our heads where they were still celebrating the Aga Khan.

In spite of the heatwave, in the PTCD Government Hotel, they served tomato soup and chips at dinner; halfway the lights went out, the fans stopped moving, and it became hotter still. I tried to sleep out on the lawn. From the direction of the river came the sound of bagpipes, as the police band, assembled in a small concrete arcade, entertained a group of visiting dignitaries who may have assumed that a visit to the land of snow would be a cool experience. The players were ex-members of the Gilgit Scouts and wore highland dress and feathered bonnets. They piped in the darkness, the sound competing with the roar of the river. Someone turned on car headlights and I glimpsed a garden of sorts, a man urinating against a wall and a line of goats.

In the daytime the heat continued to be cruel. Distant snow blocked the head of the valley on which the sun threw down burning light with a concentration of an inclined magnifying glass. People reeled with the effort of walking. In the windless feverish incandescent swelter, children cooled themselves in filthy irrigation canals, old men dozed in the shuttered bazaar, while the hippies picked their way through dust and dung to the Post Office to sift through the uncollected mail cascading out of lines of wooden boxes.

I sought refuge in the Prince's Cafe, Mohammed Beg's book-shop and the Public Library.

'I have visited the Gilgit Library and am filled with admiration for what the Librarian, Mr Ashrif Ali, has achieved. Nigel Nicolson.'

I concurred. Nicolson's visit was in January 1974, a better chosen season of the year. In July it was hot in sun and in shade. The fire breath, the dark spikes of hot air, penetrated secret places like the shadowed librarian's garden where there was a gurgling stream and yet another apricot tree.

The sun blazed on the small cemetery beside the polo grounds where a pair of skinny cows grazed among dusty broken tomb-stones, scattered pieces of paper and the remains of a charpois. Here amidst the bazaar dross were imperial graves.

'In very loving memory of our son Harold S. Eldred, Captain, Sikh Pioneers.' 'Henry Gordon Bell, July 1912. Aged 27.' 'Remember Ian and Mary Galbraith, 1939.' I found the resting place of the five members of the ill-fated Batura Muztagh Mountain expedition of 1959, and the imposing stone rising out of piles of garbage over poor Hayward's final resting-place:

'Gold medallist of the Royal Geographic Society who was cruelly murdered at Darkot . . . 1870 . . . a gallant officer and accomplished traveller.'

Clifton Old Boy, dour evangelist and servant of Empire, he died alone in the high Pamirs, having fallen among thieves. He looked for trouble; in an early photograph he is disguised as a Pathan mercenary with spear, shield and daggers tucked into his waist.

His death occurred in the mountains near Yasin among the boulders of the Darkot Pass on the borders of Chitral, closing off a bright green valley of orchards and fields where women in long, coloured dresses winnow piles of golden grain. Instead the pass is a horrible place of boulders.

> And now it was dawn. He rose strong on his feet
> And strode to his ruin'd camp below the wood;
> He drank the breath of the morning cool and sweet:
> His murderers round him stood.

Months later his body was found sticking out of the rocks, mummified in the dry air. He shared with Livingstone a demonstration of the love of faithful servants and companions. His body was hauled through the mountains down to Gilgit to be buried here, his grave the nucleus of the little foreign cemetery where the river running by roars its lament.

In the afternoon there was a stir of activity when a group of nomads with high-checked Mongol features wearing leather boots and hard round hats shining with embroidery strode through the bazaar selling jewellery and pieces of saddlery. Near Mr Beg's bookshop I noticed an old man with a look of Genghiz Khan taking a piece of cracked glass out of his pocket and facing the derision of a stall-keeper.

In the bookshop I talked to Mr Beg, who sat in the back of his shop surrounded by books, tribal rugs and antiquities he had collected over the years. He was small and rotund, wearing a smart white linen suit and karakul hat, and his kindness was well known. I asked him about the picturesque nomads.

'They are Afghan refugees. They are Kirghiz from the Wakhan.'

'Where do they live now?'

'Their camp is downriver. These poor people have escaped the war.' I had not known there was a refugee camp here in Gilgit, far removed from the pulsating refugee masses of Pathans at Peshawar. The people who had fled here were of Tajik stock, nomadic shepherds who, as far as one could tell, were unconnected with the sound and fury of Mujaheddin activities.

'You wish to meet them?' Mr Beg asked. 'You go to my friend the SP and he will give you a chit.'

The office of the Superintendent of Police was across the river. Mr Akbar Shah was a member of a family that included the former rulers of Hunza and Nagar, and like so many of the ruling stock which had originated in Persia had a fair, almost European complexion. His father had been the last subahdar-major of the Gilgit Scouts, and after the British pulled out, was instrumental in keeping Gilgit part of the new Pakistan state. During the short-lived Dogra regime Indian Kashmir had tried to claim the little kingdom. But on 1 November 1947 the Gilgit Agency became part of Pakistan, largely through Mr Akbar Shah's father, who was known, like Daniel O'Connell, as 'The Liberator'.

As a boy Mr Akbar Shah was given a Webley and Scott pistol by his father and told to flee with his family from invading Kashmiri troops. If they caught up, he was to shoot his mother and sister first. But things turned out all right.

He gave me a document and directed me to the Kirghiz refugee camp downriver, in fact in the river. The army tents were pitched on stones. Here the Kirghiz had lived and died for three years. Conditions in those khaki tents far away from the high plains and the snow of the Wakhan had killed many of them.

'I do not blame Pakistan, but the heat,' said their leader, Rahman Qul, an old man who had the reputation of being a bandit. The interpreter was competent and I learned about his tribe, which had once enjoyed one of the world's last truly nomadic lifestyles, herding sheep, Bactrian camels and yak.

These Kirghiz had wandered among the Pamirs in the panhandle of the Wakhan that divides Russia, China and Pakistan. This is an area of the world that in spite of ancient interfering politics remains remote; it retains much of the mystery suggested in Sir Thomas Holdich's description of ninety years ago. 'Amid the voiceless waste of a vast white wilderness twenty thousand feet above the sea, absolutely inaccessible to man, and within the ken of no living creature but the Pamir eagle . . . there the three great Empires meet. It is a fitting trijunction. No God of Hindu mythology ever occupied a more stupendous throne.' Beneath the great mountains among the snow plains at around fourteen thousand feet the Kirghiz had herded their animals until politics intervened.

Over the years the Russians had harassed them, restricted their wanderings, and cut off the old places with guards and wire. Frontiers which had been vague concepts became realities. Then came the Soviet-backed coup in Kabul in 1979.

Pressures on the tribe, including a conviction that as Moslems they would suffer from religious intolerance, persuaded them to leave the Pamirs well before the Soviet invasion. The exact circumstances that triggered their departure were difficult to ascertain.

'He says that as Moslems and opponents of the regime they would not have lived long when the Russians came.'

The tribe, consisting of around twelve hundred men, women and children, undertook an epic winter journey through the snow together with their animals – ten thousand sheep and two hundred yak - struggling through mountains and snow-blocked valleys down to Gilgit.

'He says that only the dogs refused to leave.'

They had lived in and around this river bed for three years, and unused to climate and altitude, they began to die. More than a hundred died during their first year here. Their flocks were sold and they had sat idly in tents provided by charity. But now things were changed.

'The Turks help them.'

'The Turks?'

'These people are all Turks. So they go to Turkey.'

For three years, as they confronted their status as refugees, the presence of the Kirghiz was noted by the international community. There was even a suggestion that the tribe as a whole might be transplanted to Alaska where it was nice and cold in a way that they were used to. But someone concluded that its unique culture would be destroyed by contact with the West.

Then the Turkish government intervened in a gesture that could be considered quixotic, considering Turkey's own vast refugee problems. The Turks recognised the Kirghiz, who spoke a language that is understood in Turkey, as brothers. They agreed to accept as Turkish citizens five thousand Afghans of Turkic stock, including Rahman Qul's people. In a month they would fly to Istanbul.

Rahman Qul was still strong enough to lead his people to a new life.

'We go to the mountains. Back to the mountains.'

'Where?'

'To Mount Ararat.'

I spent some hours wandering around the camp. The solemn children who shook hands with us looked sick and weak. I remembered the high pastures of Badakshan near the Wakhan where I had travelled thirty years before.

I sat down on a rock and the old chief-in-exile waved his hand for one of his sons to bring out glasses of tea. I learned how before their departure they were selling as many of their remaining possessions as they could. They would not return. Fortunate among the refugees of the world, they would be plucked out of the stale misery of life in tents and planted on a Turkish hillside. They would be citizens of Turkey; the language they spoke would be understood. But they would be very far from the High Pamirs.

The Kirghiz grouped around me prompted memories of the time so many years ago when I had spent a large part of my youth trying to reach their homeland. I stared at their round Mongol faces gathered in the dried-up river bed, at the khaki tents, and the clouds of tormenting flies. I remembered the time when I had set out to conquer the roof of the world.

2

NINETEEN FIFTY-THREE

'NEVER trust a Pathan,' the Colonel warned. We were standing in the shooting gallery below a well-known Dublin sports outfitters where I had just acquired a .303 rifle. Although I had fired numerous times and only grazed the outside perimeter of the bullseye, the Colonel continued to be optimistic about my marksmanship. He was a small sporty man, tweedy, red-faced and generally good-natured – but then I was a client. He was a sort that used to be common throughout Ireland and has now become extinct. 'Ireland was a land of Colonels as Hungary was a land of Counts,' my friend Arland Ussher wrote. This one had spent many years on the north-west frontier, and my family had insisted that he should instruct me in self-defence in case I came across a wily and hostile tribesman. After many more sessions in the little shooting gallery during which the .303 gradually got nearer to the target, he seemed reasonably happy that I could look after myself.

'I would be right beside you if I was only twenty years younger. Always carry a loaded revolver with you. The Pathans are good fighters and wonderful friends, if you don't get on the wrong side of them. Remember: what they really admire is old-fashioned British pluck.' In those days colonels not only still talked like that, but tended to think themselves British however long they had lived in Ireland. The year was 1953 and I was taking up a job in Kabul. If one wished to go to far-flung places, Irish was a useful nationality to be. Ireland was neutral and de Valera – never a favourite of the colonels – was a good name to bandy about. The Afghan government was looking for English speakers who were not British or American.

'I am happy to recommend Mr Peter Somerville-Large BA for one of the posts as lecturer in English in the Military Cadet College in Kabul. He had been a gifted student of English Literature for some years. He is presenting himself for the degree of BA with honours in Modern Literature this autumn, and will, I expect, do very well.' This was a kindly wish. 'He has for years been deeply interested in Central Asia and desirous of travelling there. This interest makes the post in Kabul particularly attractive to him.'

I still have the crumpled chit written on my behalf by H. O. White, my English professor in Trinity College, Dublin. Perhaps it enabled me to get the job. I took it along to the Royal Afghan Embassy in Prince's Gate, which stands opposite Hyde Park alongside the offices of the Royal Geographical Society. The tall decaying building was painted a dirty camouflage grey. (Forty years later it looked exactly the same, except the wording on the brass plate was 'Embassy of the Socialist Republic of Afghanistan'.)

The shutters of all the windows were closed, giving the place an air of mystery. No one answered the bell as I stood in the rain on an overcast October afternoon. I was about to turn away when a head peered out from a smaller building a few doors down. The swarthy face looking suspiciously in my direction was topped by a jaunty gold karakul sheepskin cap.

'Yes please?'

'Is this the Afghan Embassy?'

'Yes please. No entry.'

The head ducked back and was about to disappear, but by sprinting down the intervening pavement I managed to reach the door before it closed in front of me. The head surrendered and introduced itself as Mohammed Zafif, a Junior Counsellor. I followed the gold karakul to the Chancery where there was a spark of life – the rest of the Embassy seemed to consist of a series of disused ballrooms.

Mr Zafif went to the back of a large empty desk and sat beneath a coloured photograph of a white bearded warrior in a gaudy uniform, one hand delicately placed on a very large sword. The fact that the warrior wore spectacles did not detract from his fierceness. Later I would see this icon in every chaikhana in Kabul, a portrait of a dead man. King Mohammed Nadir Shah had come to power in 1929, a turbulent time. King Amanullah had been exiled, and his successor, the bandit leader, Bacha Saqqao, had been overthrown and publicly executed by firing squad, together with seventeen of his followers. There was a power vacuum in the country; Nadir Shah swept into Kabul, and like a reluctant Roman Emperor assumed kingship after a jirgah of his tribal army clamoured for him to be made monarch. (The same army looted government buildings and houses of the wealthy; during my stay in Kabul stolen items still turned up from time to time in the bazaar.)

Nadir Shah overturned his predecessors, made women return to wearing the chadri, reintroduced purdah and built a college for military cadets on the ruins of the Bala Hissar. This was where I was seeking employment. His death was violent, like his accession. On 8 November 1933 he was assassinated by a supporter, perhaps a son, of an executed rival, Gulam Nabi Charki. His sixteen-year-old son, educated in French lycées, succeeded him, a colourless monarch dominated by his tough paternal uncles. King Mohammed Zahir Shah reigned, but did not rule, for twenty years. His portrait did not appear very often in chaikhanas.

These facts I would learn later. Today in the chancery I was having my first experience of over-polite Afghan evasions. Sitting in a large leather armchair, I took out my letter of appointment and began to question the Counsellor closely about means of travel, accommodation, duties and so on. Mr Zafif listened politely without answering. He interrupted me to clap his hands, causing a windswept man in a grey suit that was too large for him to enter the vast room and stand silently by the desk. The Counsellor appeared to be giving him a piece of his mind in Farsi, but it turned out that he was only ordering tea.

The tray came loaded with two porcelain cups, two little decorated pots, and the first of a hundred thousand nuts, sugared like Afghan courtesies, that I would be eating over the next two years.

'Please take.'

Once again I tried to tell Mr Zafif my plans and obtain some information. When he yielded to pressure, it was only to say, 'Excuse me, I speak little English.' I asked him about visas. 'It is no problem.' But he was not forthcoming.

The tea boy came in again and stood watching me until I realised it was time to leave. I had got no nearer to obtaining my visa. The hour in the cold room, the fruitless discussion tempered by tea and nuts, was an introduction into the languors of Afghan life. Mr Zafif shook hands very warmly as I got up to depart. 'Do you know any pretty girls?' he said.

I refused to be discouraged. I saw my appointment in Afghanistan as an opportunity for exploration, and Kabul as a base for travel to unknown places in central Asia – Kashgar, perhaps, the Wakhan, the Pamirs, the Turkoman desert, perhaps even behind the ice curtain of Tibet (although the Chinese were already there).

It is impossible to recreate today the magic and promise of travel before communication destroyed it. In the nineteen-fifties the Oxus was still far distant, the Karakoram Highway was not yet a monstrous plan for opening up central Asia, and the jet plane had not conquered the world. Frontiers were closing, but it seemed possible to be an intrepid European explorer like Sven Hedin staggering across the Turfan Depression.

I read travel books: 'The Afghan character is a strange mixture of contradictory qualities in which courage blends with stealth, the basest treachery with the most touching fidelity, intense religious fanaticism with an avarice which will induce him to play false to his faith, and a lavish hospitality with an irresistible propensity for thieving.'

I read about the Great Game. I read Major Cumberland's *Sport in the Pamirs*, in which, between shooting *ovis poli*, he met Colonel Pietrow with his twenty-five Cossacks. Then he met another bearded explorer, Colonel Gromchefye, striding over the snow in fur hunting coat and giant fur mittens.

'I spoke French, but understood German a little . . . Gromchefye talked German but understood a little French.' On rival mountain-tops the decencies of civilisation were carefully maintained, and eventually 'the English party was escorted into the Russian camp by Cossacks bearing torches at the end of their lances and entertained with all that cordiality in which the Russian official is never found wanting'.

Younghusband similarly met some Cossacks under the command of Captain Grombochevsky in the Pamirs. Wearing the full dress uniform of a Dragoon Guard, Younghusband was entertained in the snows with the usual champagne, used to toast the Queen and the Czar. The Englishman was not impressed with 'their wretched apology for a tent' which compared badly with the snug little tents equipped with numdahs and groundsheets with which his own troop of Gurkhas was supplied. 'The Russians' food seemed poor and insufficient, as they lived almost entirely on mutton and ate even the entrails of sheep, and seldom had any flour.'

I read Sven Hedin's *Central Asia and Tibet*, Auriel Stein's *Sand-buried Ruins of Khotan*, Colonel Schomberg's *Peaks and Plains of Central Asia*, C. P. Skrine's *Chinese Central Asia* and Sir Eric Teichman's *Journey to Turkestan*. I read the memoirs of Curzon, Durand and Robertson. I took note of Lord Dunmore, who hunted and had trouble with Pathans, 'the most audacious and daring thieves in the world. It is said of them that they are so light fingered that they can steal the sheet off a man's bed when he is lying asleep without waking him.'

Many of the books I read were in the library of the Royal Dublin Society whose hallway was half-filled up with an elaborate statuary group depicting brave Lieutenant Hamilton falling victim to two turbaned desperadoes during the first Afghan war. In the nineteen-eighties it was removed, no doubt because someone considered it an inappropriate imperial relic. Being made of plaster, it did not survive movement, but fell to pieces, a suitably symbolic end.

Given my obsession, the opportunity of being paid to go and live in Kabul, within striking distance of the edge of Central Asia, seemed a wonderful piece of luck.

I came from a family that had its share of travellers, soldiers and servants of the Empire. The house was full of things they had brought back from abroad, heads of wild animals, swords, carved teak tables, planter's chairs, a set of Japanese ivory figures depicting torture scenes, curtains acquired after the Siege of Peking, cannonballs picked up after the siege of Sevastapol and converted into inkwells.

My mother said, 'You must be properly fitted out.' Naturally she thought I should go to the Army and Navy Stores.

I had always been fascinated by lists of traveller's clothes and equipment. Sven Hedin took a collapsible boat to Tibet to explore lakes. Colonel Alexander Gardiner crossed the steppes wearing a black Uzbeg hat, a black sheepskin coat, hair rope girdle and Turkic boots. The Reverend Theobald Wolfe walked into Bukhara in the robes of a Church of England canon. Burnaby of the Blues carried a packet of Epsom salts in his pocket as he rode to Kiva; Major Cumberland's supplies always included coloured handkerchiefs to exchange for items like sheep, milk and butter. The Earl of Dunmore never travelled without his precious posteen coat with its soft lambskin lining.

General Cruttwell, FRGS, had supplied Boot of the *Beast*. I took the advice of the Colonel who had taught me to shoot my .303.

'Don't skimp on anything, my boy.' His list included six of everything, six saucers, six plain white plates, six spoons, six forks, six tropical shirts.

'Afghanistan?' The young assistant at the Army and Navy Stores was helpful. 'We still class that under India.' He found me a mosquito net, a collapsible canvas bucket, a canvas bath and a supply of carbolic soap.

The Army and Navy still catered for people going to Aden, Cyprus, Borneo and a large part of Africa. Very soon the activities of Empire would be reduced to the flickers of a severed lizard's tail and tropical outfitters would cease to have a role. But as late as 1952 drill material (treble-shrunk), hurricane lamps and travelling baths with wicker linings were in demand.

I took all my supplies back to Ireland where I waited for confirmation of my appointment. When it came it was accompanied by a first-class single ticket on the P & O liner, the *Strathnaver*. The contract, stamped and signed by the Minister of Defence of the Kingdom of Afghanistan whose employee I was to be for two years, stipulated a salary of seven hundred pounds a year sterling which I could exchange for afghanis, the local currency. I would be lecturer in English Literature at the Royal Military Academy in Kabul.

Now I had to get my new belongings back to England. Our tractor and trailer trundled down to Dun Laoghaire pier loaded with wooden boxes marked in red letters – KABUL . . . AFGHANIS-TAN . . . WITH CARE. My rifle and a supply of ammunition under sealed cover was packed separately.

The first part of the journey was the most uncomfortable. A horn sounded, seagulls circled over the *Princess Maud*, and from the direction of Bray Head a cloudburst spattered on the heads of emigrant passengers with suitcases held together by rope and string. It was a bitterly cold March day. In the main saloon Guinness was being spilt. Elsewhere an old man took out a fiddle and some nuns sat demurely reading missals. In the early nineteen-fifties Irish nuns still wore starched wimples. Soon the weather got worse, the *Princess Maud* began to pitch and toss, children cried, the Guinness drinkers, the old man with the fiddle, most of the nuns and many of the emigrants got sick. I did not mind in the least, because I was setting out on the first stage of being a traveller.

From London I set off for Southampton with my wooden crates and my packaged rifle. The RMS *Strathnaver* made a contrast to the *Princess Maud*. Having survived wartime service, and a spell of shipping GI brides across the Atlantic, she had been spruced up to cater for the golden twilight of Empire. Once more she was painted white with yellow funnels, and she dominated other mundane ships at Southampton docks like an exotic bird among sparrows, a vast sulphur-crested cockatoo.

The great white and yellow ship enveloped me. My luggage was stowed away and my gun confiscated.

'I am afraid, sir, that it is expressly forbidden to keep firearms in your cabin.'

My employers had treated me to First-class, but not to the extent of a single cabin. I had to share with Teddy who came from Cardiff and who, like me, had brought some unusual items of luggage. Every evening he opened up a large bag and took out a couple of parcels which he opened to inspect his gold coins and pieces of elaborate jewellery.

'Chaps in the Customs are fools.'

Teddy's trumpeting snore, his throat-clearing, and his gargling last thing at night and just before the breakfast gong could not detract from the joys of First-class. I do not know what they offer nowadays to the very old and the very rich who go cruising, but I doubt if it matches the luxury of the old *Strathnaver*.

First-class accommodation took up the greater part of the ship, while the majority of passengers who could only afford Third-class were squeezed up over the engine-room and propeller. We could see them gasping behind the metal grille that separated us. On our side of the fence postwar austerity was left behind. I floated on air. Gongs sounded repeatedly for big meals smoothly served by slaves – humble, affable, charming stewards in the process of building up goodwill that would turn into large tips.

I revelled in the choice as to where to pass the long idle hours, the smoking room, the games room, the gym with its stationary bicycles, or the swimming pool where the water lapped the edges when the *Strathnaver* inconsiderately pitched and tossed, quite like the *Princess Maud*, as it plunged through the Bay of Biscay. Off the lavish main hall whose postwar redecoration persisted in reproducing old MGM opulence, were a number of bars named after governor-generals and cricketers. You did not pay for anything during the voyage, but all was put down until port was reached. It did not seem to matter when the price of a double whiskey in the W. G. Grace was sixpence.

The captain and the ship's officers were only there to please. Soon they put on tropical uniforms and their hairy legs appeared beneath white shorts. You could watch them from your deck chair, or look for the ghosts of mountains, a line of distant silver which you were told was the African Rift, or the tawny Andalucian hills, a corrugated line behind our wake. Were they mountains, or were they shadows or clouds? But there was nothing insubstantial about Gibraltar towering out of misty vapours.

'Always had a soft spot for Gib,' said one of the dozen middle-aged tea planters on board. 'Especially since 1943. It was a good moment when the convoy arrived . . . before that two of our ships had gone down.'

If you got on deck early enough you might run into Field-Marshal Slim on his way to Australia to be Governor General. With a military aide dancing attendance, he could be seen every morning making two circuits of the upper deck before breakfast. The sedentary timed them with their watches. The aide and myself appeared to be the youngest passengers on board by about fifteen years.

At Suez there were still bumboats by the hundred. We anchored during the night and next morning the great white ship was swamped in little boats tied up alongside. Here was a change from watching lascar sailors at prayer. ('. . . you'll see a lot more of that sort of thing when you get to Kabul . . .') Looking down from the deck I watched screaming figures in loose cotton gowns and fezes which Egyptians still wore in the nineteen-fifties. The comfortable rhythm of our voyage was interrupted by offers of engraved brass, cheap suitcases disguised as real crocodiles, and filthy pictures. Plenty of people bought them.

A pilot boat filled with garishly decorated Customs officials and a stowaway beggar came on board with much shouting. The beggar ran around First-class howling for baksheesh, and then appeared to be thrown overboard. Suddenly the ship was quiet again, and Suez was confused memories and some postcards passed around from deckchair to deckchair. Our stately progress down the canal was effortless. We passed a camel and a military camp flaunting a Union Jack. National Service soldiers wearing only shorts, their sunburn visible from our deck, whistled and waved in our direction.

'I don't envy them.'

We drank our whiskey sodas, our vermouths, rums and Pimms, and slowly entered the Red Sea.

After the anxiety of the last few months it was pleasant to relax in the sun. I read the Royal Geographical Society's *Hints to Travellers* which provided information on crossing deserts and dealing with polar bears. I practised my Pushtu. In London I had acquired a Pushtu manual written by a Major Raverty.

'My back itches; scratch it.' 'What language speakest thou?' 'I do not understand thee.' 'If you had half as much brain as you have beard, you would have looked before you leaped.'

Most of the words and exercises concerned military matters.

'There is no vacancy in my regiment; if there had been I would have given it to thee.' 'Sir, the soldiers are plundering my dwelling; do me justice.' 'When you are within fifty paces of the enemy, at once charge them.'

I read Major Raverty's introduction. 'We have now probably emerged for good from the Peshawar side of the Khyber.' When the gallant author, who I suspected must be another wandering Irishman, had published his little grammar in 1880, the second Afghan War had just been concluded.

My fellow passengers knew about Afghanistan. 'Did you say you were working for the Ministry of Defence? An Afghan Ministry of Defence?' The idea that anything suggesting bureaucracy could exist west of the Khyber provoked mirth. 'Never trust them. You'd better drink up.' The frail missionary lady knew the nurse who had been kidnapped by that wicked man, the Fakir of Ipi in 1930. Everyone knew the poem that began 'There's a boy across the river with a bottom like a peach.'

In the morning light the sharp hills above Steamer Point

resembled medieval paintings of hell. We were processed by Passport Control in the First Class smoking room and allowed to go on shore. Aden was a frontier town with British bobbies, a large statue of Queen Victoria in the Park, and behind the glitz of tourist shops a world of dark alleyways. I took a horse-drawn carriage from the tree lined arcades off Steamer Point to Crater City two miles away. Here was my first direct contact with the east. I sat in a small pavement restaurant full of rickety chairs and tables and watched the donkeys, goats, beggars and covered women pass outside. I sniffed pungent smells of spices and shit. I was given a chunk of flat bread and a burning yellow liquid sprinkled with nutmeg that came when I ordered tea. Around the small tables motionless men wrapped in sheets and blankets slept. Around my table ragged children kept up an endless whine.

Back to the *Strathnaver* and luxury. 'Had a good time? Aden isn't a bad place to live. You get used to the heat.' On board were new excitements, fuelled by a sense of coming climax. The ship's doctor, a jovial bearded drunken Irishman, stood up at the Captain's table and took off his trousers. A ship's officer fell in love with a German girl and smuggled her into his cabin. To make matters worse, she came from Third-class. Field-Marshal Slim appeared to be flirting with young Mrs Vigors in between circling the decks.

'I am going as a maharajah,' Teddy said.

For the last evening before Bombay strings of coloured lights illuminated the rigging, and every porthole blazed. In every cabin the maharajahs, African chiefs and Bedouin Sheiks dressed up. In the Captain's cabin the Captain put on his usual Viking horns. Mrs Prettyman disguised herself as a belly dancer.

'Bloody stupid,' said the oldest tea planter, staring at Mrs Prettyman's yashmak and navel in which she had placed a diamond as big as one of Teddy's smuggled jewels. A German pirate from Third-class had vaulted the dividing barrier and was dancing by himself as the ship's orchestra tuned up. Throughout the voyage this small elderly group had been as busy as any of the crew down below working to make the ship move through the water. The *Strathnaver* vibrated with their music, piano by day, tinkling imitations of Ivor Novello and Charlie Kuntz, and really hard work by night. Then the four men and their saturnine

leader who played the saxophone with sweeping dramatic gestures, played until long after midnight, endless slow waltzes,
foxtrots, and rumbas when they got really animated. They were
all alcoholics, we were told, worse than the doctor.

Tonight they stood on the little podium in their red jackets
making warm up noises. The German had been frogmarched
back to Third-class, the dance floor was filling up with couples
moving awkwardly in unaccustomed clothes. The barmen and
waiters were desperately trying to please everyone. By eleven
o'clock when the food was brought in, they had made everyone
drunk. Bottles and glasses littered the tables as the passengers
toyed with five courses of food. While we sipped our cherry
brandy balloons came tumbling down. We were drifting closer
and closer to India.

They were dancing the conga through the First-class Smoking
Room, the Donald Bradman Bar and the W. G. Grace Bar. The
line of kicking figures crossed the great main hall where the vast
mirrors in their Art Deco frames doubled it up so that there
were two cardinals with purple gaiters clutching two slave girls
clutching two Viking captains clutching four Nubian princesses
as they cascaded down the main staircases with its stainless steel
banisters and into the Dufferin and Ava Lounge Bar.

'Why don't we escape from all this?' Mrs Prettyman was
behind me, swathed in gauze.

Up on the sports deck the music was distant. My head ached
as I clutched at Mrs Prettyman's warm soft accessible body. The
moon lighting a pathway through the dark blue sea was almost
as bright as the *Strathnaver.*

3

Aᴿᴼᵁᴺᴰ the *Strathnaver* was a carpet of small boats, some with fishermen, others which seemed to drift aimlessly, carried hither and thither by patches of coloured sail. A few had diesel whose fumes mingled with the unforgettable rancid and spicy smells of Bombay which was still miles away on the horizon. Families gutted fish, a man squatted peeing at the stern of a little rocking rowboat, stick figures stood up against the blue sky. The shoreline took on clarity, the blinding white apartment blocks ringing Kandy beach, the Tower of Silence up on its hill. The *Strathnaver* moved in, and then there was a sigh of recognition among the passengers at the rail as the Gateway to India came into view.

Gangways were lowered, the stewards were paid off, goodbyes were said. Mrs Prettyman disappeared towards the Taj Mahal Hotel. In a few minutes the floating palazzo was a glittering memory.

In the custom shed scores of soldiers and porters shouted at each other as bags were ripped open and the babble of noise reached the roof.

'Transit passenger.'

'You have documents for baggage?'

'Excuse me, Sir . . . that firearm is not permitted.'

My gun was seized and the three crates were gently and firmly confiscated. In an office full of clerks sitting over ledgers a man with a paunch and a shiny bald head like a nut dealt with me.

'Where do you travel?'

'To Afghanistan.'

'Ah . . . !' There were gasps and whispering and laughter from the clerks who all ceased their writing for a time. The buzz continued while someone was dispatched to another room. He went off running, but twenty minutes passed before he returned with sheafs of documents in Hindi and English, all to be signed before I handed over a great deal of money so that the crates and gun could be returned to me. Then I embarked for Karachi on the British Indian freighter, the *Kowloon Spirit*. The crates came aboard as well on the backs of coolies; behind the straining procession skipped a final coolie carrying my gun. On the *Kowloon Spirit* everything was black where the *Strathnaver* had been white, and everything else was rust red. Deck class was packed so tight that it looked as if the passengers might have difficulty breathing. They were pilgrims travelling back from Mecca after the Hadj. There were old men, women, youths and cripples. Some were cooking on deck, others had stretched out on rugs oblivious to noise or discomfort. Some were praying. Seeing so many pushed together for a purpose for which the majority had been saving up all their lives was chastening for the only first-class passenger.

The ship's officers and crew kept to the main living quarters which also contained First-class. Here the solitary passenger passed the time reading the man who would soon become India's most popular author writing in English – P. G. Wodehouse. No one else used the ship's library which otherwise consisted of engineering manuals and a book on how to play the harmonica.

At mess I sat at the Captain's table with the other officers while the engineers and mechanics formed another group at the other table. We ate steak and chips, peas, HP Sauce, Tomato Sauce, Malt Vinegar, Branston Pickle, fruit salad and tinned cream. From where I sat I could see the pilgrims wedged white around the bow. The Captain introduced the Paddy who was going to Afghanistan. Sparks mentioned the wogs whose greatest pleasure was to shoot someone and then carve off his balls. Number One recited the poem about the boy across the river with a bottom like a peach. The conversation soon changed to Everton, Arsenal and Manchester United.

Everyone here had his duty and his time off with smokes and eats, sunbathing, listening to the BBC, watching the shoals of flying fish, writing letters home. The *Kowloon Spirit* regularly crossed the Arabian Sea to Jeddah, Mukhalla, Hodeida and other bloody hot, filthy boring places.

After two days I left ship at Karachi, the only passenger to do so, and stood with my luggage on the quay beside a row of corrugated sheds. There were a few cranes and a number of rusty waiting ships that moved with heatwave; young soldiers stood with rifles topped with bayonets, scarecrow coolies eyed my things. After an hour two officials appeared out of a shed, one of whom pointed to the baggage with his swagger stick.

'From where are you coming?' When I told him that I was in transit to Afghanistan, his face became stern and his carefully brushed moustache bristled.

'Please follow.' He picked out some coolies with his stick, and shouted at them to gather up the crates and suitcases and stagger in single file towards the shed. The interior was big and echoing, filled with bales of cotton, and other crates. Some officials were drinking tea as my things were deposited, or rather, dropped onto a bench.

'Your invoice, please.'

At first nothing was said as the list was handed around and scrutinised.

'From where do these things originate?'

'London.'

'I have to ask you to open these cases for examination.' There was more pointing with the swagger stick and a long pause until two men appeared with a crowbar and a claw hammer. The wooden lids were splintered and opened and the contents disinterred from wood shavings, the crockery, saucepans, knives, forks, parcels of food, medicines and other things that the salesman at the Army and Navy had told me that I could not do without. I was worried that I would miss my train. 'What is this?' The collapsible bathtub. 'You have chit?' The invoice was consulted.

The boxes of ammunition and the rifle caused great excitement. The military man took it out of its canvas bag and peered down the barrel. He tested the loading mechanism, adjustable sights, cartridge dispenser and alignment. Then the other custom officers did the same, each examining the weapon carefully, firing imaginary shots into the air and passing it on to a colleague.

'How much did you pay?'

I told him.

'Very good.' He retired to his office, and I waited for an hour. Elsewhere fumes of factories, incinerators and cars formed a tin smog over Karachi. A long time passed before I was summoned to the office.

'It will be two thousand rupees and the rifle is confiscated.' His eyes did not flicker.

'Three hundred pounds?'

'You pay or everything is kept here. And naturally there will be a monthly charge for storage.'

I did not have three thousand rupees. Should I offer him a bribe? Very likely.

'But I am not staying in Pakistan. I am on my way to Afghanistan.'

'That is of no consequence.' There was something like contempt in his voice. Perhaps he felt strongly about the feud between Afghanistan and Pakistan that was raging at the time. He may have felt that the Pathans did not deserve a homeland to be named Paktunistan. Or he may have been hinting at a payoff.

And then suddenly it seemed a good idea to leave behind the dinner and breakfast sets of china, white edged with gold, the box of Huntley and Palmer biscuits, the tropical shirts, bottle dispenser, the bars of carbolic soap, the bucket and the bath. I didn't want the rifle either.

I left them all behind and never saw them again. Eight years later I received an enormous bill from Pakistan customs which I didn't pay. The rifle was not listed among surviving effects.

I took my bedding roll and my great-uncle's cricket bag which carried my surviving personal possessions and sought the Frontier Mail. For generations of English soldiers and officials the Mail had been the quickest and safest means of travelling to the north-west frontier, where the Pathans feuded and fought. I had read of warring Waziris and treacherous Afridis from numerous soldiers and statesmen who had taken the Mail for a visit or a campaign. Back in 1877 Lord Lytton, the Viceroy, wrote on the problems of confronting Pathans. 'I believe that our North West Frontier presents at this moment a spectacle unique in the world; at least I know of no other spot where, after 25 years of peaceful occupation a great civilised power has obtained so little knowledge of them, that the country within a day's ride of its most important garrison is an absolute terra incognita, and that there is absolutely no security for British life a mile or two beyond our border.'

A place of adventure and slaughter, where there was a constant threat of violence, although the early Fifties were comparatively quiet years.

The Frontier Mail consisted mostly of Second-class carriages with hard slatted wooden seats, a few Third-class, and one First-class at the far end. Once again I would be travelling in luxury. There were bars on all the windows and everything was covered in dust.

At the last minute I was joined by a middle-aged man wearing a dark buttoned-up frock coat, loose white pantaloon trousers and a silky grey karakul cap. He greeted me formally in English while his servant placed a bedding roll in one of the two bunks before disappearing to sit on a hard seat for two days. People were running up and down the platform in clouds of steam, men carrying enormous packs, women in bright clothes, small boys, beggars, and vendors selling betel nut, purple paste and small clay bowls of tea to be broken after use. The platform was strewn with shards.

The carriage door was locked, and we were imprisoned. After false starts punctuated by blasts from the train whistle and tremendous hisses, we moved slowly out of Karachi. The journey was half an hour of shacks and hovels and two days of a vast tawny wilderness. For most of the time Mr Abdul Khan, who was a lawyer, read his briefs. Occasionally he would address me.

'You know in Pakistan we still like Englishmen.'

'Actually, I'm Irish.'

'Better still. Eamonn de Valera. The first country to gain its freedom from Great Britain.'

Mr Abdul Khan had brought along a big basket of supplies, little wafer biscuits that tasted of curry powder, honey, salted preserves and almond cakes. At intervals he would spread them out on the seat, place a napkin over his knees, hand me another and invite me to share.

'Eat up . . . you are still a young man.'

There was no way of refusing him, so I enjoyed my first experience of eastern good manners. When dusk came and we pulled into a terrible crowded station, his servant ran down to lay out his bedding roll. After he departed and some official had come along and locked us in again, Mr Khan stirred, unfolded his hands from where he sat opposite me in the jolting carriage.

'Excuse me . . . please go to corridor while I change my clothes. I will turn over when you go to bed.'

All night and all day the train rattled through a flat empty land. From time to time it would stop at a station and absorb yet another gesticulating mob crammed into Third-class. We sat comfortably behind our locked doors listening to the hawkers and tinkling bells, waving away the contorted faces that peered in at us. At larger stations like Multan or Lahore wizened sweepers would be let in to agitate their little twig brushes and move the film of sand and dirt about. The sand got into hair, clothes, shoes and mouth. Occasionally Mr Khan would scrutinise his face in a little hand-mirror, take out a handkerchief and, tut-tutting, remove some specks of dirt. Outside the train would stop again, and if I bothered to look out, I could observe desperate people being hauled in through carriage windows.

When we said goodbye at Peshawar station Mr Khan said, 'Take my word for it, Dean's or the Military Club are the only possible places to stay.'

Set among smooth green lawns, Dean's proclaimed its long links with polo and hunting with the Peshawar Vale Hunt, of being a place of refuge for officers recuperating from confrontation with Pathans. A tonga drove me up the gravelled drive and an enormous bearer, made taller by his crested turban, led me and my cricket bag past airy verandas and huge dark rooms full of rattan arm chairs and planter's chairs. I ordered a whiskey soda.

Later I was taken up to my bedroom where a bowl of scarlet flowers had been arranged on the table beside the big window through which I caught sight of my first orange tree studded with golden fruit. The bathroom attached to the bedroom was a place where a cockroach would lie down and die for the cleanliness. After two and a half days on the Frontier Mail the pleasure of a bath in this big clean room, followed by relaxation on the planter's chair by the open window with a cigarette and whiskey, gazing out at the orange tree, were deeply satisfying.

Peshawar was a wonderful little town with narrow streets and bazaars which exuded passion and life. Beggars were hardly to be seen (or at least were discreet), Pathan tribesmen lived up to expectation and swaggered, and all the bicycles were decorated with coloured plumes. The place was cool. There was none of the dragon's breath of Karachi and Bombay. You could walk eastward to the edge of the town where thirty years later the plain would be covered with refugees' tents housing three million people. Now it was empty, stretching to the horizon where a ghostly line of mountains appeared against the light blue sky. Peshawar's suburbs were high mud walls surrounding gardens filled with fruit trees and singing birds. In those days when there was only a little dope to be distributed and no one had heard of Kalashnikovs, the tribesmen still carried ten-rupee jezails.

My appointment to the Royal Afghan Military Academy was due to be taken up in the second week of April, which gave me five days to reach Kabul. Up until now my journey had been straightforward, but now no one could tell me how to proceed. I only had travel tickets this far. In London, Bombay and Karachi I had been told that I would find ways of crossing the frontier once I had reached Peshawar. But now I could not find out where to go next.

After repeated enquiries I learned that there was one man who could help me. The Afghan Agent occupied a neat little office in the main bazaar over one of the many small restaurants and tea shops that crowded the street. To reach him I passed by displays of sizzling kebabs, rice, freshly-baked wafers of golden nan, and sights and smells of fruit, sliced pilaus and curries. At the house where the Agent resided a particularly rich medley of smells poured out into street from the open door. Inside diners crowded around small tables covered with saucers and bowls of brightly coloured food, tribesmen with shoulder-length hair dipping their fingers into sauces and licking them with grunts of satisfaction. A servant wiped his nose with the end of his turban before passing over a dish of curried *maki* fish; an old man was smoking a hubble-bubble which made a little burp each time he drew in his breath.

The Agent's office on the second floor was reached by ascending a ladder to a door beside which a tarnished brass plate was inscribed with the royal Afghan arms. A volley of Farsi greeted me as I gingerly opened the door and peered across a sea of waiting figures to where I could just make out the grey stubble of the Agent's chin. He was sitting behind a huge desk piled with ledgers and papers; across the ceiling were lines of discarded invoices and letters strung up like Christmas cards.

'Salaam aleikum.' In spite of Major Raverty, they were just

about the only Farsi words I knew, and in that hubbub of noise and smoke the foreigner's voice created a stir. I pushed my way through the crowd up to the desk where the Agent was twisting the stalk of a red rose between his teeth. He looked up and smiled, a small flat man with a habit of squeezing up his eyes when he was addressed. His handshake was damp.

'Very good, very good.'

The rose twitched as he stood up, lowered his head, dropped my hand, brought his to his heart, and spoke with what appeared to be passion. Tea was brought in by a servant.

'I wish to go to Kabul.'

'Very good, very good.' He smiled and offered me his chair. We drank several glasses of tea while I produced my passport and Afghan visa, my contract and a photograph of my mother. Nothing was any use. The rose swivelled aimlessly back and forth in the Agent's mouth.

'Is there a bus   a car?'

'Inshallah.'

'I speak no Farsi.'

'Hub! Hub!' That, I knew, meant 'Good!'

Two soldiers came in escorting an important-looking official who demanded the Agent's notice. I was getting nowhere, and for the moment I left, squeezing through the crowd and down the ladder. In the restaurant a musician was playing a rebab, and tinny chords of music quivered above the diners. Out in the street a man was arranging daggers for sale on the ground, murderous curved blades arranged for clients who wore crossed bandoliers studded with brass bullets. A woman enveloped in a dark blue sack was clutching a pile of flat loaves of nan between her hands like so many plates.

Dean's Hotel offered a painless translation to eastern life. Outside its gardens was noise and confusion, where from every alley and medieval street came the sounds of thousands of people struggling to keep alive, hawkers and tonga men, shopkeepers, potters and tribesmen down from the hills, and behind them all closed doors and shutters keeping the women inside.

Dean's was a formal placid contrast where instead of the shouts and wailing music, the only sounds were birds singing. The staff was immense – surely there couldn't have been more servants than this in the noonday of memsahibs and the Raj? In the morning I watched the head gardener's procession coming down the gravelled path. First came the head gardener himself, an old man dressed in baggy trousers, flapping shirt and waistcoat, his white hair covered with a corkscrew turban into which he had tucked the essential notes and messages for the day – water the front lawn . . . cut back the rhododendrons . . . bring out the baskets full of seedlings . . . cut rose blooms for the hotel . . . make sure Azif collects the camel manure. Behind him came a procession of gardeners like janissaries, carrying their own special tools and implements – a spade, a fork, a special knife for trimming the edges of the lawns. Little boys without these emblems would be dispatched to weed the paths, and as evening approached it would be time for all hands to reach for the watering cans.

Inside I encountered the same abundance of servants which was very striking to someone coming from postwar England. In every one of the reception rooms downstairs was a bearer like a museum attendant. He stood there waiting for your orders. The intricacies of social grading meant a downward pattern developing between an order given and an order carried out.

'Sahib!' intoned the gold-braided, moustachioed princeling summoned from his sentry post.

'Beer!'

'Very good.' He would clap his hands and a lesser man would come and receive instructions. This one in turn would pass them to the barman or kitchen boy through a chain of command eventually down to one of the innumerable ragged men whose duties seemed to be confined to wiping down the bottle. Eventually I would receive my glass of Murree beer on a salver.

It was a process that amazed me, although I knew it to be a continuation of Imperial tradition. In early days *Punch* had noted the young officer with his great retinue of servants: 'And who is this important official? Why it's Captain Smith of the 24th Punjabi Infantry on his way to join his regiment.' During the first Afghan war each officer in the Army of the Indus was allowed a minimum of ten domestic servants, not counting the grooms for his camels and the six bearers he needed if he was prepared to ride in a palanquin. Many thousands died in the bloodstained snow as they retreated from Kabul.

For three days I mused about Afghan wars, ate chicken curries and drank beer. The Pakistani officers who came to Dean's were Captain Smith's successors. Did I really hear them say 'spiffing' and 'jolly good'? Certainly they called each other 'old man'. And there was the irate major bellowing across the expanse of the dining room. 'Those blighters have brought me the wrong drink! The service here has gone to the devil!'

Struggling to find any transport that went in the direction of Kabul, I discovered that I needed special permission and chits even to visit the Khyber Pass. There seemed to be no way of travelling up to the capital except in the train of an official delegation of some sort.

I was lucky. On the third evening a dusty green station wagon containing an Afghan driver and two young English passengers drove up to Dean's. Sam and Diana worked in the British Embassy in Kabul.

Diana had a migraine and went straight to bed. Sam, who was a cypher clerk, had a job to do.

'The beer's run out.'

They had driven hundreds of miles over the mountains, through the Khyber following the route of a slaughtered army, and across the Jalalabad plain to replenish supplies.

The arrival of the station wagon seemed miraculous. 'Any chance of a lift?'

'I don't see why not as long as there's room. Beer first, passengers afterwards, you understand. You'll have to squeeze in the back. It's your life.'

Sam was small and sandy-haired, wore glasses and seemed to be in a perpetual rage which made me wonder if he was suited to the diplomatic life. We dined together, and I have rarely seen a man so devoured by thirst. We drank three bottles of wine – two for him – innumerable whiskeys, a beer or two, and the dignified bearer was kept busy scurrying backwards and forwards for replacements. Sam inveighed against Afghans, his Ambassador – 'a drunken clot' – dirty drinking water, fleas, the bleeding country, his bleeding driver who would not listen to him and take it easy over the effing bumps that had given Diana her headache. He didn't think much of my prospects.

'How do you know the bastards will pay you?'

'I have an elaborate contract. They paid my fare out here, First-class.'

'Means nothing.' He polished his glasses and put them back
on his nose. 'You might think it's none of my business, but it's
quite on the cards it will be. At the Embassy we have to deal
with people like you all the time.'

'How do you mean?'

'You know, the usual sort of consular stuff, but out here it
lands in our laps in the Embassy. People arrive, lose their money,
get sick. The other day we had a bloody fool who had broken
his leg. And there's always some stupid woman who's got herself
married to an Afghan. A month or two stuck inside a house in
Kabul with another wife for company, and they're whining
about how they're being treated and wanting to go home. Of
course there's absolutely nothing we can do.'

'It seems bad luck.'

'Nothing to do with luck, just stupidity. If I had my way I'd
pass a law forbidding English women marrying wogs.'

'Do you live in the city?'

'God, no! We're out at the Embassy, all of us. Guarded by
Gurkhas. They'd give the Pathans what for if the need arose.
We have our commissariat and Indian *hakim* . . .'

'Hakim?'

'Doctor. Not a bad bloke. There's a swimming pool.'

He lit his fifteenth cigarette. 'You'll have difficulties if you
find yourself landed in trouble. There can't be an Irish diplomat
nearer than the Vatican.'

Next morning we started off for the Khyber. I sat in the back
among the beer crates and other less essential supplies. The
vehicle was eccentric, putting me in mind of mid-Thirties races
across deserts. A homemade wooden framework surrounded
the Armstrong Siddley chassis; the windows were covered with
curtains. Instead of the sphinx the radiator cap was replaced
with a large gold crown. The driver had been smoking hashish
much of the evening before.

It was a beautiful cool morning and we drove out of the green
Peshawar valley clinging to the remnants of spring towards the
strange khaki hills that are the homeland of the Pathans. Nigel
Nicolson wrote how the Khyber has 'a cutlass ring about it',
while another traveller, G. Griffiths, observed how 'Nature has
conspired to create a backcloth appropriate to the character of
the area's inhabitants'. I had read Mountstuart Elphinstone on

the Pathan character: 'their vices are revenge, envy, avarice, rapacity and obstinacy; on the other hand they are fond of liberty, faithful to their friends, kind to their dependants, hospitable, brave, hardy, frugal, laborious and prudent; they are less disposed than the nations in their neighbourhood to falsehood, intrigue and deceit.'

'Some of the finest fighting material of the Indian army comes from the Pathan tribes, both on the British side of the frontier and across it,' Dr Pennell, who worked here as a medical missionary, wrote, 'and very pleasant some of these Pathan warriors are.'

The Embassy wagon with the crown over the radiator cap and the cargo of beer passed by old regimental crests carved out of the rocks by the roadside and under toy forts. There was indeed an outlaw air about the tawny countryside, an expectancy of whistling bullets. At midday we reached Landi Kotal, a few shops and corrugated shacks. In spite of the driver's pleas he was not allowed to stop.

'Bloody fool's got a sore head. So have I.'

'Isn't it dangerous to let him drive?'

'Oh I don't think so. You'd never get anywhere if you worry about that. All Afghan drivers live on the stuff.'

The road twisted and turned, and above us spires and pinnacles of rock shot up and the old railway line went in and out of tunnels. No one, not even a Pathan, seemed to live in the harsh landscape. Then came Torkham, the Pakistani frontier post, which was a patch of green and a few trees.

'You make a big mistake taking a job in Afghanistan,' the Customs officer told me. This was a moment when the Pakutuni otan issue loomed particularly large. 'Those dirty people will kill you.'

At least the frontier was open. This was because the Pakistanis had grown a little nervous since Afghanistan had turned to Russia as an ally.

The Customs officer produced a feast and entertainment in our honour. Sitting under an awning of branches we sucked grapes and nibbled nuts, while he invited over a group of hermaphrodites who had been sitting on the other side of the road to dance for us.

'Look, they are good,' he said as they shuffled around in the dust. We watched them in drowsy silence; Diana read a book.

At last they had finished. 'How much?' Sam asked the troupe leader.

'Forty rupees.'

'Too bloody much.'

'Give him twenty,' said the Customs officer, and it was done. We went halves.

'That is the correct amount unless they take off their clothes. Naturally they would be dearer if they were boys.'

All the way from Peshawar we had followed the tarmac road into the frontier hills. The thin black coil had squeezed between the railway and the traditional route along which conquering and defeated armies had marched back and forth. There was a chain across the road with a sign in English: 'BEYOND THIS POINT ALL TRAFFIC IS FORBIDDEN'. This seemed to be a relic of the Paktunistan conflict because we went across without trouble. On the other side was the same fawn landscape pitted with rocks, but it was more difficult to see now, because the road raised such a lot of dust.

'Wait for it.' Sam turned around to me as the first jolt hit the station wagon and the driver changed down into second gear. Diana groaned and the beer bottles rattled like bell-chimes, as I leaned forward to watch him spin the wheel to avoid the first rock, and then spin it the other way to avoid the first crater. From then on it was slalom all the way through the Khyber. Rocks littered the road as if an avalanche had just occurred – or – one's instinct was to look upwards to the tops of the pale cliffs on either side for warriors waiting to ambush.

The potholes were deep and as frequent as the rocks. Moving along zig-zag on the reflexes of a drugged chauffeur was a slow progress, like the days of early motoring. We could have done with dust-coats and goggles. This was a pace just a little faster than that of an unsprung coach and four that took eighteenth-century travellers through Europe. It was no wonder that the impressions of those on the Grand Tour were sharp and clear; they had all the time in the world to gain them. I counted the bushes, watched a lizard flick its tail, and felt the sensation of being driven over a knobbly dried-up river bed. The beer bottles rang out; I was in Afghanistan.

In fact the Afghan border post was some miles from the actual frontier, and we were cruising through a no-man's-land from the dancing hermaphrodites until we met the first representative of the Royal Afghan Kingdom, a young soldier wearing a thick brown overcoat, carrying an old-fashioned rifle. Could it be a Lee-Enfield? He came out of a mud hut and peered into the station wagon. He seemed good-natured and simple. He took my passport and handed it to a group of men wrapped in sheets who squatted in front of the door. One by one they examined it, every single page, turning each one over, and pausing for a long time at the visa decorated with a lion and a sword that had been stamped by their London Embassy.

'They can't read,' Sam said.

We gave them cigarettes and they seemed pleased and waved us on. From here to Jalalabad took two hours of infinitely slow, twisting driving through barrenness. There were colours in the rocks, blues, yellows, purples and a constant pychedelic pink, and all these colours moved in the shimmering heat. The heatwave induced a feeling of moving through liquid at the bottom of a lifeless sea. However, I saw a few people, like the solitary shepherd, a chocolate-brown figure carrying his stick, standing in the midst of his flock. Once we passed a line of caravans piled with baggage and tents, the men striding out in front and disappearing into the haze.

Coming to the Jalalabad plain was like reaching an oasis. Lines of poplar and mudwalled gardens appeared, and every few hundred yards we passed a water course. In the town we continued to swerve to avoid hens, donkeys, sheep and goats. We stopped briefly at a teahouse, one of many along the main bazaar, where we sat on a dais of cushions raised above carpets and drank tea from a brass samovar stamped with the two headed Imperial Russian Eagle.

Naturally I thought of Dr Brydon slumped on his pony, feebly waving his forage cap as he approached the garrison. He was not the sole survivor of the Army of the Indus, but the only one who was neither killed nor captured. A merchant called Baness, said by Brydon to be Greek, also managed to reach Jalalabad, but died almost immediately of lockjaw and the effects of exposure. And some sepoys got through, but they didn't count. The horse, immortalised in Lady Butler's picture, was given to Brydon by a dying subahdar. 'Sahib, my hour has come. I am wounded to death and can ride no longer. You, however, still have a chance; take my horse which is now useless to me, and God send you may get into Jalalabad in safety.' According to Brydon, the poor animal 'directly it was put in a stable lay down and never rose again'.

A year later when a force marched through on its way to Kabul to demonstrate Imperial displeasure by blowing up the main bazaar, the regimental band of the Somerset Light Infantry stationed here at Jalalabad played 'O but ye've been long o'coming'.

Many years later Sir Mortimer Durand stopped at 'a dirty little place, surrounded by dead donkeys and camels whose essence makes the live air sick'. However, by the nineteen-fifties the town was famous for its mild winter climate, its fruit and its reputation as a resort for rich Afghanis.

We did not see any of these, only the inquisitive crowds whom Sam could not shoo away. Not only did they stare, but they examined us physically, and old men in night shirts, children, and shameless young men pressed to feel around our bodies and clothing, checking and examining shoes, socks, trousers, shirts, and most importantly, any watch. At least Sam and I were not pinched the way Diana was. The stares and gropings were much worse for her; she said you never got used to it. No wonder she was so bad-tempered.

After Jalalabad we drove back into the mountains, bumping along hour after hour, raising clouds of dust that settled over everything. I dozed and woke as we passed through Sarowbi where Sam told me a dam was being built on the Kabul river, but we saw no sign of it. This was a German undertaking, evidence of how Germany had completed its postwar recovery. I was lulled to sleep again as we ambled along through peppery scents of flowers and bushes and always the dry golden dust.

When I next woke it was getting dark, with the last glow of light fading over the mountains. It was instantly cold, and I understood why the few men we had seen passing us had carried rugs and sheets. Above the dark shapes of mountains the stars shone out with great force and brilliance. It got colder as we climbed towards the Lataband Pass where the Panshir Valley joins the Kabul Valley.

Sam was passing around some beer which even Diana drank, in spite of her headache. The driver perked up at the thought of reaching Kabul, and lit his special brand of cigarettes whose fumes were sweet and sickly. I was not yet experienced enough to recognise hashish fumes.

'Do you see anything?' Sam's voice called from the front.

We had crossed the Lataband and now the darkness was total. Looking out past the jerking beams of the headlights I could see a crown of stars. Only they were too low for stars.

'There's Kabul.'

The word was like magic, like Lhasa or Samarkand. But where? That little ring of lights could not be illuminating a city. Where was it?

'The king only lights up the palace and those two bloody hills. No one lives on them.'

'Where do they live, then?'

'Down below where it's dark.'

'But it's pitch dark – there doesn't seem to be even one light.'

'That's Afghanistan for you.'

4

THERE were lights, of course, but they were concealed in the dark streets where the glow of lamps and candles provided a gentle illumination as we bumped through. A dog barked, or it could have been a wolf strayed down from the hills. Sam had talked a lot about wolves. We crossed a bridge and pulled up outside an imposing building; on the front door I made out on a tarnished brass plate the words 'Hotel de Kabul'.

'Best of luck,' Sam called out and the station wagon roared away into the night. Standing outside the closed door carrying my cricket bag, I wanted a nice clean bed. Through the grill I could make out a man lying on the floor under the reception counter who took a long time to respond to my shouts and thumps on the door.

'*Salaam aleikum.*' He yawned. I could see the dirty coconut matting on the floor, and even in the dim light of an oil lamp clouds of dust moved. On the wall above the reception desk was a Pan Am calendar with a picture of a Super Constellation.

'A bed . . . *zud.*' I would be saying '*zud*' a couple of million times before I left the country. It meant 'quick'.

He blew his nose on the end of his turban and said in English, 'No room.'

'*Zud!*'

Very slowly he burrowed in the drawer of the reception desk for a candle and a large key. A dark passage ran through the hotel and I followed him to the far end where he unlocked the door.

'*Hub.*' But it wasn't so good. The bed was unmade, the floor and table were covered with dust on which were scattered scraps of paper like dead leaves. There was a smell.

'*Hub.*' I nodded and he was gone, back to his hollow under the reception counter. I did not mind the candlelight, the smell, or the iron framed bed with its thin mattress. After ten hours and two hundred weary miles, I was offered the luxury of sleep.

In the morning I was woken by the sound of thumping feet. I opened the door and peered out to meet the same night porter running up and down the corridor spraying the dust with a watering can. By daylight I could take in the details of my room, the thin sagging curtains, the lack of sheets on the bed, the stains on the mattress and the marks on the walls which appeared to be excrement. Outside the window I could hear shouts, bells, music and the bray of a donkey.

I went to the dining room which was furnished with a bright red Afghan carpet and the same tinted photograph of Zahir Shah that I had seen in the Embassy in London. The watchful eyes behind the spectacles followed the viewer around, the same stern ghostly gaze which looked down on his subjects in every teahouse and public place in the country.

The waiter brought in a dish containing something yellow and cold.

'I wouldn't eat that, old fellow, it's an Afghan death trap.'

A bald young man sat at the next table which was covered with bottles and tins. I noticed New Zealand butter, apricot jam, Spam, some German sausages in a glass jar and vitamin pills.

'Welcome to the damned. Take my advice, old man, and stick to the bread.'

The bread was flat and dry, but little by little Joe handed me titbits from his table, including two hard-boiled eggs and a vitamin pill, so that in the end I ate well.

'Can't see you starving on your first day, old boy.'

The old boys, old mans, jolly goods and rippings came in every sentence. Back home in Istanbul Joe's family had belonged to the old ruling Ottoman caste before Ataturk took over. Where he learnt his English was not clear. He smoked gold tipped Balkan Sobranies in an amber holder and made his living as a carpet dealer, regarding the Afghan merchants whom he did business with as rum characters you couldn't trust.

Other guests were spaced out all over the vast dining room each with tins, pots and bottles laid out on the table before him. A Japanese business man got up and bowed. An elderly Italian nodded in my direction; he was the colonel who ran the Afghan air force, whose main duty was to look after its half-dozen old biplanes and see that they flew relatively safely on National Liberation Day.

The meal was eaten in silence except for the occasional sharp handclap from one or other of the solitary seated figures. The clap was a signal for a servant to push his head out from behind the screen that covered the kitchen door.

'This plate is dirty.'

'Bring jam.'

'How am I expected to eat this?'

Sometimes a servant was sent to the bazaar to buy an essential tin. While the dining room was silent, there were perpetual sounds coming from behind the screen, quarrelling, retching, coughing, and quite often the crash and tinkle of breaking china and glass.

The Hotel de Kabul – the 'de' a vestige of old times when French was spoken widely by the upper class – had been built, or rather half-built, as part of a chain during the years when King Amanullah was encouraging progress. There were other hotels at Mazar-i-Sharif and Herat, and no expense had been spared to give the illusion of luxury and modernity. The hotel at Herat had Windsor chairs, marble-topped tables on which were spread white American cloth, and a gramophone.

Robert Byron was one of the first guests at the hotel in Mazar-i-Sharif. 'Every bedroom has an iron bedstead with a spring mattress, and a tiled bathroom attached, in which we sluice ourselves with water from a pail and dry our feet on a mat labelled BATH MAT. The dining-room is furnished with a long pension-table laid with Sheffield cutlery and finger-bowls. The food is Perso-Afgo-Anglo-Indian in the worst sense of each. The lavatory doors lock on the outside only. I was about to point this out to the manager, but Christopher said he liked it and wouldn't have them touched.'

He and Christopher Sykes were the first guests there, 'judging by the excitement of the staff'. They paid 7s 6d a day, 'which is not cheap by local standards'.

Amanullah's reforms were short-lived, and after he went into exile Westernisation was no longer encouraged in Afghanistan. The hotels soon lost their initial gloss. Ben James, an American, visited Kabul in 1935, a time when drinking wine had returned to being a capital offence. ('The approved manner of dispatching the tippler into a parched hell is to set him upon a high wall and, without ado, push him off.') He found that the only hotel in Kabul had already assumed a familiar air. 'Floors and stairs were carpetless. A couple of Afghans were taking a nap on the billiard table from which the cloth was worn. The dining room had one long table in it; the rest of the room looked like a barn with its wide planks of rough-hewn timber. The only furnished room in the hotel was a tea-room having a dozen tables spread with dirty covers. In the music room was a battered piano with an earthenware crock for a stool.'

Fifteen years later piano and billiard tables had gone, but it was recognisably the same place. A few years after I stayed there, the Hotel was not improved, according to the evidence of Edward Hunter, another fastidious American correspondent. The building was still unfinished, as I remembered it. On arrival he received the customary greeting, 'No rooms. All filled up.'

So little had changed. 'The narrow winding steps at the side were a booby trap. My foot caught in the tear of an old green carpet, the kind seen in the narrow stairways of boarding houses in the West! An importation into a land famous for its rugs! Torn spots had been sewn over and over again. This must have been the original carpet dating back to the opening of the hotel.' Not so, according to James' account, but the same carpet that I remember well, which also tripped me up.

Since my appointment with the military authorities was in a few days, my first duty was to contact them straight away. After breakfast I emerged from the dark and dusty interior of the hotel and stood on the steps. Here was the main street with its tea houses and pastry shops which led down to the bridge and river. The only tarmac road in the city, probably the country, it flaunted the only cinema and bank, and was the location for the two dancing policemen in conventional blue uniforms and white hats who constituted the traffic corps and directed the camels and horse- and ass-drawn vehicles as well as the very occasional car, bus or lorry.

For a time I stood watching the swaggering tribesmen with their guns, who really did dangle roses from their lips as nonchalantly as if they were Woodbines. I watched the hawkers, itinerant letter-writers, small boys in their embroidered pillbox hats, a man in a striped silk robe like Joseph's coat carrying a bird in a cage, and countless women rippling past in chadris. Then I took a tonga to the Ministry of Defence. Since there was so little motor traffic, the tonga had great importance. It was generally a cheerful-looking vehicle – forget about the horse – consisting of steps leading up to a high wooden carriage with back to front seats. There would be a bicycle bell that worked like a pedal and the whole would be much given to ornament, curly brass handles, plumes, mirrors, paintings and paper garlands.

I chose the most picturesque out of the scores that were available, climbed up and sat on a seat under which was a sack of hay, and the driver went off whipping his horse and screaming insults at other traffic. Like a shark in the ocean, the tonga driver had few natural enemies, his main danger coming from the *jueys*, or freshwater canals that lined the roads. It was a common sight to see the wretched bits and pieces of a tonga submerged in the green slime of a *juey*, the sort of accident that occurred almost as often as the overturning, when passengers were thrown out as a result of a chassis or axle breaking, or a horse being injured.

I can't think of a more delightful way of seeing a strange city where there is next to no motor traffic, perched on the back of a tonga, which put me in mind of the dog cart at home, with the sun beating down. It was a good time to have arrived. April was a month of pale blue skies and roses and the rustle of paper kites flying over the city. All around Kabul the fields were turning green and the fruit trees were in blossom. It was the season of floods when the snows melted and lambs were being born in the wintery fields of the Hindu Kush. The nomads were returning from the Indian sub-continent with their long strings of camels, stopping for a short time in Kabul on their way to the high pasture lands of the Hazarjat. Spring was coming and a renewal of life after the long lethargy of winter.

Kabul seemed undistinguished, an overgrown village between two bare hills. Most of the original town, including the great bazaar, the old fortress of the Bala Hissar and quantities of pleasant houses had been destroyed by the avenging English. The subsequent construction in the nineteen-twenties of the grandiose palazzo that was the British Embassy was an act of Imperial arrogance. What was left of Kabul after so much was blown up and pulled down was a mixture of flat mud-roofed houses, bazaars, and one or two newer suburbs. Then, at the end of a great avenue, where a few tumbledown buildings were all that remained of Amanullah's planned new city, was his unfinished palace at Darul Aman.

The tonga came to a suburb and the driver pointed with his whip at an ornate gateway where two sentries stood beside a couple of old cannon. This was the Ministry of Defence. He accepted the agreed fare without complaint and drove off, something, although I did not realise it, that was most unusual. No doubt the veiled threat of the military presence made him nervous.

Beyond the impressive entrance the ministry was a big two-storey building with a corrugated tin roof and its share of Kabul dust. Here I spent a long morning walking up and down dust-clouded corridors seeking details about my appointment. In due course a languid officer sipping tea under the king and the flag gave me some vague orders. I was directed to a rendezvous with other teachers and officers from the Military School at the crossroads near the hotel where the bridge crossed the Kabul River.

Next day, I was once again in the thick of the city crowds, a medley of ragged children, beggars, porters and a group of shrouded women, shrill quarrelsome voices emerging like smoke from the corded grill in front of their faces. A boy was cleaning fruit in a particularly filthy *juey* before putting it out for sale, a shouting herdsman was trying to keep his donkeys in line, bicycle bells and music from the chaikhanas competed with the roar of the muddy brown river flushed by melting snows. A smell of ferment from rotting fruit wafted into the pale blue sky.

Among the waiting military men, a tall fair-haired figure in a purple duffle coat contrasted with the dark little figures in drab khaki uniforms. I was astonished to learn that he was another Irishman. Warren Shaw and I had never met, but we soon placed each other and found mutual friends and relations. Back home, we too had our tribes. If you got a very large piece of paper and laid it out on a ballroom floor and wrote down the family trees of every Protestant in Ireland you could connect the lot.

Warren had arrived well after me, and looked pale and tense

having suffered a nightmare journey with his Italian wife and two young children.

'Have you ever taught before?'

'No.'

'I've been boning up on my Farsi.'

We did not know yet that we need not have worried about our abilities as teachers, since our appointment was purely ornamental, a consequence of our nationality. The Irish lacked imperial and colonial history; on the world stage they were doggedly neutral. We were a discreet choice of Westerner. Our presence represented a suitable step forward in the slow process of modernisation which had gone so badly wrong when King Amanullah had tried it twenty years before. But although we stood for change and progress, we were not expected to play a direct part in either.

In the next decade during Prime Minister Daud's long flirtation with the Soviet Union before he and his family were machine-gunned, we would be replaced by Russians.

We noticed a group of grim men who stood apart carrying brief cases and wearing belted mackintoshes and topees. These were Turks who had also come to Afghanistan to teach. Already they hated us. One of the Afghan officers, a perpetually smiling man, detached himself from the group lounging under the trees. His uniform was identical to that issued to officers in the British army – perhaps some entrepreneur dealing in army surplus had been at work at the Ministry. The only difference were the pink tabs on his lapel and the four gold stars on each shoulder.

'How are you, my Sire? It is very good and happy.' Our presence was a heaven-sent opportunity for Captain Amin to practise his English. The Turks looked very angry. He continued polite and painstaking banalities until a rusty brown bus emerged from the encircling pedestrians, horses and tongas, sped along beside the *juey* and pulled up with a blast from its trumpet-shaped horn. It had no proper doors or windows, and inside, peeling paintwork surrounded a lopsided arrangement of broken seats. Here was the Military Bus designated for officers, which would take us to work every day.

The order of boarding was controlled rigorously by a list of names pasted up behind the driver's seat. Warren and I were let on first and given the important seats in front, which didn't suit the Turks at all. They came on next, scowling at us where we were smugly seated. Their spokesman, a feline little man with a Hitler moustache, began to shout. We sat rigid as the Afghans pushed past with protestations of politeness and stood at the back.

The bus could not go, the Turks were still complaining. A compromise had to be reached, a matter of honour. At last Captain Amin issued a judgement of Solomon. I would sit with one Turk, Warren with another. Everyone was satisfied, the shouting died down; soon passengers were seen to be smiling. The driver, an old man with a forage cap hanging limply over his face, gave the signal to start with a blast from his trumpet. After a fierce grinding of gears, and we shot forward, bursting through crowds of Waziris, Afridis, Hazaras and dense coils of horse-drawn traffic.

This was the first of many journeys through the heart of Kabul out to the Military School. The route would always fascinate me. For the first few hundred yards we followed the gorge between the Sher Darwaza and Asmai hills, their steep bare escarpments dropping to the river that would eventually join the Indus three hundred miles away. I remember the carpet shops, and how in summer the banks were covered with the brilliant splash of carpets left out in the sun to dry. We crossed a second bridge past a blue and white Wedgwood mosque and the Russian Embassy behind huge mud walls. Beyond the gorge the tarmac ended and in a few moments we had left the city, passing the turnoff for Amanullah's beautiful avenue that stretched straight for four miles towards his unbuilt capital. The white-stemmed poplars lining the road had grown to maturity since Robert Byron saw them newly planted. From here were the bumps and potholes that I had encountered on my journey from Pakistan, as the bus passed a few booths and heaps of mud bricks drying in the sun, offered us a distant view of snowpeaks, and swerved to avoid black and white goats and squatting figures along the road's edge.

The distance was about seven miles. I was thoughtful as I sat beside the uncommunicative Turkish major gazing out of the window and wondering about the future. We crossed a humped bridge beside a burial ground where ragged prayer flags stuck out from dried mounds of earth. A few more squatting figures and another chaikhana with its charpois, samovar and lines of decorated pots.

As a large black Chevrolet passed us at speed, I caught a glimpse of a decorated military figure lounging in the back seat, who raised an idle hand. This was a signal for agitation behind us.

'The Commandant, Sire,' called out Captain Amin as the Afghans all stood up and saluted back, stooping since there was a headroom of five feet. Neither the Turks nor ourselves moved. Piedogs lay in the hot dust and I noticed a pair of vultures. The bus drove towards a group of buildings surrounded by long white walls flanked at each corner by towers. A group of sentries lounged outside the main gate; inside a squad of cadets was marching up and down to a bagpipe band.

When the bus came to a stop the Turks and the Irishmen were brought out ceremoniously through the front door while the Afghans toppled out of the back. We found ourselves in a large square centring on a flagpole and lined with mud-walled huts. As the bagpipes played away I had a look at the sweating cadets in their thick army coats and heavy boots. They had shaven heads and they varied in age from children to grown men in their twenties.

5

I HAD given little thought to what the Royal Military Academy would be like, apart from forming a vague picture of an eastern Sandhurst attended by a camel corps. There was nothing eastern about the barrack square bordered by austere tin-roofed huts. A victory column stood in the centre, a cluster of loud-speakers fastened to its concrete laurel wreath. Inevitably the victory it celebrated was against the British. A few flowers scattered among some spindly poplars of the same species as those that formed Amanullah's magnificent avenue did nothing to relieve the sadness and drabness.

Our arrival was noted at once, and straight away the topee-hatted Turks and the two Irishmen became the centre of a bitterly contested confrontation. Groups of cadets, all holding up notebooks, jostled and fought to get our attention as we clambered down from the bus.

'What is Philistine meaning, Sire?'

'Chasm please?'

'Samson?'

'Circumcision?'

An old soldier appeared and beat them all back with a stick. Warren and I had little time to wonder at these strange questions as we followed Captain Amin to the guardroom near the main gate. A map of Asia was pinned on one wall and facing it another of Paktunistan, coloured pistachio green. The uniformed royal portrait frowning at our entrance was not the usual representation of the martyred Nadir Shah, but of his son, King Mohammed Zahir Shah. Zahir Shah had been young when his father was assassinated, and for years the country had been ruled by his uncle; he had only recently begun to flex regal muscles. It might well be that we were here as a result of his personal decision.

Captain Amin said, 'The Commandant welcomes you to the Military School. To have you here is a great honour.'

Colonel Azif, sitting behind a large desk twiddling a pencil, was recognisably the jowly man we had glimpsed from the bus sitting in the back of the Chevrolet. As head of the Military Academy he was in a position of supreme authority; everyone from his immediate subordinates to the smallest shaven-headed twelve-year-old cadet felt a sense of terror whenever he stepped out and strutted across the barrack square. Everyone except us. The foreigners were a political imposition, an irritant in the smooth running of his fief.

For the moment he greeted us courteously in Farsi which Captain Amin translated, rolling the words around his mouth like sunflower seeds. The affability lessened when Warren took out of his briefcase an intimidating list of questions about our job. He spoke with a slight stutter, clenching his fist and dragging out words which the Captain translated slowly. To each question he got a brief reply, the same one.

'How many classes will we be teaching?'

'The Commandant says there is no problem.'

'How much time should we devote to language and how much to literature?'

'The Commandant says there is no problem.'

'About how many cadets will there be in each class?'

'The Commandant says . . .'

Warren persisted while the Commandant became more surly. We should have struggled harder to make our position plain and to find out about our duties. But neither we nor the Turks, who threw in a couple of querulous queries of their own, could penetrate this stone-walling. In the end Warren put away his questions, and the Commandant smiled for the first time as he dismissed us.

The cadets were formed in line across the square and stood stiffly, their arms raised in salute as we passed. We were led towards a hut marked out from the others by the sentry guarding the door.

'From today this will be the teachers' room.' The Captain took out a key.

'For all?' cried out a Turk peering in.

'Yes please. Do not worry yourself. Very good.'

We crowded in and there was just room for all of us to find a place sitting on one of the cane chairs that surrounded a long wooden table on the hard mud floor. Immediately the door closed behind us, the body of cadets outside broke ranks and rushed towards the windows which looked out on the square. Noses were flattened against the glass which rapidly misted over from the effects of concentrated observation of the foreigners. The Turks began to grumble and the Captain tried to shoo the observers away, flicking his hand. He gave up and took out a cigarette, an action which aroused a sigh of comment from outside.

The Turks were still smarting from their inferior treatment in the matter of allocation of seats on the bus. There were four of them, dark little men with moustaches, anxious eyes and melancholy expressions. They had come here on loan from the Turkish army. Turkish military advisers had been in Afghanistan since Amanullah first wished to emulate Ataturk and modernise his army as well as his country. For this aim the Military College was created with the intention of being held in high esteem. Zahir Shah had come here for part of his education – most of the rest was in France – together with the children of leading Afghan families.

As a nation Turkey had continued to be admired, the more so recently since her soldiers had gained a reputation for exceptional bravery during the Korean war. Turks had always been on the staff of the Military College. However, the present contingent had been most reluctant to come and live in such a backward place as Afghanistan. To persuade them they had been given, not only financial inducements, but higher ranks – captains had jumped to majors, majors to colonels. But nothing could shake them from their deep misery at being exiled from their home. Sadly they, too, lit up cigarettes.

In contrast Warren was looking forward to his new job and had carefully prepared himself for Afghan life. He seemed to know a good deal about food, health, sanitation, the position of Moslem women, the Paktunistan question and other matters of which I was ignorant.

He asked, 'What method do you intend to teach?' and was nonplussed when I admitted my ignorance of any method apart from mere survival and the imposition of discipline.

'From what I can see the main problem will be the army mentality. These soldiers have had no opportunity to liberalise their minds. I have worked out various courses which should get them thinking again.'

The time came for us to be teaching much sooner than we anticipated. A soldier outside blew a loud bugle call and before the last notes had died the cadets at the window had run off and Captain Amin, who had left the roomful of foreigners a few minutes before, reappeared grinning with embarrassment.

'Your classes are waiting for you.'

Warren jumped up and pointed an accusing finger. 'I've never heard of anything more ri . . . ridiculous . . .' His stammer increased in his anger. 'We . . . ve had no dis . . . discussion about timetables or books or even subjects . . .'

The Turks muttered among themselves until their spokesman got to his feet and, seizing the Captain's arm, began twisting it while the others stood blocking the doorway. Warren sat down again and folded his arms determinedly. The Captain wrenched his arm away and continued to smile, occasionally shrugging his shoulders.

'It is better that you all come. Yes please. The Commandant has ordered it.'

Another officer was waiting outside to conduct us to our classrooms. The others peeled off one by one to their allotted rooms, until I was left on my own to follow him down a corridor. From either side of me came the drone of boys' voices learning by rote.

'This is for you.' The officer indicated the last door in the corridor, and after measuring it with his eyes marched up and kicked it open. From inside came a yell of command and a clatter of boots and I was conscious of shaven heads bobbing back into the distance and bodies standing to attention. The officer mounted a rostrum and spoke rapidly in Farsi, but all too soon he finished, saluted, shook my hand and marched out slamming the door.

I was alone with my class for the first time looking over the ranks of cadets standing three abreast behind rough wooden desks staring back at me. Indoors they still wore the belted overcoats they had on outside, and I could see at close quarters how closely the thick material resembled carpet felt. I could also see once again how these youths varied in age. Some were little children, others husky grown men. What was the reasoning behind the composition of this class? It was impossible to deduce. Intelligence? Had they been grouped by tribe? Evidently not – here in front of me were examples of every diverse Afghan feature from dark eyed Pathans to Mongol Tajiks.

I regretted that during the idle weeks I had not worked harder at Farsi. Major Raverty's Pushtu grammar would have only been of partial use here. Farsi united dissident tribes; Pushtu was the language of the Pathans. 'Show me the defences of the city.' 'Bring me the brown riding horse.' None of it had stayed in my mind. No one had asked if I was qualified in the language or demanded that I should know even a few words.

'Sit down,' I said in Sahib's English.

No one moved. I repeated my request, changing my tone so that it was almost pleading. Beads of sweat were breaking out on my forehead as I stepped forward and tried to push one of the bodies down. It rose up again like a cork.

'Please my teacher, my name is Mohammed Yussuf, head of eleventh class. Hello. How are you?'

I picked out a grinning face from the first row of desks.

'Can you tell the class to sit down?'

'Good morning my sir. We are very well. Yes sir. I sit, you sit, he sit.'

It took another five minutes to get them off their feet. Now they were looking up at me blankly. I felt envy for Warren down the corridor, who had surely prepared himself carefully. I wondered about the Turks. In the first moments of panic I drew a map of Ireland on the blackboard and another of Afghanistan, and linked the two together with a line of chalk.

What connections did the two have? I thought of poor Captain Hamilton fallen to long Afghan knives. There was little Bobs. Better not to emphasise that I was the same nationality as the conqueror of Kabul, a native of Waterford.

'Kabul was at our mercy, the Amir was in my camp, ready to agree to whatever I might pronounce . . . It will be a just and fitting reward for such misdeeds if the city of Kabul were now totally destroyed – its very name blotted out; but the great British government ever desires to temper justice with mercy and I now announced to the inhabitants of Kabul that the full retribution for the offence will not be exacted and that the city will be spared . . .'

In my classroom Ireland was unknown and the presence of an unbeliever with a red beard speaking through Mohammed Yussuf's dubious interpretation did not inspire confidence.

Textbooks were produced, a medley of loose pages and bad print. The pages were covered with smudges and there were blank spaces where the text had failed to appear altogether. I made out a passage which appeared to concern Abraham.

Mohammed Yussef snatched up a page and began reciting. 'And the children of Israel did evil in the sight of the Lord. And the Lord delivered them into the hands of the Moabites.'

There were also extracts from Milton. The compilation was a splendid source of the English language, perhaps not well suited for Moslem boys. This was evidently the reason for the curious list of words we had been presented with on our arrival.

The origin of the anthology remained a mystery forever. Had it been written by a missionary with a sense of humour? By Colonel Raverty of the Pushtu grammer? It was someone who considered that Samson Agonistes and the fall of Jericho had relevance for the future leaders of the Afghan army.

Before Mohammed Yussuf tackled 'Doth God exact Day Labour, light denied?' I made them put away the shabby little books for the time being. For the remainder of the morning I drew pictures on the blackboard.

'This is a tank . . . this is a gun . . .'

Twice the door opened and an officer looked on at more than fifty cadets staring at my attempts to depict military hardware. Occasionally they would bend and write something down.

The hour passed slowly. Towards the end Mohammed Yussuf took over, lecturing the class by repeating every word of English he knew and then occasionally bursting into a harangue of Farsi. I gave up drawing pictures and listened to him; there was no blackboard duster and my fist had become sore with rubbing out; the few broken stumps of chalk were worn down.

The chalky room was crowded solidly with lines of desks and cadets, and from where I stood I could see that they were divided by two gangways so narrow that they had to be negotiated sideways. I stepped down, leaving Mohammed Yussuf to continue his talk, and made my way to the back of the class where I was invisible and could project a form of secret authority, looking over brown shaven heads like seals. All the windows were closed and the fudge of bodies, thick woollen uniforms and coats generated a foxy smell.

Through the wall behind me I could hear a roar of voices like waves breaking over rocks. Sometimes there was a brief silence followed by the distinct sound of a slap. A door would creak open and there would be a heavy tramp of boots. I walked back to the dais where Mohammed Yussuf had stopped talking. I picked up a smidgin of chalk between thumb and forefinger and drew another aeroplane, the sort of picture I used to draw when I was six years old.

I noticed that the smaller brighter boys were all crammed together in front, while the back rows contained the leviathans – youths who appeared to be well into their twenties. The more I looked, the older they seemed. A number had moustaches. They were husky giants who kept to themselves, rarely speaking or even moving. They could have been asleep.

At last came a lovely sound. Outside the entrance to the hut the same tattered soldier blew a trumpet call that never reached the top notes. The cadets jumped to attention, a small boy knocking over an inkstand that dribbled across his desk. Tomorrow I would get them all to write something with their pens and nibs.

In the sanctuary of the teachers' room the Turks sat in a little group whispering unhappily to each other. Warren looked distraught.

'Did you have Milton and the Old Testament?'

'Yes.'

'We'll have to insist on getting some proper books.'

'How did you manage?'

'Not too well. The buggers can't speak any English.'

Outside the window cadets watched us dispassionately.

Our appointment was yet another indication of the Government's awareness of the importance of education. As far back as the great Amir, Abdur Rahman, who against the odds had died peacefully in his bed in 1901, there had been valiant and well-meaning attempts to modernise the country with the aid of foreign experts and advisers. Education was a priority in these efforts and the foundation of various foreign-language schools soon became a part of the process of enlightenment. The first, Habibiya College, founded by Abdur Rahman's son, Habibullah, modelled on Aligarh College in India, had English as the medium of instruction in some higher classes. French was taught at the Istiqial Lycée founded by French professors in 1922, and German at Nejat College, founded two years later. In 1932 Kabul University had begun with a Faculty of Medicine affiliated with the University of Lyons. Now it taught law and political science.

For many years anti-British feeling had ensured that French and German had been the foreign languages taught in prestigious schools, while privileged Afghans spoke French. Now this was changing.

The nineteen-fifties were the years of American influence, helped by massive economic aid. Morrison Knudsen were building new roads and had begun their ill-fated Hilmand Valley project which undertook to bring profound changes to the land area beside Afghanistan's largest river. The problems involved in dam-building, cooperation between Afghan and American engineers, the disturbance of two or three million people and the mushrooming expense eventually became factors that undermined America's dominance and gave the Soviets their opportunity. That was in the future; meanwhile English, the language of the Americans, was in favour.

During Amanullah's brief stormy reign, education had been one of his enthusiasms, becoming the keynote for changing traditional ideas in a feudal and undeveloped country. Schooling became compulsory and free, promising students were sent abroad, girls were taught for the first time, and a new and highly esteemed 'Medal of Education' was instituted. But out in the countryside few peasants thought that literacy was desirable even for their sons. In spite of every effort, when I arrived in Afghanistan in 1953, it was estimated that four-fifths of the population had never been to school and could not read or write.

What was the position of the Military Academy in regard to standards deserving a Medal of Education? Abdur Rahman had sent his son there, and Amanullah had also attended as a boy and received the rudiments of military training. (This seemed unbelievable to Warren and myself.) After Amanullah's downfall, when Kabul was besieged by the brigand, Bacha Saqqao, students of the Academy helped to defend the city beside troopers of the King's Bodyguard.

Today the Academy reflected current progressive trends and struggled to keep up with the times. A proportion of the students were literate, perhaps as many as half.

One of the main problems teaching them was the lack of supplies. Very soon Warren and I were making nuisances of ourselves, pressing demands for pencils, rulers and proper books.

'Do not worry,' the Director would tell us unhappily, his anxious twitching face reflecting the only object in his life, which was to avoid upsetting the Commandant. He did not mention that we were to be paid a lot more than the Afghan officers and teachers who did their work without complaint on their meagre salaries. The Afghans never grumbled that they were able to teach something to their pupils with no other aid than half a piece of chalk.

The chalk crumbled to pieces as we wrote on blackboards, and even further supplies of that appeared to be unobtainable. As for the Biblical and Miltonic extracts, there was not one copy in the whole College that possessed a full quota of pages.

'Please write a report.'

In the first week we wrote a score, none of which were looked at. Our duty was to take five periods each morning and keep quiet. I attempted dictation, reading and drawing without much result. The brighter boys endlessly repeated the few words of English which they knew, but the great majority were inarticulate. Many cadets were sick. Every day I would notice several dozing in the back of each of the five class rooms where I taught, whose leaden face and general inertia suggested that something was definitely wrong with them. But when I mentioned this to the Director, he laughed nervously.

'Do not worry your head, Sir, about this little matter.'

'They should see a doctor.'

'It is not important.' He could not quite ignore us. We were the latest fashion.

The Academy was a melting pot of Afghan races, and the boys were carefully chosen as representatives of their tribe or area. Not all attended willingly; many were press-ganged. Every summer the Commandant and his senior officers toured the provinces picking out likely candidates for officer material. The chosen boys, who were around ten years old, would be picked on the basis of who they were related to. They were hostages to their fathers and uncles, and their sojourn away from their families would be more or less permanent. The Commandant had chosen them for a military career. The fate of those who were considered unsuitable to become young officers was to linger on at the Academy far into their twenties.

Most cadets were Pathans, but there were Tajiks from the north and a few strange stolid Nuristanis from the remote eastern valleys up near the Pamirs. The tradition that these big blue-eyed giants were descended from Alexander's soldiers seemed unlikely; their profiles, emphasised by skinned heads, gave them a look of Easter Island statues.

After the Commandant had made his rounds and picked out his recruits, these small boys were taken away from their homes at a time when they had been most cosseted and spoilt. Most of them would only return home as visitors.

Initially army life meant years of misery at the Academy, enduring a harsh regime with wretched living conditions. Much of the daily routine was taken up with fatigues and square-bashing to bagpipes. The education syllabus had nothing to recommend it.

The first bugle call of the day would announce eight hours of routine as the NCOs stationed themselves outside every hut armed with sticks. Stragglers who did not obey the bugle quick enough were whipped ferociously. Then came the monotonous hours marked out by the bugle's clarion of being herded into class rooms or lined up to march outside.

The cadets had one day off, the Moslem Friday when, dressed in special uniforms, a light grey decorated with pale blue stripes, they were allowed to go into Kabul and wander about. Most of them had little or no money; their families were far away. I would come across them in the city and they would always give me the same exaggerated grinning salute. The older boys, or rather men, looked particularly wretched and sad. With few good roads communications were primitive and letters from many places were delivered by runner. Some of them had not heard from their families for years.

On one day in early summer I climbed up the Sher Dawaza hill which had traces of the old battlemented walls and found four cadets sitting on the summit gazing towards the distant mountain-tops to the north. In the clear bright light they could see lines of orchards and fields running towards mountains lapping the horizon which appeared as rippling khaki folds. Below us was the city with its mud-brick walls, its mosques and hidden alleyways, and the river which we could see reduced to a thin brown trickle in the heat.

> Kabul town's a blasted place –
> Blow the bugle, draw the sword . . .

I handed round cigarettes, one of the Russian brands with long filters that were sold everywhere in the bazaars. I knew they had no money and that smoking was forbidden at the college. They grinned with pleasure as they sat in the sun puffing away contentedly.

'Where do you come from?' I asked the oldest, who was well into his twenties. He made a great sweeping gesture northward towards the khaki mountains. They might have been the mountains of the moon.

I wonder how many of my students have survived the next tumultuous thirty years.

One morning, about a month after I had begun teaching, a man darted out from behind a grove of poplars as I walked to my class. Middle-aged, he wore a tight-fitting blue suit patched at the elbows and a black karakul hat pulled down over his head.

'Good morning my sir . . . good morning.' He opened his mouth, showing uneven yellow fangs. 'You are my teacher.' The teeth and the long face made him look like a wolf. From a briefcase he produced a printed form for my inspection which was signed by the Commandant. Apparently he was ordered to accompany me to all my classes.

From that day the Wolf never left my side. His role was never satisfactorily explained. Was he spy or inspector? Was my incompetence so glaring that he had been detailed to write a report? What made me uneasy was that neither Warren nor any of the Turks had been assigned a similar minder. Perhaps he thought it would be easier to learn English from someone like myself. For his passionate desire, he kept telling me, was to learn the English language, and there was nothing in the world that he would rather be doing than listening to the golden trickle of words that fell from my lips.

Was he in love with me? I was reasonably young and a lot better-looking than Warren. All around the compound people were falling in love. Cadets walked hand in hand, exchanging traditional greetings with sighs, fluttering eyes and exaggerated protestations and simpers like Victorian maidens. The smallest Pathan boys with the biggest black eyes flirted shamelessly; it was like my old school.

If I spent too long talking to a student, the Wolf would complain. If I dropped a piece of chalk he would rush to retrieve it. Everywhere I went, he went too; he accompanied me into the teachers' room and sat there grinning. In the briefcase which he carried tucked up under his arm was my teaching schedule for the day. Whenever we arrived in a classroom he would bring it out and consult it.

'Lesson One. Milton, my teacher.' He would smile disarmingly. Later he would recite in a slow ponderous deep voice. 'The BRUTE and BOISTEROUS FORCE of VIOLENT men.' Each syllable was pronounced with slow clear emphasis; at the end of each line he had a habit of blowing his nose violently and squeezing the tip between two fingers – no handkerchief.

In each class he would stand behind me as I read. Everything I said was taken down in shorthand in his grubby notebook. Questions would be asked.

'Who is Delilah, my teacher?'

'She is a bad girl.'

The mildest joke could be a risky business. If a titter arose from the class – a nervous titter, since women were never supposed to be spoken about directly – the laughter would vanish rapidly as a spasm of rage would contort his features. To be insolent to a darling foreign teacher was bad; to laugh in class while the Wolf was present was worse.

It was hard to associate my meek and overpolite minder with the maniac who rushed up and down the rows of desks savagely twisting ears and rapping hands with a ruler. When he returned to my side smiling sheepishly, the only evidence of the storm that had just raged through the classroom was the spectacle of the victims rubbing their wounds.

I had no need for him to display his frenzied authority. The rumour that had arisen back home in Dublin that I could have any student who disobeyed me taken out and shot was not true. But army discipline, an austere regime, tradition, and the fact that so many of the cadets were subdued by ill health ensured that I had little trouble keeping order. Moreover Warren and I were foreigners, Europeans from the west, which automatically placed us above any Afghan officers – apart from the Commandant – or any Turks.

Although I resented the Wolf's continual presence, his nannying and his terrifying bouts of temper, I found his usefulness outweighed his nuisance value. Since he was a man of some importance, however indeterminate his rank or position, and had the ear of the Commandant, we were always treated with particular deference. In time my Farsi had improved, but there was so much that I still did not understand which he would translate. He tried to make himself useful in every way. If a student was reading an extract from the abominable compilation and came to a missing page, he would find one from the book of another cadet. Sometimes at his request I would retell a story and he would translate, slowly spitting out the words.

Perhaps sometime in their lives it would be useful for these young men to know that Samson was very strong, but Delilah cut off his hair when he was asleep and that made him weak, so that his enemies, the Philistines caught him and put out his eyes.

'And then, my teacher?'

And seventy cadets sitting in front of me would learn

how Samson broke the pillars of the temple and killed his enemies.

I began to wonder if someone had chosen these particular texts because the Pathan code of Pushtunwali had something in common with Old Testament laws. With its emphasis on an eye for an eye, and death to enemies, adulterers and many other people, it was a harsh code for harsh people whose lives were harsh.

Those who follow the laws of Pushtunwali, grimmer than the Ten Commandments, must:

Avenge blood.

Fight to the death for a person who has taken refuge with them.

Fight to the death for any property entrusted to them.

Provide for the safety and property of guests – to the death.

Refrain from killing a woman, a Hindu, a minstrel or a boy not yet circumcised.

Pardon an offence on the intercession of a woman of the offender's lineage, or a holy man. But the offence must not be murder.

Spare a man who seeks sanctuary with a mosque or shrine of a holy man – so long as he stays within its precincts.

Spare a man in battle who begs for his life.

Kill adulterers.

A coward killed running away from battle will be barred from Paradise and will wander for ever a wretched ghost.

The Army of the Indus struggling in the Afghan snows in 1841 perished as a result of Pushtunwali. Recently the Russians also discovered the sterner aspects of a code that makes vengeance a divine law which asserts that death is the only suitable punishment for enemies.

The first division of the eleventh grade consisted of children who had been specially recruited from Paktunistan in the mountains to the east. At the college learning Pushtu was compulsory for everyone except Warren and me. The Paktunistan question, where Afghanistan claimed large areas of the territory known in the days of the Raj as the north-west frontier, was at its height in 1952. 'Afghanistan Unjast; Paktunistan Unjast!' was heard on all sides.

The issue of Paktunistan was a frontier argument which began in 1893 when the British sent a mission headed by Sir Mortimer Durand, the Indian Foreign Secretary, to do what it could to create a buffer zone in a troublesome warlike area. The result was the Durand Line, an example of imperial map-drawing with a blithe disregard for ethnic considerations which has plagued the world since empires decayed.

This particular artificial political boundary sliced through the Pathan area, giving half to Afghanistan and half to British India. The Amir Abdur Rahman considered that he was coerced to accept the frontier in 1919 when the Treaty of Rawalpindi reaffirmed it. With the emergence of Pakistan the question of territory became strident, since the Pakistan government had no intention of changing what the old servants of the Empire had devised.

Just before my arrival the issue had shuddered towards war. Pakistan had tried to push roads through territory claimed as 'Paktunistan', a Pakistani aircraft bombed an Afghan village, while the Afghans convened a Jirgah and gave support to Paktunistan irregulars. In 1951 an Afghan exile was reputed to have assassinated Pakistan's prime minister, Liaqat Ali Khan.

Surprisingly, considering the warlike nature of the parties involved, the issue did not give rise to wholesale bloodshed. Instead the weapon continued to be propaganda and nuisance. The propaganda war was strident, even though the rest of the world had lost interest in this little feud. The Afghan government might shout for the creation of an independent state called Paktunistan, the land of the Pathans, lying on both sides of the frontier. But Pakistan could win the trade war.

When I came to Kabul this was being waged furiously. After 1947 the Pakistanis subjected Afghan imports to endless delays, limited the number of railway cars transporting goods north from Karachi, and refused the Afghans permission to re-export goods. My own little difficulties with the Pakistan Customs arose because my destination was Kabul.

In vain did Afghanistan cast the only negative vote when Pakistan applied for membership of the United Nations in September 1947. In vain did the Kabul government supply the Pathans with weapons for the armed struggle. Pakistan held the key to Afghan prosperity, and in 1950 cut off all supplies of petrol to Afghanistan.

In due course, frustrated by Western indifference, increasing United States aid to Pakistan and the Paktunistan stalemate, the Afghans turned to the Soviet Union for support. The alliance with the old enemy began in July 1950 when Afghanistan and the USSR signed a four-year agreement during which Soviet petrol, cotton, cloth and sugar were exchanged for Afghan wool and raw cotton. The Soviets offered a much higher exchange rate than any capitalist country, and the Afghan dependence on the Soviet Union had begun.

At the Military Academy every classroom had its bright green map showing the putative area of Paktunistan which included a considerable chunk of west Pakistan. And all the boys recruited from the Afghan side were adored by everyone from the Commandant down. They were handsome little fellows and would be watched rapturously as between classes they marched around the main square in their oversized army coats gravely saluting everyone in sight. Other cadets, not so pretty, endured lives that were made a misery for them. But these little Pathans were heroes (until they reached puberty).

The Wolf was in ecstasy over them; nothing was too good for them. Not for him the opinion of the great seventeenth-century poet Khushhal Khan: 'No good qualities are there in the Pathans that are now living; all that were of any worth are imprisoned in the grave.' When he brought out from his bag a gift of sweets, he would tremble and smirk as each wide-eyed child came forward and dipped his hand in the bag.

He was a lot less loving when I lectured the left-overs from previous years, the boys who had grown ugly, great hulking youths who had not succeeded in graduating into the army. Education had passed them by, and it was impossible to get even the simplest ideas into their heads. There was a dreamy look in their eyes as they gazed across the classroom into the square and brooded on their families and villages far away from the chalk dust, bugles and weary tramp of marching.

Nothing I could do would shake them from their inertia as they sat for hours in their ill-fitting clothes staring straight ahead.

'They are no good, my teacher.' The Wolf was quite ready to

declare himself defeated by these rows of stone heads. Textbooks remained unopened as they waited for the slow hour to pass and the welcome sound of the bugle.

At the end of every morning's grind the Wolf would escort me through the ranks of cadets to the military bus. There we would make a formal farewell, behaving like mandarins, bowing slightly to each other as we clasped hands.

6

I HAD been in Kabul a month. One morning after the usual breakfast consisting of stale nan or unleavened bread, and the soup they called shorwa made from ghee, sour milk and anything that came to hand, the manager of the hotel called me into his office. Hand on his breast, apologising from the bottom of his heart for any inconvenience this might cause me, and quickly offering me tea and a cigarette, he came round to the problem that was worrying him.

'Paisa.'

I guessed as much. Since arriving at the hotel I had paid nothing. He held up a dirty piece of paper stamped with the seal of the Hotel de Kabul, full of scribbles indicating the cost of my room, the food I had tried to eat, a service charge, etcetera. He declared that his nation was hospitable, and so far as he was concerned, dear friend, I could stay for ever. It was never a question of throwing me out . . .

The cloud of politeness that baffled foreigners had for once been dispelled by a hint that went beyond the customary diplomacy. As the days went by and the hotel began to starve me out, I noticed how my daily plate of pilau contained less and less meat or chicken. In due course I got nothing to eat at all, and the boy who waited at the tables indifferently refused my requests.

'Halas,' he would say. Finished.

'Don't worry, old boy,' Joe reassured me as he shared one of his precious tins. 'They often do this.'

Since my arrival I had received no salary. Every time Warren and I mentioned the question of money someone had shrugged.

Things were far worse for Warren who had a family to support. He had taken a house and also employed a cook. He had to buy things like powdered milk, tins of Quaker Oats, pistachio nuts and jars of yoghurt. There were all the numerous hidden expenses in setting up a household. To save money his wife had taken to wearing a chadri on her shopping expeditions and pretending to be an ordinary Afghan housewife. She may have gained some bargains in the market, but she was pinched black and blue. Warren became haggard with worry.

The fact that we were fellow countrymen and that we were destitute strengthened our resolve to strike. The day came when, after finishing classes, we decided to take action.

'Either we get our salaries now, or we don't teach.'

We marched to the Director's room followed by the Wolf and an agitated retinue of officers. As we reached the door which was guarded by two sentries, the Wolf became hysterical.

'Please my teacher – please my teachers – it is better not to go inside!'

One of the sentries lifted up an enormous hand to stop us. The Wolf blew his nose and cried out, 'The Director is not in!' But we pushed past. Behind the desk decorated with a cannon ball and a lean-back photograph of the King, the familiar pock-marked face looked very startled at this lèse-majesté. He hastily shouted at one of the soldiers at the door to bring tea.

'We don't want tea.'

The Wolf slithered in. 'He say everything will be all right. He say please return to your class.'

We continued to put our case in broken Farsi and mime. Had we gone too far? We knew very well that no one else on the staff would have dared to behave in this way. And we appeared to have achieved nothing. We retreated, the Director glaring at us, the Wolf looking afraid, and nothing settled.

In the teachers' room the Turks greeted our action with their usual mistrust. They would not tell us whether or not they had received their salaries, but we assumed they had, since they seemed so untroubled. But strike action was a western notion, outside their experience or that of our employers.

We went back to Kabul where for three days we languished in a state of acute anxiety. At the hotel the manager refused all my pleas to extend credit. At such a moment the warm comradeship of the other guests was very welcome.

'Please take from my plate.'

'Can't let you starve, old fellow.'

'There's plenty of food here.'

I was given boiled eggs and tinned Spam by Joe and Mr O'Hoy, the Japanese offered me sweetened rice, while the Italian Colonel smuggled pocketsful of nan out of the dining room. Unlike Warren and his family, who were on the verge of starvation, I was never hungry. But I could not buy a packet of cigarettes.

On the fourth day of our strike, as I returned to the hotel – having spent the day wandering around the city far from the manager's eye – I found a note at the desk. It was a message from the Director to say that our money had arrived.

In the morning we took the bus together with the Afghan teachers and the Turks. We were driven along the familiar road to the Academy where the bagpipe band, the marching squads, the Wolf and various officers were waiting for us under the poplar trees. As we descended at the front, the Afghans as usual getting off at the back, someone blew a whistle and we were joined by a soldier carrying a bulging leather satchel. From all sides of the square men and boys came running over to watch. After a while almost the entire personnel of the Academy looked on murmuring as dirty Afghan notes were counted out one by one into our hands.

'You are happy, my teacher?' The Wolf grinned as I stuffed them into my pockets with difficulty. 'It is very much money.'

Our salary, which worked out at about seven hundred pounds sterling a year, was colossal. A colonel or even a general received far less; the few civilian teachers here had to supplement their incomes by taking on extra work. We knew the Turks, even with their inducements, earned less than us. After the bag had been emptied, the audience lingered to watch us signing a form declaring that we had been paid, and the soldier saluted and walked off, we never went on strike again.

In the dining room of the Hotel de Kabul where Nadir Shah, wearing his astrakhan busby and his jewelled sword, looked down from peeling walls, my own table took on the look of the others with its group of tins and sauce bottles to relieve the tedium of pilaus. The cook house stood at a distance, far enough away to ensure that the food would be cold by the time it was carried across the little yard. In the heady days of the nineteen-thirties when the hotel opened, a German chef had been employed. Nowadays his place was taken by a general cook, a two-dish man (chicken or mutton) who was to be seen wearing baggy trousers and shirt and crouched over a mud stove fanning charcoal embers. His small kitchen was lined with rusty pots and pans which were washed out by a boy whose days were spent among scattered piles of sheep's offal and chicken heads. Now and again the protest of a chicken being killed could be heard.

After the first night I quit the terrible room I had been first assigned, which was usually reserved for three unfortunate Indian aircrew when they arrived in town during their occasional flights up to the capital. I was given a room on the first floor overlooking a main street where the usual barrage of street noise was reinforced by the uproar from loudspeakers sited outside the cinema. Those who could not afford the price of a ticket could listen for free to wails from Indian melodramas, deep-pitched Russian choruses and hoofbeats and bursts of gunfire from American westerns.

In our bedrooms along the upstairs corridor the residents banded together, sharing national meals cooked on little paraffin stoves. These get-togethers formed an essential part of our daily routine. If the Japanese tinned fish and beanstalks proved unappetising one evening, there was the prospect of a kebab or a pasta next time.

'What is your national dish?'

I served them an Irish stew with tinned American potatoes, carrots and peas.

'May I make a suggestion, old chap?' Joe said. 'Next time check the meat. Shake out the maggots.'

Sometimes we were joined by some outsider who was visiting Kabul, like the Indian doctor, a specialist in VD, whose delicious curries could be sniffed all down the corridor. After him came a small piece of international social history – the arrival of the first hippies. I saw the bearded Englishman and his wife – girlfriends were less common in those days – standing outside the hotel beside their motorbike and sidecar, surrounded by a gawking crowd. The journey from London had been gruelling, endless breakdowns, a precious camera stolen, a near-rape in Turkey. They continued eastwards on their journey, and two years later I met them again in a back street in Delhi wearing the same clothes, standing beside the same lopsided vehicle, stared at by a different mob. Subsequently, because the hippy trail was uncrowded in those days, I learned they reached Singapore and there she left him.

Another arrival at the hotel was an elderly Afghan who boasted of being over ninety. He had a long bushy white beard, carried a gold-topped walking stick, and his fingers glittered with jewels. When he was young at the turn of the century he emigrated to western Australia to work as a camel drover among the new gold mines. This was his first time back home. News of his arrival swept around Kabul. Not only was he a millionaire who at an advanced age kept up a thriving practise in homoeopathic medicine (the camels had long gone wild), but he had recently married a white girl in her twenties.

'It's like this, mate,' he told me, nodding his head significantly. 'A man of my age needs some bloody relaxation after years of work. Am I right?' They held a levee in the hotel's large drawing room where all the sofas and chairs were pushed against the wall in the Afghan way. Any conversation had to move longitudinally from mouth to mouth. Surely most of it was about the star attraction, sitting demurely beside her patriarch wearing dark glasses, gloves and a piece of white cloth wrapped round her head.

'This sheila comes along to see my town. We have a big bloody good house in Adelaide to return to . . . too bloody right . . .'

I explored Kabul in the evenings, the best time, wandering through the catwalks that made up the different bazaars, absorbing the old-fashioned and unpretentious atmosphere of a place that had not yet come to terms with the twentieth century. The entry into the modern world was proceeding slowly, and for the first time the citizens were learning at first hand about trucks, buses, electricity, radios and even whiskey. It was still a place which retained ancient Moslem custom and values. Its previous experience of the outside world had come from the English who twice burnt down the great bazaar. But the English occupations were only tremors in Kabul's long turbulent history and the Soviets were yet to come.

I remembered Robert Byron's comparison of Kabul to 'a Balkan town in the good sense of the term' as I wandered among the shadowy bazaars, past all the shop booths and chaikhanas. A medley of people pushed past, squint-eyed workers from Hazaristan, descendants of Ghengiz Khan's pillaging armies, nomadic Kuchi women who did not wear chadris, Uzbegs from the north, and every assortment of quarrelsome Pathan carrying guns and roses, walking about in twos hand in hand. All their burnt brown faces contrasted with their glittering unreliable smiles. The picturesque unshaven people wearing embroidery and brocade and leather and sheepskin and huge white turbans went about unhurriedly. And everywhere were soft moving cotton sacks rippling past, madonna blue, ox blood, fawn or aubergine.

Louis Dupree, the eminent authority on Afghanistan, wrote on the chadri's two functions: 'It put all women in public on an equal basis (a plain rayon chadri would cover the most expensive clothing) and it kept women (i.e. personal property) from being coveted by other men. However, some chadris were made in the richest silks, and also used for clandestine assignations, thus defeating the original purpose . . . ' Since then the chadri has developed a further function and women are bundled up as an assertion of religious and national allegiance like wearing a flag.

But like many others I found that the mystery of the pleated chadri simply set a man's heart racing. Their delicate anonymity suggested certain headless Greek statues – were they perhaps another legacy of Alexander? Here was the Victory of Samothrace bustling along, alive and faceless, femininity suggested by movement within the tented framework, an angle made by an elbow, a little hand appearing holding a basket, a little foot in serviceable shoes, and the voluptuous curve of a bottom which needed a crinoline to conceal it. They greeted, gossiped, quarrelled and bargained through the grille in front of their faces.

Everything was a bargain, a piece of silk, a sequinned hat; vegetables and fruit in piles in the road; nan from a tray carried on a boy's head; money from a money changer. Everything must be negotiated with signals, the shake of a head, an upraised finger, and if you could show your face, a scowl or a crafty smile. The bargain would be eased along with the glass of tea. Everyone was polite, politeness was a national obsession. They would kill you with good manners. Bearded old men were polite, so were the ragged boys greeting each other formally. The beggars holding up their bowls had none of the hysteria of Indian beggars; they made a formal and courteous request for alms.

Along the catwalks one lane sold embroidered hats and shoes ranging from tough leather chaplis with soles made from rubber tyres to delicate traditional slippers covered with leopard skin. Around the corner were the new foreign goods, many smuggled in from Pakistan on the backs of horses and mules following the same route used more than thirty years later for machine guns and Stingers. The transistor had not yet taken over the world.

Each bazaar had its own speciality and items such as Russian broadcloth, American army uniforms, ancient Greek coins, or Japanese pressure cookers were roughly divided into animal, vegetable or mineral, to be found in the cloth markets, the metal bazaars of the little shops whose proprietors were hidden behind pyramids of tins, a great many of which had been purloined from the American Embassy.

There was a smell everywhere compounded of excrement decomposing piles of fruit and vegetables, and wafts from the fetid *jueys*. Children ran about with baskets collecting dung and droppings to be used later for fuel or fertiliser. A public letter-writer would be squatting in the dusty street laboriously writing down something for a wrapped-up woman, a boy would be selling sherbet kept cool with blocks of dirty ice, a funeral procession would pass, the corpse wrapped in a sheet. Once or twice a week a line of braying donkeys loaded down with panniers of rock salt would charge through the crowd trying to escape the wild beatings of their driver, usually a wizened Hazara. *Burro! Burro!*

One day I was walking in the city to discover that children were on display. On Children's Day shopkeepers paraded their children in front of their shops or stalls or windows. A small boy's face would be peeping out from under an enormous turban of Bokhara silk, his eyes made huge with kohl; another would be wearing an intricately stitched waistcoat blazing with sequins and patterns of gold thread. And girls would also be on show, rows of immobile little girls with braided hair wearing jewellery, scarves and bright silk dresses squatting like Bhuddhas above the noisy streets. Their faces were powdered white round their big dark eyes, their podgy hands were tattooed or painted with henna, and perhaps a gold zarnik or dot would be placed on their forehead. For the time being, perhaps for the last time, they were the object of universal admiration and attention before they were bundled away.

In the hotel the summer dust rose in every room and corridor in golden clouds and settled on sofas and chairs, on hair and clothes; sheets, glasses and plates were covered in it; it crunched underfoot. The residents escaped as much as they could. One favourite way of getting out was to organise an evening's tonga-racing round the river. The course, which took about twenty minutes to circumnavigate, had become a tradition – down from the hotel, across the bridge, and back past the Russian Embassy. The winner got a prize of sequestered whiskey, or, if times were hard, a bottle of Murree beer. Unlike the diplomats in their embassies we considered any sort of alcohol to be an unexpected luxury.

Choosing a particular tonga from the hundreds that roamed the streets took expertise comparable to selecting a National Hunt winner. The majority of pitifully thin ponies could safely be ignored. But there were about a dozen which for an inexplicable reason were sleek and well fed. We each had our favourite. The start from the hotel was always chaotic as half a dozen tongas would be lined up on the road, the drivers flicking their whips, the residents crouched behind, holding on. We would go off through the cool evening, the wind in our faces, the drivers shouting and stamping on their bells as the ponies galloped past the carpet shops and the carpets hanging down over the river wall. At the far bridge there was a sharp turn, and our chariots, if they were racing two abreast, would threaten to collide. There were accidents; my tonga lost a wheel. Once Joe Aslam fell into a *juey* and had to be fished out. The Japanese tonga ran over a chicken and Mr O'Hoy had to be rescued from a crowd of angry women.

On Fridays we sometimes indulged in a favourite Kabuli pastime and went on a picnic. A few miles outside the city was the tomb of Babur, the first of the great sextet of Mogul Emperors. He had adored Kabul: 'The climate is extremely delightful, and there is no such place in the known world.' He was fastidious and scholarly, and had an interest in nature; according to records he identified sixteen different kinds of wild tulip flowering in spring around Kabul. He deserved his memorial, this pavilion

in a garden erected in 1640 by his grandson, Shah Jehan, now
a place for all to enjoy with its great plane trees, view of the river
and hills covered with roses and meadows filled with the same
sort of flowers that the Emperor had recorded. It was pleasant
on a hot afternoon to linger among the trees watching passerby,
a man riding a horse like a figure from a miniature, a procession
of women walking down to the river balancing jars on their
heads, a shepherd with his flock, a boy singing to himself.

General Roberts from Waterford, 'one of the most popular
and greatest men in England', had been an obtrusive visitor
during his occupation when, in between taming the city, he came
out here for recreation. 'On the 6th of December a large picnic
was given by the General near Babur Badshah's tomb . . . to
which all the officers were invited with their knives and forks.
After the picnic there was a paper chase, which finished up near
the ground over which our cavalry was to charge so desperately
a few days afterwards.' They knew what to expect after the chase,
which was remarkable for the number of falls owing to the
difficult nature of the ditches, the banks of which were lined with
willows and poplars, just as I saw them, whose branches whisked
off several paper-chasing riders on the route which the serious
cavalry charge would soon take.

There were casualties during the charge. Afterwards Roberts'
acting Political Secretary, Sir Henry Mortimer Durand, another
rum Empire-builder ultimately responsible for the Paktunistan
problem, wrote a poem:

> Aye, we have found him, the fair young face,
> Turned to the pitiless Afghan skies,
> The frost bound earth for a resting place,
> Dead – with the horror of death in his eyes.
>
> Lying alone there, out on the plain
> Where the desperate charge of our horsemen broke;
> Foremost fighting and foremost slain,
> Gashed by many a murderous stroke . . . etc.

Another picnic destination outside the city was King Amanullah's half-completed palace and parliament buildings at Darul
Aman which still looked the way they did when they affronted

the fastidious Robert Byron: '. . . and then, at the end, O God, appears the turreted angle – not even the front – of a French Municipal office, surrounded by a French Municipal garden and entirely deserted. While below it, occupying the very centre of the whole four-mile-vista stands a match factory in the ferro-concrete farmhouse style . . .' and so forth.

In the nineteen-fifties the buildings had remained untouched after thirty years. The large palace was unfinished, and the windows had no glass. Scattered around the main hall were unopened packing cases filled with miscellaneous equipment that had come from Europe during the great tour that had brought about Amanullah's ruin.

Amanullah's touching enthusiasm for reform arose from his famous journey outside his austere landlocked primitive country in 1928. To the cheers of the world he underwent certain common experiences with which he had been totally unfamiliar. He travelled in trains, embarked on ships (where he enthusiastically took up deck tennis and quoits) and walked on asphalt pavements in crowded industrial cities. The contrast between the circumscribed life in his Kabul palaces and his novel process abroad was exhilarating. Most gratifying was the impressive welcome that he received in England.

After visiting Italy, where he met Mussolini, and France, he arrived in England for a state visit at the end of March 1928. For weeks English newspapers had been praising his achievements and aspirations, lauding his desire to see western civilisation at first hand. *The Times* compared him to Peter the Great.

The state visit began with a drive through London in an open carriage with King George; now and again snowflakes fell on the stout soldierly figure in his grey-green cloak, dark khaki uniform and red shako. Crowds cheered him, and also his queen, the lovely Soraya, the first oriental queen to accompany a consort on an official tour abroad.

Amanullah not only endured, he enjoyed the ceaseless entertainment. At no point did he find the programme tedious. Eager for information and novelty, he attended the Boat Race and the Grand National, visited Windsor Castle, went down a coalmine, toured air force establishments and watched tanks performing military manoeuvres. ('They would be no good in my country.')

At Portsmouth he examined the *Victory* and asked detailed

questions about the working of the ancient cannon; subsequently
he boarded a submarine flying the Afghan colours and was taken
for a tour of Portsmouth harbour. When it submerged he fired
two torpedoes at a practice ship and dispatched a telegram to
his wife over the radio: 'I send you my best wishes from below
water.'

With unabated enthusiasm he inspected a small arms factory
in Birmingham, motor works in Coventry, railway yards in
Swindon, and took an unregal joyride in an aeroplane over
London. At Oxford he received an honorary degree and the
Vice-Chancellor described him and Queen Soraya as '*sol alter et
luna altera.*' Before he left Claridges where they had been staying,
the king indulged in his hobby and entertained the staff to a
display of conjuring tricks.

With the praises of Europe ringing in his ears, he made his
way home via Moscow and, fatally, Turkey. Ataturk was in the
midst of his shakeup. He had abolished the Caliphate, brought
the power of religious leaders under control, replaced the spidery
Arabic script with a Latin alphabet and urged on Turkish women
in the drive towards emancipation.

One reform struck Amanullah in particular. In Turkey not
only was the wearing of the fez prohibited, but a revolution in
dress was under way. In 1925 Ataturk had declared to his people:
'A civilised international dress is worthy and appropriate for our
nation, and we will wear it, boots or shoes on our feet, trousers
on our legs, shirt and tie, jacket and waistcoat, and, of course
to complete these, a cover with a brim on our heads. I want to
make this clear. The head covering is called "hat".' The Turks
listened and donned shabby western clothes.

Impressed by Ataturk's success, and also during a final visit to
Iran, by Reza Shah's similar efforts with his people, Amanullah
arrived back in Afghanistan determined to bring in a programme
of modernisation. But fatally he lacked what Lord Kinross saw
in Ataturk as 'an uncanny sense of the psychological moment'.

A month after his return, during the celebrations of Afghan
independence, in addition to the usual parades he introduced a
series of innovations. Films were shown publicly in Kabul and
the first theatrical performance took place. The European cast
was terrified by the disapproving and threatening audience, but
nevertheless, in good theatrical tradition, persisted in putting on

their music hall bill which included a female contortionist.

At the same time the Loya Jirgah, consisting of one thousand tribal and religious leaders, assembled to be addressed by the king. In the gardens of Paghman near the plaster Arc de Triomphe a corner was fenced off with barbed wire and fitted with wooden seats. Here the delegates assembled after they had removed their beards. Most of them had been shaved by soldiers, in many cases roughly and forcibly so that inches of stubble remained on their cheeks. They wore European clothes that had been run up hastily in the bazaars. Photographs exist of these proud unhappy leaders of the Ghilzai, Manghal, Afridi and other warrior tribes, shorn of their robes and turbans, and sitting in lines wearing long black coats, black ties, boots and, on their heads, soft homburg hats.

There was further outrage on the subject of clothes when it came to the Queen's behaviour. Conservative Afghans had been enraged by her conduct abroad. She had gone unveiled; her close fitting cloche hats had not concealed her face to foreign eyes. She had also worn European dress. Not only had she behaved shamelessly in Europe, but now, amid a crescendo of criticism, declared her independence in her own country. A few months after her return from abroad she attended a government reception where, amid nervous applause, she dramatically tore off her veil.

Amanullah lacked the backing of an army, and unlike Ataturk, he had no reputation of being a military man. 'If only he had waited for two years and built up his army as Ataturk advised, what might he have not done?' his Turkish adviser, Mahmud Tarzi lamented as the opposition of his furious subjects ousted their reforming ruler. The King fled to Kandahar in his Rolls-Royce (given to him by King George) before the advancing army of the brigand, Bacha Saqqao, the water carrier. Behind him the frozen streets of the shattered city were filled with pyres of burning European clothes. Reform in Afghanistan was set back indefinitely.

In the empty windowless rooms of his palace I found the bathroom tiled with precious lapis lazuli from Badakshan and thought of the young Amanullah lying in the soapsuds planning his strategy of innovation. But no, that could not be right, for the rubble-filled bath still waited for taps to be fitted.

Kabulis boasted that you could find more than a hundred

different kinds of grape around the city. But not one was turned into wine. Hash was acceptable, alcohol never. For the half-dozen foreigners who were not attached to any Embassy this created a serious problem. In the Hotel we regularly tried to swallow down the latest homebrew distilled from grapes or apples bought in the bazaar. Then the manager would complain that the apparatus of pipes, valves and clips hanging above the one hotel bath would have to be dismantled. A few weeks later we would start again with a new batch of pipes.

There were two ways of getting a drink. You could be invited to an Embassy, or you could buy one at the French club. For obscure motives, whether altruistic or cultural, this establishment opened its doors every Friday evening. It was situated down a leafy lane in the new fashionable suburb of Shahri Naw. A policeman was stationed outside to prevent Afghans from slipping into the forbidden garden. Sometimes, in spite of vigilance, someone would succeed in getting past, and once he was safely inside the front door he would be handed a glass of wine at once. It would be hard to exaggerate the pleasure the poor wretch showed as he gulped it down.

Even though they had stacks of alcohol back at their embassies, diplomats came regularly to the French club, no doubt to relieve the boredom of routine. But it was the tongas of the hotel residents the French lived in dread of. At the sight and sound of us the trays of drink would have a habit of vanishing. Sometimes one or other of us would succeed in sneaking off with a bottle.

Apart from the drink, the entertainment ranged from classical music to dancing, both provided by the wind-up gramophone. The dancing was a mixed pleasure; there were always far too many men.

'I'll take the dark one, old fellow,' Joe would say. 'Your turn for Martha.'

Martha was the secretary from the American Embassy who smelt of camomile, herbs and disinfectant. We stumbled around the small overcrowded room to Victor Sylvester and Charlie Kuntz until at last Martha departed with the rest of the embassy crowd. The stalwarts from the hotel would remain until the drinks cupboard was finally locked. Usually we had done well; the Italian colonel would have collapsed behind one of the tables and would be snoring, Joe would look like a corpse, I would be staggering and Mr O'Hoy would be bowing to his reflection in one of the Club's mirrors.

Finding our way back to the hotel was always a struggle. If we were lucky there might be a tonga waiting at the little crossroads of Shahri Naw. If not, we tottered back through the empty streets. The hotel would be closed and the lights would be out. Hours would pass before our knocking, accompanied by the midnight chorus of piedogs, would wake the porter. There would be a rattle of keys and we would be greeted with the usual smells of urine and dust. Upstairs, looking out of my window, I would find the world quiet; even the noise from the cinema had ceased. The stars sparkled very brightly above the unlit city.

Abdul Karim, one of the civilian teachers at the Military Academy, was a small neat man who always wore a mackintosh over his blue striped suit and bowed every time we shook hands. His obsession was to visit America and England. 'Tell me about London!' he would cry with the passion of the man who has never been abroad. He had never heard of Ireland.

As a frustrated traveller he understood my desire to see more of Afghanistan than the confines of the capital. There was a public holiday and time to get away. 'What about a trip to the Panjshir?'

The Panjshir valley was about fifty miles from Kabul, and the only way of getting there was by lorry, the country's sole means of general communication taking goods and passengers wherever there was a road. Since there was no set price, every journey had to be bargained for.

Carrying the briefcase containing his pyjamas, Abdul Karim strode through the confusion of vehicles, shouting men and donkeys, and piles of abandoned luggage quickly gathering dust in search of a lorry bound for the Panjshir.

'The driver tells me one hundred afghanis, but I laugh at him and offer sixty.'

'That sounds reasonable.'

'When they see you are foreigner they charge much more. It is cheapest to be woman. You see those' – he indicated the shrouded figures at the back shrieking at each other as they adjusted the draped sheet that would conceal them from men's eyes – 'they only pay thirty.'

He had negotiated for the two most expensive seats in the driver's cab. Elsewhere every spare piece of room was taken up, including the cab-top above us where three tribesmen squatted; others were crowded behind a mound of luggage. And then there were the ladies behind their sheet and some sheep thrown in by a laughing Hazara workman in a greasy posteen. Hung over the back wheels the bacha or driver's boy clung on, waiting to begin his duties which would start with collecting fares – later there might be a wheel to change or lives to save by jumping down and pushing a special wooden wedge behind a wheel when the lorry hesitated or stopped on a mountain slope.

Mountains were depicted all over the lorry's cab which was elaborately decorated with pictures of snow-capped peaks and views of lakes, rushing rivers, waterfalls and bright pink blossoming orchards all under solid fleecy clouds, some with a little curl in them like those in Persian miniatures. The tastes of this particularly fierce-looking driver were tranquil, and soothing in comparison to other restless murals in other lorries which might cover every possible available piece of cab space with the thoroughness of tattooing. Subject matter ranged from crossed swords and scimitars, guns, mosques, minarets, hands holding the Afghan flag, plenty of trains and aeroplanes and Rousseauesque bestiaries with smiling lions lurking in jungles, fighting cheetahs and snow leopards and *ovis poli* perched on mountain peaks. The effect was painstaking, jolly and juvenile, like the work of talented small boys.

Idealised mountains and landscapes around me, below the windscreen before me was a nest of red paper roses arranged on a bed of sequinned embroidery. We turned north past the great white British Legation in its walled compound facing Legation Hill. The classically inspired building was built after the Treaty of Rawalpindi in 1919 on a grand scale; like Amanullah's Darul Aman, it was designed to impress. It would finally blot out the savage memories of the old Residency at the Bala Hissar and its sacking when poor Cavagnari and every member of his Embassy were murdered: 'the floors were covered with blood stains, and amidst the embers were found a heap of human bones'. It may be imagined how British soldiers burned at such a sight. So the Bala Hissar was razed for a second time. Years later the Legation was designed to impress, to assert the role of the great neighbouring Empire. Mostly it invited derision; it has been called a mini-Versailles, absurd, pretentious, a caravanserai with a touch of suburban Guildford, Lord Curzon's Easter Egg.

Scarcely had it been built and occupied than it had to be evacuated following Amanullah's flight into exile. In February 1929 all the British residents and foreign communities departed in a spectacular airlift, the first of its kind. The flight of the foreigners from the advance of Bacha Saqqao is a forgotten episode of history which contained some of the elements of the siege of Peking or the siege of Lucknow.

Bacha Saqqao, the water carrier's son, brigand, outlaw and housebreaker (he had spent eleven months in jail for burglary) was a fearsome folk hero. Stories were told of his bravery and cunning; he robbed the rich to help the poor; a mullah prophesied that he would become ruler of Afghanistan. In the winter of 1928, when Amanullah's forces were wavering, he advanced on Kabul with an army of two thousand men, reaching the outskirts of the city on the fourteenth of December.

Standing directly in his path was the gleaming white portico of the British Legation. The self-contained compound with its tennis courts, bungalows and newly planted gardens was not only a bulwark against the tedium of Kabul society, but suddenly a tempting target for the crossfire of rebel and royal guns.

The rebel forces captured the Koh-i-Lula forts that stood between the Legation and the city, and seized their stocks of ammunition. Then they established themselves on the Asmai heights overlooking Kabul and directed their guns at the royalist troops. The smart new Legation was in the way. More than sixty shells and thousands of bullets rained down on the unfortunate Legation staff which huddled behind a barrier of hastily erected sandbags. 'Today even billiards becomes an unhealthy game,' Lady Humphreys, the Ambassador's wife, wrote in her diary for 20 December, 'bullets in the squash court, three in the bedroom, three near my bed, three in our own bathroom, one missing the Minister by six inches.'

It was not the gunfire that disturbed the diplomatic staff so much and alarmed the Europeans rushing to seek shelter within the Legation's commodious confines. It was the memory of old massacres. For once the British were strictly neutral, and both rebel and royalist forces agreed to the evacuation of foreigners – excluding the Soviets, who remained, the foreign minister later claiming that his presence in Kabul prevented slaughter.

Since all roads leading out of Kabul were blocked or cut, the only way out was by air. The war in 1919 had proved that planes could cross the Khyber. In this operation a decade later pilots took off from Peshawar and travelled the hundred and forty miles to Kabul, a four-hour journey over some of the most dangerous flying country in the world.

The planes were mostly Vickers Victoria bombers which had been taken over from the British forces in Iraq. They had to be stripped of all surplus equipment to enable them to gain necessary height, and of all arms to preserve a front of neutrality in a war that did not concern Great Britain. They were flying in winter, and the winter of 1928–29 was particularly severe. Kabul was covered with a deep layer of snow and ice; cold winds brought the temperature down well below freezing, affecting the running of engines. In order to avoid snipers' bullets most members of the foreign community had to be smuggled aboard the planes by night. The first plane that reached Kabul bringing a wireless transmitter to the beleaguered Legation landed with fourteen bullet holes in its fuselage and had to be abandoned.

In the circumstances it was remarkable that this two-month-long airlift was accomplished without the loss of a single life. Between the end of December and 25 February 1929, more than five hundred people were evacuated on a total of eighty-two flights. Women and children were the first to leave, and the last man out was the redoubtable Sir Francis Humphreys. The evacuation of Germans and French together was taken prematurely as evidence of the reconciliation of Europe.

Outside Afghanistan the operation was hailed as an achievement, coming at a time when the potential of air power was beginning to be recognised. The pilots were described as 'knights volant' and were given a civic reception in Delhi by the Viceroy. King George sent the young Royal Air Force a telegram of congratulation.

As I write during another harsh Kabul winter, February 1988, the staff at Curzon's Egg are closing up the Embassy (long promoted from its Legation status). After a final dinner of army rations and champagne they are taking part in another airlift. In 1927 the snow on the airfield had to be tramped down and Lady Humphreys tore up Legation sheets to be used to make signals to the pilots. In 1988 the evacuation had to be halted for days because of heavy snow.

In the summer of 1953 when I journeyed by lorry to the Panjshir I knew little about the place and its lurid reputation (no doubt false) as a palace of luxury and idleness, where the staff did nothing but swim and play tennis. Opposite its walls I noticed a small Kuchi encampment consisting of half a dozen brown tents and herds of grazing animals. A nomad caravan on the move was a common sight, the animals weighted down with tents and equipment, the men striding ahead, the women following in their colourful clothes.

Then we were out of the city, driving among orchards and streams whose banks were lined with willow, and fields of flowers seen through the lorry's dust cloud, no doubt including Babur's tulips. Wherever the eyesight may be directed, says an Afghan poem, all are flowers, flowers in front and flowers behind, flowers on every side. At Gulbahar, where the Panjshir river debouches out of the green mouth of the valley to join the Kabul river north of the Lataband pass, we left the lorry on its way to the north and found a chaikhana full of somnambulant figures.

Outside a group of children, ragged boys wearing shining pillbox hats, small girls wearing red dresses and silver jewellery like chainmail, surrounded an old pedlar who was sitting under a tree with his bear, making it dance for a few Afghanis. He pulled its chain sharply if it tried to sit; one of its legs had a dirty bandage. The foreigner was more of a spectacle. They left the bear and the pedlar and came over to watch me as we sat, mimicking the way I squatted, the way I held the thin porcelain tea-cup, my strange voice. It took time for them to go back to the bear, who was jerked once more onto its hind legs. We continued to sit in the shaded cool porch of the chaikhana before the lines of decorated teapots and the pair of samovars with smoke curling through their tarnished brass funnels.

The word panj means five, and five rivers combined in the floodwater that poured down from the surrounding hills. For a time we sat on a rock listening to the roar of water and watching the changing patterns of light on the small terraced fields divided by stone walls. There were groves of walnut trees whose leaves still had the pale shining green of spring. The orchards were in full bloom and the colours were nearly those of the painted landscapes in the lorry cab that I had been studying for hours. Below the trees a canopy of butterflies hovered over the flowers. The Panjshir valley would offer some of the fiercest resistance to the Soviet occupation, and would be bombed and bombarded for years during the nineteen-eighties.

We followed a track along the river past orchards, where peasants were working away in the sunlight. Later, as the first blue shadows crept down the valley, we stopped at a village above the gorge, a place of high mud walls, secret lanes, sheep and smells of strange cooking. Abdul Karim knocked up one of the houses to negotiate a night's stay in one of the mud towers we had seen against the skyline. A series of rough wooden ladders led onto the roof where we had our dinner brought up by a panting old woman – rice, tiny freshly caught fish like minnows and fermented milk. We were given quilts and braided cushions and smoked cigarettes under the stars. Only a bus ride out of Kabul, and I seemed to be on the brink of the sort of escape that I had dreamed about all my life. Central Asia was just over the mountains. What was there to prevent me carrying on walking, instead of going back to teach at the Military Academy?

A year later Eric Newby and his companion would pass this way en route for a short walk in the Hindu Kush. In the morning I looked down from the tower into the heart of the village and watched the day begin, the picturesque rural routine – a shepherd in his rough woollen cloak, a dog scratching itself, women washing clothes in a roaring white stream, lines of donkeys led out to the fields. Again I rejoiced to be out in the country. Later we followed the river along the track to Ruka, the main town in the lower Panjshir. Before the MiGs and the bombs, the sheltered valley with its fruit trees and gushing rivers, its villages perched on high bluffs, was considered by Afghanis to be a place of particular beauty.

For most of the day we walked towards the mountains which closed off the valley to the north. Ruka was a spreading town of squat mud houses blending easily into the landscape – they seemed less man-made than natural features until we penetrated them and found ourselves in the bazaar where lines of open

booths sold piles of fruit and vegetables. But nothing else to eat
-- in Paradise there was not very much food.

We had not eaten since the night before, and were hungry as
we sat down in a teahouse demanding a meal. A child was
dispatched to find us a hen, but it seemed that nowhere in Ruka
were hens to be found that day. After a good deal of commotion
a little bird was produced which managed to escape. There was
pandemonium within and without the teahouse before a shifty
man with a rusty knife caught its leg and hacked off its head.
Two hours later we ate a few scraps of meat accompanied by
nan and were the best fed people in the Panjshir.

Next day it was time to return, and we trudged back through
the deceptively beautiful valley to a rendezvous with our lorry
and back to the city. After my return the Panjshir chicken had
its revenge and I became sick with well-known symptoms. There
were no lavatories in the military college, and now many times
a morning I was forced to join the people who squatted in lines
under the poplars. Only the staff assembled here; the cadets
defaecated elsewhere.

My arms and legs ached. I had no energy, and my body felt
like molten glass. In class, even with the Wolf beside me, I found
concentration impossible and forgot to read out whole passages
of text. With an aching stomach it was hard to explain the
difference between scribes and Pharisees, Gentiles, Moabites and
the Children of Israel. Rows of shaven heads looked up, nut
brown faces stared as once again I excused myself and ran for
the trees.

The Afghans did not use paper, but brought along jars or
bottles of water. As emancipated modern Muslems the Turks,
whose stomachs appeared to be as weak as my own, carried their
own rolls of paper. Even out here, always squatting – standing
up to urinate was offensively discourteous – the Afghans managed
to be dignified.

'Hub as te! Dhur as te?' No one omitted the polite formula of
greetings. I exchanged courtesies with the white-bearded mullah
balanced on his toes to my left, and more to the Captain on my
right. Large black birds waited and moved in to peck at what
they could find under the trees; groups of piedogs, more timid
in their approach, likewise waited to make their moves. From
my position so near the ground I was close to nature; I watched

a line of ants scurrying past me over the thick white dust – was their mission the same as the piedogs? The two sentries at the gate seemed like Gog and Magog; the sun blazed down. I heard the call of a bugle and around me the staff of the Military College, groaning and cursing, staggered reluctantly to its feet.

Back at the hotel I took to my bed. My body had melted away in a pool of prickly heat, my lips and mouth were parched, and a weight pressed down on my chest. Visitors peered into my room. Mr O'Hoy peeped through the door.

'You sick?'

'Yes.'

'Afghanistan *harab*.' *Harab*, meaning bad, was the one word we all knew.

Joe nursed me, sending away any servant who attempted to bring in something hot.

'He doesn't want any more of your filthy food, you swine. *Harab! Harab!*'

My head ached and my vision was blurred. It was the height of summer, and during the day my bedroom heated up. Even if the one small window was shut the metallic noises, larded with shouts and shrieks from the street and hoofbeats and gunshots from the cinema, seeped through. There was a small cupboard, a single chair, an iron frame bed with jingling springs. The lavatory, at the end of the passage, was dangerously far away and had no light.

I knew I was delirious when I woke one morning to see a middle-aged woman in a linen suit arranging a vase of roses on the cupboard.

'How are you feeling?' The voice was upper-class English.

I gazed at her as she picked up my clothes which were scattered round the room and folded them. My temperature was taken.

'You must stop eating things from that awful kitchen. I have given instructions to my servant to bring you some proper food.'

She changed the sheets on my bed. She induced the sluggish porter who spent the day in a haze of hashish to clean up my room. Then she vanished, leaving faint scents of talcum powder and eau de cologne.

Joe appeared looking awed at the sight of my clean quarters.

'Who was that?' I asked.

'Didn't you recognise her? She's the British Ambassador's wife.'

'Oh. I wonder why she bothered. I'm not even English.'

'I suppose you're a white man, old boy.'

In later years scores and hundreds of tourists, backpackers, hippies and overlanders would lie delirious in rooms like this without a cool, soothing, well-bred hand feeling their foreheads. I lay between clean sheets with the table beside me loaded with bottles of lemon barley water and a tin of shortbread biscuits with a Tartan pattern on the lid. I had a good night's sleep, and next morning the Embassy *hakim* appeared, an elderly Indian doctor with a fussy bedside manner. Once again my temperature was taken, my chest was tapped, my eyes peered into with a torch, and my urine examined for cloudiness. There was nothing wrong with me apart from a dose of KT – Kabul Tummy.

Later her ladyship sent round some cheese biscuits from Fortnum and Mason, a tin of consommé and a promise of further culinary delights. Seldom have I felt such an overpowering sense of gratitude; if she had reappeared I would have kissed her shadow like a soldier at Scutari.

7

PERHAPS KT is fiercer than its equivalent in Delhi, Egypt and elsewhere. One consequence of my week in bed was a permanent revulsion to the squalor and camaraderie of the Hotel de Kabul. I suddenly found it strange that so many residents preferred to live out their stay in Afghanistan in this place, and endure its discomforts for as much as two or three years until their contracts ran out. If you pressed them there would be head-shaking and references to all the disasters that could befall those foreigners foolhardy enough to consider setting up in a house of their own. Kabul town's a blasted place. There were problems of thieving servants, outdoor lavatories, mud roofs that dissolved in the rain and snow of winter, shortages of fuel during the cold months, and Afghan xenophobia. The Hotel might not be the Waldorf Astoria, but it was safe.

I did not know how to set about finding a house in a country where there were no advertisements, or estate agents and news of rented accommodation such as there was had to pass by word of mouth. It was an opportune time to attend a party at the British Embassy where the Ambassador's wife dismissed my effusive thanks with a matron's brusqueness. In spite of my heightened sense of gratitude, I found the party deadly – just like the functions at the French club, it was attended by a mixture of nationalities without any common interest apart from putting away as much drink as possible.

The drink was finished earlier than usual. Meanwhile I had spent my time detailing the miseries of the Hotel de Kabul to a Swedish businessman who listened to my complaints with growing horror. When we rose to leave he handed me his business card – Carl Schmit, Director General, General Traders, Import-Export. He added that there was plenty of room in his house at Shahri Naw. If I liked I could avail myself of his hospitality and escape the life I had been so vividly describing.

I did not hesitate. Next day I took a tonga to his house, which was situated near the French club and a small well-stocked bazaar whose chaikhanas and shops had an air of affluence unlike the crowded seedy excitement of the bazaar I had explored during the last months. It was difficult to pinpoint the difference which perhaps was merely the fact that there were rather less people about. From a doorway came a smell of kebabs roasting over charcoal and nan hot for the oven. A nomad woman in red pantaloons and a black silk dress festooned with silver jewellery that seemed to make her bend under its weight was selling bowls of yoghurt. Fat-tailed sheep were being driven past piles of fruit and vegetables that were high as houses . . . With a tinkle of bells we swung round the traffic intersection and down a narrow street darkened by the branches of trees which grew across from behind garden walls and touched each other.

Shahri Naw was fashionable, a place for rich Afghans or Embassy people. It was secluded, away from the city's bustle where noises were restricted to the cry of a Hazara water-seller carrying his goatskin bag or the jingle of a tonga. We stopped at a studded door with a brass plate on which was written in English and Farsi the identical legend on the card I had received the evening before.

I banged for some time before a bolt was drawn and a sour manservant let me into a garden full of fruit trees and roses. He led me past a broken fountain, across a vine trellis that had collapsed over the path to a modern two-storey house painted pink. My host was there to greet me, wearing pyjamas topped by a padded silk smoking jacket and carrying a long cigarette-holder like a Noël Coward character.

He indicated the scowling servant who had let me in.

'This is Nabi. I have not entirely convinced him that you are Irish and not English. Naturally he has not heard of the Emerald Isle. He cannot countenance the English since he was valet to the German Ambassador before the war.'

Carl was in his thirties, a man with sandy-coloured hair and heavy lips which gave his face a sullen expression when he was not talking. This was seldom; he spoke excellent English nearly all the time.

'This house is really too small.' He showed me over the sumptuous interior, the bathroom with plumbing that worked, the spacious bedrooms, the large sitting room leading onto the *gul khana* or flower room overlooking the garden. The kitchen, where the cook was asleep with a dishcloth covering his face to keep off the flies, was as filthy as most.

The most important room in the house was the long room where Carl kept samples of his wares displayed on a long wooden table as if they belonged to a museum. There were glass bricks, nails, a primus, pieces of plastic, trade catalogues, a pair of army boots, an assortment of Swedish clothes and even a model of a jet aircraft engine.

'My firm is one of the biggest in Sweden.' He led me into the sitting room where he poured out lethal measures of bourbon. 'Those are a few of the things that we hope to introduce into this country.'

He took a deep breath. 'You know that Sweden is the most advanced country in the world, and we are realising that here in Afghanistan are great opportunities for us to bring advancement. Roads first, then industries, then who knows? Perhaps oil.'

'What about America? Aren't they doing the same sort of thing, reviving the economy?'

'The Americans may as well give up since they insist on supporting Pakistan.'

'And Russia?'

'Oh, there is nothing to fear from the Russians.'

'And your company is tackling all that?'

He looked at me pityingly. 'You do not get grasp our ideas, our scope.'

He took down a sheaf of trade brochures from a shelf and arranged them like a hand of cards. 'Take one, each will tell you something different.'

I pulled out a plan to build a monorail linking Kabul to Peshawar across the Khyber. He burrowed in a cupboard and produced a model of an opaque house made from what looked like polythene. 'You remember I have just showed you my plastic bricks? I am planning to build a model plastic house in Kabul and then everyone will want to buy.' The next brochure concerned a health programme which would rely on contracts with various Swedish pharmaceutical firms; it included a scheme to supply contraceptives to the Afghan army. He also wanted to supply the army with boots – there were a couple of bulky samples laid out on his table. I understood his motives in inviting me to share his house – he saw me as a good contact. My humble position at the Military College might be a means of influencing the Defence Ministry when it came to tendering for military supplies. Just about the only Swedish firm I had heard of was Bofors, but thankfully Carl made no mention of arms.

'There is the army and the airforce, which we would like to see improved, and after that there are all the mineral resources to be developed . . .'

In the days to come I heard a good deal about the destiny of Afghanistan under the guidance of his company. He lectured me on how during the Second World War this backward country had been further isolated from the rest of the world, and even now in the nineteen-fifties serious shortages in basic goods continued to tie in to the past. Here was a mind which would have appealed to Amanullah. Postwar trade may have revived first with America and now with Russia – Carl dismissed the importance of the 1950 border agreement and the exchange of oil and textiles for wool and cotton. He based his plans on the belief that Afghanistan must come to prefer a neutral country for a trading partner. And Sweden and Swedes would be able to cash in.

I moved my things from the hotel the same day. For the first time since arriving in Kabul I was able to appreciate how pleasant life could be for the foreigner. Instead of the constant roar of noise which helped to make life at the Hotel de Kabul hideous, there was the shaded garden. There was fresh fruit from the quiet bazaar. Carl was generous with his supplies of bourbon and shared other imported delicacies like Swedish butter, chocolate and American cigarettes.

I saw him seldom; I went daily to the Military College leaving him to his problems. On holidays he would sometimes emerge from his sample room where he was presumably working to further his business interests, and start to complain about poor communications or Afghan depravity or his headaches.

We shared dinner, pilaus which Nabi would bring in after brushing off the flies and slices of pink harbooza bought from a nearby stall sopping with liquid likely to bring on further attacks of KT. Then a few whiskeys, and I would learn about the failed match factory in Thailand and the failed ping pong ball company in Hong Kong. A lack of liquidity had been the problem. There was the failed nightclub which had fallen victim to the extortions of a Chinese gang.

He saw many mysterious visitors in his business room. Meanwhile I entertained friends from the hotel and we sat among the roses drinking canned Swedish beer and eating nuts and raisins. Filled with envy and amazement at how I had managed to escape the Hotel, they were too tactful to voice their suspicions that Carl was my lover.

One Friday afternoon my siesta was interrupted by a banging at the door. I took no notice, as quite regularly a pedlar would bring around antiques and precious stones which would be irresistible to Carl. Any old handful of brass or silver coins dating back to the Greeks, a piece of glazed pottery dug out of a tepe, or a Nuristani carving would be considered as the pedlars stopped here, only one destination on the steady round of foreigners, particularly diplomats who might well want to smuggle out the occasional artifact in their handy bags.

Usually if the door remained closed – as when Carl had his headaches – the pedlar went away. This time it did not happen, and the banging continued until Nabi, grumbling, went down and opened the heavy door. There was a shout and a woman ran in. She wore a loose white headscarf over her shoulders and a striped cotton dress.

'Help, help!' she cried in English.

Her name was Anna and a few years before in London she had met a handsome Afghan diplomat and been swept off her feet. It was the usual sad story. When he brought her to Afghanistan, she found he had another wife and plenty of children. She only discovered this little by little; at first she and her husband had lived together in Kabul, and only later was she thrown in with the second family. The charming foreigner she knew in England turned into a standard Moslem husband when he was at home, and was overbearing in his efforts to persuade her to yield to the cultivation of modesty and self containment. She was a prisoner, confined to a woman's quarter of the house, with a servant sleeping outside her door at night. When her husband took her out, they used different sides of the road.

'I've got no money.'

'What do you want from us?'

'I want to go back to England. I want to go home. Oh, Mum was right!'

'Have you tried the Embassy?'

'They won't touch me. I've lost my British passport. I'm a bloody Afghan!'

'You poor child!'

Although Carl was clearly flattered to be asked to take part in a mission of chivalry, he had no intention of helping her. His negotiations with the Afghan government were at a particularly delicate stage, not to be jeopardised by giving sanctuary to a runaway wife. There was far too much to lose. But he was quite prepared to spend the afternoon listening to her troubles. 'A chadur, can you imagine? He insists. . . . My mum didn't like him from the start . . . People like him shouldn't be allowed to marry English girls.'

However, he would not give her practical assistance. 'It is best, my dear, that you should return to him.'

'Ooh no! I need your help . . . please.' But she soon grasped that she had knocked at the wrong door.

'Could you give him a job, then? He's a good cook.'

'I thought he was a diplomat.' Carl was visibly shaken.

'I thought so too at first.'

'I do not need another cook.'

'You won't help?'

'I will make enquiries.'

They left it at that – no plans for sanctuary or for employment – and in due course Anna departed meekly. I felt desperately sorry for her, but Carl was hard-hearted.

'Foolish little English girl.' He opened another bottle of bourbon. 'In every place you find them. They listen to some story from the handsome hawk-faced foreigner and think they are marrying a sheik. A diplomat! Hah! You even hear of Swedish women committing stupid errors as to marry Arabs and suchlike. To cut your throat is better. They should pass laws forbidding such marriages.'

There were quite a few foreign women married to Afghans, poor things, he told me. In Kabul he knew of an American in similar circumstances, various Turks – they didn't count – and he had heard rumours of three French dancers who had come to Afghanistan, had vanished down some bazaar in Kabul and had never been seen again. This story greatly took our fancy as the bourbon emptied steadily.

Carl said that he had only ever heard of one happy marriage between an Afghan and a foreigner, a cockney lady who had been here for forty years, who had become so Afghan in her lifestyle and habits that only the most knowledgeable could make out in her Farsi a certain chirpy London intonation.

I mentioned the Australian girl married to the camel drover.

'If a woman must marry an Afghan, it is better to wait until he is ninety or more – he cannot live for ever. . . !'

Later that day I read my favourite author, Major Raverty, retired Bombay Army. This time I dipped into his *Poetry of the Afghans* 'Literally Translated from the Original Pushtu', and found a selection of the poems of Khushhal Khan Khattak, the great warrior poet and hero who lived in the seventeenth century ('Khushhal Khan was the father of fifty-seven sons, besides several daughters; but with the exception of four or five of the former, they do not appear to have been particularly worthy of their parent's affection'):

> All woman-kind are of intellect deficient;
> And the voluntary causes of all life's ills.
>
> Thou mayst be straight and even with them;
> But they are crooked and wayward with thee.
>
> Do them a thousand benefits and services;
> Yet, at a single word, their hearts sulky grow.
>
> They become poison unto thee, and kill thee –
> They, whom thou deemest a healing balm.
>
> They have no fidelity in their composition:
> They are naturally unto perfidiousness prone.
>
> Created indeed, in the figure of mankind;
> But in reality with no humanity in them.
>
> In all things they are fickle and changeable:
> Tame in tongue* but untameable in heart.

Say no more about them, O Khushhal!
It would be better had they never existed!

*Not always, at least as far as the tongues of most
    Englishwomen go. (Major Raverty's note.)

We did not meet poor Anna again, but her fate became
part of Kabul gossip to be discussed whenever foreigners met.
Rumours abounded; she was dead, she had never existed, she
was seen walking out of the British Embassy followed by a
bearded man carrying a gun. Gossip was important in the
lives of foreigners in whatever circumstances we congregated,
whether it was Bastille Day, American Armed Forces Day or
whatever occasion we were invited to where the poverty of
the foreigner's spirit of adventure was enhanced by the dreary
round of drinks.

We did not participate in the event that marked the zenith of
American influence in Afghanistan, the visit of Vice President
Nixon. (In the streets of Kabul passengers crushed in buses were
ordered to crouch down so that only those who were seated
comfortably were visible to his passing motorcade.) But we
enjoyed the British Embassy's attempts to welcome in the new
Elizabethan Age.

In 1953 Britain had a new Queen and Everest had been
climbed. For weeks before the coronation the front of the Embassy was covered with strings of coloured lights showing a large
illuminated crown. Since the rest of the capital was in almost total
darkness, this made a singular impression on passing nomads.
For once, in spite of three ferociously unsuccessful wars against
Afghanistan, British prestige counted for something.

Standards had fallen since Robert Byron's time when the
Legation employed a staff of ninety. However, on 8 June 1953
entertainment was put on with a certain style, as every foreigner
in the city – and some Afghans – made their way out through
the darkness at the edge of the city towards the shining crown.

Guests were herded under the great white porch into the
hallway with the lifesize portrait of the young Queen, a blue
ribbon across her breast. There were Indians, Pakistanis,
Americans, Chinese, Russians, and just a sprinkling of self-

conscious Afghans nursing glasses of lemonade. There was the Ambassador to queue up and shake hands with, all that a British Ambassador should be – tall, blankly good looking, a scholar of classical Persian, and no doubt Pushtu, who could surely read Afghan poetry without Major Raverty's help.

The live-coal-like ruby in her nose-jewel is fire itself;
And the red bulak, like unto a spark of fire is placed by
its side.

The Ambassador stood being charming beside his wife, the good woman who had saved my life, at the head of the steps, while two secretaries tried to sort out sheep and goats.

'Diplomatic or non-diplomatic?'

Champagne was for the diplomats, cheap plonk for the rest. But the Indian businessmen, the Polish engineers, the Russian advisers, all the Hotel habitués and unclassifiable people like myself refused to be classified. In the end the staff gave up and there was a rush through the double doors into the ballroom where a little Afghan band broke into a quickstep variation of *God Save the Queen*.

Soon, however, the reception divided up more or less naturally in the way that had been originally planned. The diplomats congregated to exchange pleasantries with the Ambassador, while the rest of us followed Sam – who had brought me and the Murree beer up from Peshawar in the Embassy station wagon. Sam had done better this time, and had secreted away a number of magnum bottles of Embassy champagne. After a few dutiful waltzes with the secretaries under stern-eyed portraits of more royal personages, we all retired to a back room.

The atmosphere was like that of an undergraduate ball. Drunken sounds floated over the tennis courts and swimming pool, across the herbacious borders and rose beds, past the Gurkha sentries into the Afghan night. Someone got sick on the Aubusson carpet. Sam kept running down a passageway to fetch new supplies. The military attaché, a bristly-haired Scottish colonel, stuck his head in and complained about the noise. One of the secretaries passed out.

The diplomats had long gone home – no one bothered to see them out with the national anthem. The Ambassador and his wife went to bed. The non-diplomatic stayed on until dawn. Outside the window I watched the first flicker of sunlight creep over the hills from the direction of the Khyber Pass. The Gurkha sentries were changed, while the Ambassador's favourite Afghan hound was being led out from his kennel by the gardener for his morning run. This was a true *tazi*, not the bird brained creature bred in the west, but the noble beast that is so highly regarded by Afghans that he is considered a superior beast altogether to the usual miserable piedogs whose name *sag* always seemed appropriate. Watching the graceful and pampered creature sweeping across the Embassy lawn, I recalled how the *tazi* traditionally sleeps in his master's tent and wears a quilted coat in winter. He hunts by sight rather than smell, making a beeline for the doomed gazelle trying to throw him off with a complicated zig-zag trail.

The Ambassador's *tazi* disappeared behind the roses. Five thousand miles to the west the Queen was being crowned.

PART
TWO

8

THE earth cracked and dust settled inches thick on the valleys and the hills slowly turning them from green to brown. Hot air smothered the city and every day violent dust storms obliterated the streets. Every morning lines of men armed with special wooden shovels would rhythmically sprinkle water from the *jueys* in a vain effort to keep the dust down. Each day was hotter, the flowers shrivelled and the river turned to a thin fetid trickle between its rocky banks. Blocks of ice brought down from the mountains, wrapped in straw, exhaled odours of rotten fruit and filth. The bare brown hills under which we all lived gave off heat like hot coals.

During the five morning periods it became an increasing effort to keep students from slumping over their desks. They responded less and less to Milton and the Old Testament. When it came to bringing English to the Afghans, perhaps a mischievous spirit was at work. A decade after I was teaching at the Military College Bruce Chatwin was amazed to see at the British Embassy quantities of copies of *Animal Farm*, an obscure atheist parable full of pigs which, sanctioned by official approval, was awaiting general distribution throughout the education establishments of the country.

I hardly did better by abandoning Milton and teaching with the aid of nursery rhymes and fairy tales. Old King Cole and the Grand Old Duke of York were yelled out. Bluebeard was well received; perhaps there were similar traditional folk tales with which the students were familiar. Most popular of all was Little Red Riding Hood. I was careful not to draw parallels with the wolf the heroine met in the wood and the Wolf beside me, ever eager to translate. Any story in which girls were mentioned was considered to be a good joke.

Otherwise progress was fitful.

'He is donkey.' 'I am brave boy.' 'Abdul is fool.' In due course sentences became more complex.

'Soon I journey to mountains.' 'God bless Afghanistan, also Ireland.' 'Today is holiday, so Commandant is good man.'

The chance of their speaking good English seemed as remote as the cure for dog bite in Major Raverty's manual: 'Sir, if you would be cured, take a bit of bread and dip it in the blood of the wound, and give it to the dog that bit you.'

The Wolf, ever diligent, continued at my side asking me lists of words. After the classes were over, and my voice was still hoarse from teaching, he would produce an assortment of articles from his pocket for me to identify. Out would come a piece of string, a walnut or a dead grasshopper which would go back into his pocket after its name had been carefully recorded in his notebook. He must have filled five or six of these during the school year.

Although the brighter boys could speak a few words, the great mass was still inarticulate. Head jerking, running round the classroom, bawling out the names of objects achieved very little. Then, in order to escape the overheated classrooms, I introduced rugby.

From the teachers' room I had watched strings of students shuffling around to the shouts of the two overworked sports instructors. I saw a golden opportunity to exchange the dusty classroom for the open air. It seemed ridiculous that so little attention was paid to physical exercise; that the future backbone of the Afghan army with its tradition of steely endurance was so out of condition that it could scarcely jog around the parade ground.

I culled an impressive array of facts from a manual of athletics borrowed from the American Embassy Library, and wrote a report mentioning a running track, high and low jumps and a football pitch. Weeks passed before I got an interview with the Commandant.

I entered the office with its guards outside, rifles and bayonets forever fixed, and was greeted by the plump figure with pudgy shaven head and gimlet eyes, who with solicitous gravity waved me to one of the easy chairs placed round the room. He was always punctiliously polite to foreign teachers. The school director might fear him, so did the sixty or so Afghan teachers, and all the pay clerks, ordinary soldiers, cooks and trumpet blowers. But we were free spirits.

Captain Amin the interpreter stood beside him in his kid gloves and impeccably tailored uniform. He had been on a training course in England and Sandhurst had left its imprint. In off-duty moments he would recall nightlife around Piccadilly.

Without wasting time I explained my plans and how I envisaged myself in the role of chief instructor for physical education. I mentioned cricket, rugby and hockey – and perhaps a commando course with wire obstacles, water jumps and other novelties which the British military attaché would tell me how to make.

The Commandant listened intently as Captain Amin translated, occasionally gazing out of the window at the Paghman mountains. Then he spoke rapidly, punctuating each remark with a vigorous nod.

'The Commandant says he wishes to know what the game rugby is.'

I gave Captain Amin a lecture on rules and tactics which he passed on. Then, after some doodling and fiddling with a paperweight, the Commandant gave his verdict.

'There is no objection to your organising athletics provided they take place in your free time.' That meant an end to my afternoons which I usually spent recovering from the ravages of teaching English.

Captain Amin continued, 'The Commandant considers that rugby football would be the most suitable form of athletic activity of those you have suggested. The Commandant thinks you would do well to start off with some of the men from the twelfth class. He will see that arrangements are made and some men are chosen for you as demonstration teams. How many? You would like to begin tomorrow afternoon? Then two o'clock on the parade ground.'

A football. An elliptical rugby football. Where was I to find one before the next afternoon? I spent the rest of the day combing the bazaar, asking the British Embassy, the Ghazi High School, the Habibiya High School and the Institute of Technology. Again it was the American Embassy that came to my rescue, producing an American football, which had the right shape, even though it was too small. In the evening I tried to remember rules and to invent simple Farsi equivalents for 'scrum' and 'kickoff'. To begin with we would have to do without goal posts, although perhaps I could plant a few sticks in the ground.

Next morning after classes, instead of returning to Carl
Schmit's, I joined the other Afghan teachers for lunch which was
held in the communal mess, a small unadorned room packed
with wooden tables and pews. I swallowed a few mouthfuls of
rice and mutton fat served off a tin plate, and then hastily went
outside where I found the two sports instructors with the cadets
who had been specially chosen to play rugby. They were the
pick of the school, but through an oversight, instead of the thirty
I had asked for, more than a hundred were assembled.

'The Commandant has ordered. They must play.'

We walked over to the wooden shed which served as the sports
store. One of the instructors unlocked the padlock while the
cadets crowded around jostling each other to gain a view. A
groan went up at the sight of a few burst football bladders and
the torn remains of some jerseys.

'The rats have eaten. Bad, Sir.'

Although it was very hot, the cadets wore their winter uniforms. I had a blackboard brought out from one of the classrooms
and set up in the corner of the parade ground. I tried to explain
the fundamental ideas of the game – that one ran with the ball
instead of kicking it, that one had scrums, tackles and lineouts.
A few minutes of watching the cadets' faces setting into masks
of boredom made me rashly decide to dispense with further
preliminaries.

To my dismay all the senior officers turned up to view the
spectacle, sitting on a line of chairs arranged along the pitch.
Roughly dividing the cadets into two sides, I placed the ball in
the middle of the field and kicked it into the air, blowing my
whistle at the same time. The ball rose up in a high arc, and as
it descended the hundreds of other cadets who had strolled up
to watch joined in. The field became a battle ground as figures
in belted overcoats tussled with each other.

In due course the game degenerated into a massed kicking
punching fight. I blew my whistle in vain; the ball had vanished
behind the clump of trees where the familiar figures squatted.

'Very good rugby,' one of the instructors remarked with unpar-
alleled generosity. 'Soon we have new army team.'

I tried again two or three times with very little improvement.
It was a relief when the heat made the pitch hard as iron. We
all agreed there was a danger of broken legs and collar bones,

perhaps even death from heatstroke, and rugby was postponed until the winter.

Some months later a proper Austrian sports instructor arrived. Trained as a coach in the American army, his ideas of gyms, running tracks and sports equipment were even more ambitious than my own. But with no equipment athletics were severely limited, and he would talk wistfully of sporting life among Americans. Every day I watched his progress as he arrived in the teachers' room to change into his flame-coloured track suit. Followed by hundreds of cadets, he took his 'working out seminars', circling the parade ground at a slow jog. These expeditions coincided with marching practice and were accompanied by the bagpipe band and the thumping of drums.

At last the cadets discarded their winter uniform for summer khaki. A new ordeal awaited – Ramadan. Tempers flared, and it was harder than ever to keep the students awake. Shamelessly I hid nuts and chocolate in my pocket.

'For God's sake don't eat anything in public,' Warren advised. We brought magazines into the teachers' room and, ignoring the Turks, and suppressing our guilt, we nibbled behind them.

All the hot day the cadets had nothing to eat or drink. Each morning there were anguished looks, exaggerated sighs and a deep renewed feeling of despair, far exceeding the usual low-grade depression that pervaded the institution. The lunch hour was mockingly retained, when the cadets wandered around vacantly, and then there was more teaching, more torture throughout the afternoon. Learning English was further than ever from the thoughts of those waiting for the mullah's liberating evening cry to be amplified through the loud-speakers.

Halfway through Ramadan we were told that an inspection would take place by the military attachés living in Kabul. This surprised us very much, since activities inside the Military College were secretive, and appeared to concern only the Defence Ministry. In general the authorities were obsessive in their desire to avoid publicity; perhaps they were ashamed. But now the desire to exhibit their ramshackle institution to international scrutiny seemed more puzzling still. Perhaps, Warren and I guessed, they felt that it was part of the penitential spirit of

Ramadan. Perhaps they wanted to keep all the spies in foreign embassies occupied harmlessly.

Military attachés in Afghanistan held an unenviable position. Their task was to help and advise the army, but any advances in this direction were invariably regarded with mistrust. India and Pakistan as neighbours, England from force of habit, the USA and the Soviet Union because they were ingratiating themselves with Afghanistan, all maintained MAs in Kabul. In addition, the US and Soviets, as the main rival powers, kept large military staffs and courier planes stationed at the airport. Not unnaturally the Afghans considered that the only reason for all these colonels and assistants was to spy out the country. In point of fact they were almost entirely confined to their embassies. Inspection of the Military College was a day out.

Teams of soldiers appeared armed with buckets of whitewash who scrubbed down classroom walls. Windows were cleaned and outside flowerbeds were weeded and raked. A special colour party in new uniforms and helmets practised standing to attention just inside the main gate; one or two fainted. A notice appeared in Farsi and English:

'It is forbidden for foreign teachers and officers to make use of nature facilities. Order of Commandant.'

This meant that the familiar poplar grove was prohibited as the teachers' WC. No alternative was given.

As we tumbled off the bus on the day of the inspection we had difficulty recognising the place. Gleaming whitewashed walls sparkled in the sun and around the main square – empty of cadets – rows of annuals had been planted in the red, black, (actually purple) and green of the royal Afghan colours.

Wearing a brand-new uniform, the director hurried up, giving instructions that we should go to our classrooms straight away. There was no time to waste.

'The Commandant has given instructions that until the military gentlemen are gone, no one is to move.'

In my classroom the windows had been firmly shut, and the surface of the floor and the desks was covered with a thick coating of DDT. So were the shaven heads of the cadets, crowded in three to a desk. The stench of the powder and the spectacle of sixty and more apathetic boys, their sorrowful eyes looking out from whitened eyebrows and snowmen's heads, awaited the international inspection.

A system of signalling like beacons on hilltops had been developed so that at the first approach of the *ferenghi* officers we could immediatcly spring into action. We had been warned that the cadets would have to show off their English, and there was plenty of time to prime the more lively of them with passages from the texts. 'There entertain him all the saints above.' 'What language speakest thou? I do not understand thee.' 'There hath not come a razor upon mine head; for I have been a Nazarite unto God from my mother's womb.'

The day was hotter than ever. I could not bring out of my pocket the melted chocolate I had secreted there and eat it under the gaze of sixty boys who had had nothing to eat since dawn, and would have nothing more for another seven hours. Worse than the hunger was the thirst; the DDT fumes parched the throat. By eleven the cadets had begun to fall asleep, and little trickling snores could be heard all round the classroom. Outside on the parade ground the guard of honour in German helmets and the bagpipe band sweltered away in the full glare of the sun. Through the white cloud in the classroom I could make out beyond the window the Director and the Commandant standing together waiting by the front gate.

They waited for five hours. Long before then, the vast majority of boys in my classroom had fallen asleep, and I too was nodding off. No doubt the DDT was having some of the effect on us as it had on flies; one by one the students dozed and the snores multiplied. It was like the story of the Sleeping Beauty (sniggtr, giggle, my teacher, a sleeping lady) and her entourage which I had often related with the aid of the Wolf. Today the Wolf was not here to prod people awake, shake them by the shoulders and pull their ears. He was away elsewhere doing something important involving the arrival of the distinguished visitors.

Who still did not come. The guard of honour wavered as the hours passed; the Commandant and Director, showing military qualities of endurance, stood their ground with only the odd brief look at a watch to mark a departure from the exigencies of military discipline. At last, a few minutes before one o'clock there was a call to arms from the main gate and the band began a drone of welcome. Scurrying figures moved around the MAs descending from their bus, and for a few minutes we caught a brief glimpse of gold-braided dress uniforms. Then they all vanished into the Commandant's private suite in the tower; we did not see them again. They were spared a tour which might enable them to write a report on military education, and were spared a demonstration of my pupils' English. Someone at last had seen sense and the bugle sounded for the dismissal of classes. Windows were flung open, doors slammed and six hundred white-headed figures rushed out into the sunlight shaking DDT from their heads.

Ramadan continued its weary way through the hot weather. Each day the torpor and the resistance to learning increased among the cadets as they thought about sunset and food and water. To schedule the year's exams just three days after Ramadan came to an end with the festival of Idd seemed to be another example of military inefficiency.

The Commandant invited us all to a sad lunch where everyone spoke with polite whispers of respect, during which we were informed that every cadet was expected to pass. There could be no exceptions.

Warren was horrified. 'I don't see why we should grovel. There have to be some standards and these boys simply aren't up to it. In my third class I should say at least half of them ought to be sent home for good.'

Warren still took his job very seriously, keeping meticulous notebooks, developing his own methods for educating the boys, in which Milton had long been discarded. He had devised certain rules which he considered essential, and proclaimed that no one, not even the Commandant, would make him depart from his well-tried procedures.

The Defence Ministry had stipulated that, in addition to a *viva*, three different sets of exam papers should be prepared for each class and one would be chosen. 'How pathetic that they should worry about cheating. Perhaps they toss a coin.' However Warren was slowly modifying his principles and was working out an ingenious system for his papers whereby, while no three questions were the same, a single answer would be sufficient for each.

My own papers were of shameless simplicity. Is Delilah a man? Please comment. Did Samson lose his hair? How? (A difficult one.) Is the story of Little Red Riding Hood true? After consultations with the Director and Commandant the pass mark was reduced to three out of ten.

The Wolf would also be taking the exam and had begun to memorise, not only whole sections of the badly printed pages of Milton, but the fairy stories, which he had taken down word for word as I had related them.

On the morning of the examination the classrooms were chaotic as the cadets milled about filled with frenzied anxiety. 'They try very hard, my teacher,' the Wolf said, pointing to bare arms and legs on which were scribbled long lists of English words and phrases.

Boys ran up to my desk bearing notes containing personal entreaties. 'My name is Abdul Faizi. I am twenty years old and very beautiful. Please pass, my teacher.' I was handed a verse of the poet Mahmud Warraq:

My beauty, I cannot exchange you for the cash of my life.
You are priceless, I will not sell you so cheap.
I hold your skirt with both my hands,
I may loosen my hold on my life, but not my hold on your
    skirt.

A rumour had got round that the examinations would not be the usual formality, since the foreign teachers were not to be trusted, and might even insist on standards. This was not the case at all. I was more than willing to collaborate and pass everyone with the highest honours. So were the Turks, although their teaching methods appeared to be very basic, particularly during the past week. The occasional anguished roar came regularly from the direction of the class rooms where they taught. By this time Warren had yielded to eastern duplicity. Why should we make these boys' lives harsher? Our instinct was to do our best for them.

They were given their examination papers and for an hour or so scratched away, occasionally folding up a shirt sleeve in search of an aide-mémoire recorded on the forearm. Other pieces of helpful information were written on scraps of paper and passed around.

For the fifth class worse was to come. Instead of a nice cosy *viva* witnessed only by the Wolf, at the end of the written examination the Commandant, attended by his senior officers, made an unexpected appearance and demanded to listen in. I felt nervous myself, but among the boys the sight of the familiar jowly figure inspired terror, and in a number of cases, tears.

A room had been set aside for the ordeal, and one by one each cadet marched into where I sat flanked by the inquisitional panel. Standing to attention, looking straight ahead, each boy shouted out his name and then with a murmur of prompting, any words of English that he happened to know. Numbers, days of the week, months, seasons and the odd 'good morning', 'hello' and 'goodbye' poured out in a roaring monotone.

After each candidate had finished and marched out, the Commandant would lean across and inspect the mark I had given. If it was high, that was a matter of handshaking all round; if it was low, the cadet had to be called back and re-examined until a satisfactory mark was given.

At last they had all been examined to the satisfaction of my superiors. Not quite all – I had forgotten the Wolf, who had been fingering his notebook and now came up to the blackboard. He, too must undergo the same ordeal as the cadets. For the Commandant and his officers this was clearly the star performance of the afternoon. The Wolf could remember everything, the stories of Bluebeard and Little Red Riding Hood word for word, and the whole of the last verse of 'On His Blindness'. He smiled with delight as I congratulated him before the applauding audience and, beaming, we all bowed each other out of the classroom. Everyone was pleased; everyone had got a prize.

After the problems and discomforts of teaching it was pleasant to return to the garden at Shahri Naw. Carl was planning to start a regular air service between Europe and Afghanistan. Our original cordiality had become strained as I struggled not to show scepticism and boredom at his repeated grandiose plans to equip the Afghan army (without my help) and get contracts for building Swedish glass brick palaces.

'You will see, Peter, when I tell you these things are not jokes,' he said over his bourbon. 'In this very backward country they are longing for our expertise so that they may develop and come into the twentieth century.'

As the days of August succeeded each other, I showed no surprise that his Afghan contacts were exasperated because no aeroplane had arrived from Sweden.

'They are like children with no patience.' Carl dismissed the whole Afghan nation. 'They do not realise that the plane will soon arrive in Kabul and it will have our director, Mr Hoffman, on board. Mr Hoffman could buy up this whole city.'

Mr Hoffman and his plane failed to appear, a fact which I suddenly realised was important – there was no reason for me to be bored and plenty of reason for Carl to be petulant. He had obtained a good deal of credit on the prospect of his fabulously wealthy and influential impending arrival and now it became hard to placate his grumbling beneficiaries. The shopkeepers in Shahri Naw could not be paid, nor the various merchants with whom he had already done deals. Worst of all, the bank froze his money.

He stopped seeing all visitors and spent the day in bed. There was very little food in the house, although the stocks of bourbon had not quite run out. The servants gave up their usual duties. Nabi was sent on a foraging expedition to his old village and returned with a small goat which wandered round the garden. No one had the energy or the heart to kill it. The cook managed to increase his intake of hashish and went around the house with a smile as if he was dreaming of choirboys dressed in white singing like nightingales. The house, filled with dirty plates, unwashed coffee cups and empty whisky glasses, became repulsive, and I even began to regret my decision to leave the hotel.

But there was still the garden with its shaded walks and flowers that persisted in blooming in spite of the midsummer heat and the fact that they were never watered. 'If a man would be happy for a week,' runs a Chinese saying, 'he would take a wife; if he planned happiness for a month, he must kill a pig; but if he desired happiness for ever, he should plant a garden.' There was no dust in here, and the heat was dissipated a little by the broad green leaves of the trees.

One afternoon, as I was sitting under a plane tree correcting examination papers, the goat not far away eating roses, I heard the sudden drone of an aeroplane. A few minutes later I caught sight of a small silver plane that darted across the trees and vanished.

Carl rushed into the garden in his pyjamas, hopping around with glee.

'My God, now you see people should believe me.' And everyone did. This was thirty years before the menace of Russian MiGs and helicopters, and the noise and spectacle of one little plane could attract the attention of the whole city. All the shopkeepers of Shahri Naw saw it pass overhead and suddenly were prepared to give us more credit.

Soon Carl was hurrying out to the airport in a large American car supplied by his Afghan agents while I was left to try and clean the house and obtain food from the bazaar – which in an instant had become an easy task.

When the car returned, Carl, all smiles, ushered in three very tired-looking men. Here was Hoffman, the boss of the company, whose existence I had doubted, stout, well-preserved, with shrewd blue eyes. He was dressed, not altogether successfully, like an American, in a crumpled lightweight blue suit set off by a very bright tie and an oversize stetson. The two members of the crew wore uniforms specially designed for the new Swedish airline, light blue, their peaked caps perched at a jaunty angle. Within a few minutes of entering the house they began polishing off one of Carl's few remaining bottles of bourbon.

For my benefit the Captain spoke English, the lingua franca. 'They say, Sven, my boy, you are to fly to Afghanistan, and it is another chicken hop. My God, I tell them something when I get back. This is the worst trip of my life, I tell you. No navigation aids, nothing.' He talked a good deal in a raucous voice as the whisky circulated. The plane, a Lockheed Lodestar, had developed engine trouble over the Persian Gulf so that they had been forced to sit around in a small sandy sheikdom for three weeks until new parts had been flown out from Europe. It had been very hot. Sven got up from his chair and repeated the exact temperature a number of times, both in Fahrenheit and Centigrade; he was very sure of it, because he had nothing to do but record it morning, noon and evening, every day he spent there.

At last the parts had come and the Lodestar was able to fly on to Kabul. It was the first flight of its kind to the capital which had last seen serious foreign aerial activity in the winter of 1929.

Our circumstances changed dramatically as the shopkeepers continued to insist on offering the household unlimited credit. Watermelons, grapes, fruit, vegetables and legs of stringy mutton were brought up from the bazaar in gratifying quantities after weeks of near-starvation, which had recalled to me my first month at the Hotel. True to his American persona, Hoffman, and the crew as well, spurned the bazaar food and the delicacies brought by ingratiating Afghans intent on doing business with the Swedes. Instead, in order to reduce the risk of dysentery, they would only eat the supplies they had brought with them. I helped Hoffman to unpack the tins of pâté, sauerkraut and frankfurters which were to be the mainstay of our diet so long as the crew of the Lodestar stayed with us. This would be for as short a time as possible.

All day visitors knocking at the garden door with samples of goods for sale were received by the two servants, now dressed in American-style khaki uniforms bought in the bazaar to give a military air to the household. But no business could be done for the time being. The Swedes had made the mistake of arriving at the time of Afghan National Independence Day which celebrated victory in the third Afghan war of 1919. For a week everything closed down, while from every part of the country tribesmen piled into Kabul for the festivities. These included an elaborately disgusting game of *buzkashi* where the King and Prime Minister and all the most important in the land assembled to watch three teams of thirty horsemen fight over a huge bleeding goat whose head had been chopped off just before the game began.

My friends at the Military Academy assured me that the game was played with traditional ancient strategy ('like chess') and that some of the heaving, shouting, bearded thugs on horseback were stars of a scientific game – particularly the snatchers – who were recognised and cheered on by the crowd. Halfway through, the carcass more or less fell to pieces and the equivalent of 'new ball' was called by the umpire, an army officer on horseback who had been ineffectually keeping things under control with his whistle. Hastily another animal – a calf this time – was beheaded and the game began again.

Other festivities included a lot of men with wild black hair dancing in the National Stadium and stick wrestling, which I was told developed good swordsmanship. Two or more men, each holding a stick in either hand, whacked at their opponents' sticks in an age-old rhythm. If someone missed, his fingers were battered to a pulp. Then came the fly-past of the air force, the three old biplanes in the care of the Italian colonel staying at the Hotel de Kabul.

The grand climax of the week was the military parade in which the guns captured from the British were adorned with flowers and pulled in triumph past the saluting stands. Even the fiercest anti-English observer had to admit that the British Ambassador, dressed in formal dress-coat and top hat, took the occasion in a good-humoured way, and as the guns passed him, he was seen to smile.

The week of national celebration was the time that the Defence Ministry arranged the graduating ceremony for the final-year cadets. The location for these proceedings was another light-hearted example of anglophobia: Amanullah's monument to independence which featured broken British cannon and British lions in chains. (Perhaps now a couple of chained bears will join them.)

I was instructed to put on a dinner jacket to attend the ceremonies that were enhanced by the colour guard in German helmets and a band ('this is our symphonic orchestra') that played the 'Eton Boating Song' over and over again. A number of generals ate and drank cakes, tea and sherbet, and made long speeches. The proceedings were modelled on passing-out parades at Sandhurst and West Point, except that there were no applauding parents present to witness their sons' success.

The postponed departure of the Lodestar meant that supplies of pâté and frankfurters became low and the visiting Swedes, who had already suffered in the Arabian deserts, became increasingly bad-tempered. When at last Independence Day and its attendant junketing drew to a close and a departure date could be fixed, Carl suddenly suggested that I should take the opportunity of flying in it back to Sweden, from where it would be a short hop to Ireland. 'Plenty of room. No trouble at all.'

The military College was on vacation, and it seemed a brilliant idea to leave Kabul for Europe and return a month later. Or a fortnight later, if I preferred, since soon there would be a fortnightly service between Sweden and Afghanistan concerned with import-export.

'I shall write to the Managing Director introducing you as my very good friend,' Carl said munificently.

'What Managing Director?' It was the first I had heard of him.

'Naturally he arranges everything at the Swedish end. He is based in Stockholm. I will tell him of our friendship and of all your work for the army.'

A free trip back to Europe to see my family within eight months of leaving Ireland seemed an incredible piece of luck, so much so that I ignored the uncertain nature of the import-export business. Anyway it seemed to be on the up and up. Not an hour seemed to pass without some important officials coming to the house. Some carried away the army boots; others collected the glass bricks so that they could eagerly hand them around at ministries and government departments with a view to transforming Kabul. A couple of men arrived with a load of the best sort of karakul skins to be carried back to Sweden. A portly ex-minister was appointed official Afghan agent of the company, crested writing paper appeared and a new even more impressive name plate was fastened to the garden door outside which a pair of policemen had taken up duty.

It was a significant moment in the fortunes of the company, one which the transformed Carl greatly enjoyed. 'Now you can see, Peter, that I was not joking', he would say watching the latest consignment of goods being carried up the garden path.

The day before the plane was due to take off for Kandahar on the long flight back to Sweden, Mr Hoffman invited well wishers to a banquet to celebrate the Company's success. It would be held outdoors at Paghman, the favourite resort of the royal family and the Kabul rich, situated about twenty miles from the city on the edge of the mountains. Amanullah wanted to turn it into a summer capital something like Simla, and left another monstrous piece of debris beside the winding irregular streets twisting up the mountainside through a haze of orchards and walnut trees – a half-completed summer palace equal in grandiose futility to the ruins at Darul Aman.

The banquet, hosted by Hoffman and Carl, was held in a walnut grove with a river running by. Long wooden tables were heaped with half a dozen varieties of pilau, fruit, pickles, freshly caught fish, champagne, and fruit juice for believers. Servants were drafted in to wait on the guests who included the ex-minister and a number of prominent Kabuli dealers. The meal progressed in a leisurely civilised fashion, interspersed with congratulatory speeches by Carl and various Afghans expressing admiration to which Mr Hoffman, half-asleep, nodded in acknowledgement. I was feeling equally drowsy, having drunk a quantity of champagne, and found myself dozing in the filtered sunshine, when I was woken by two soldiers and an elderly official waving a piece of paper who rushed shouting into the garden.

The paper turned out to be a government writ stopping the plane from leaving Kabul.

Carl went into a picturesque fury, shouting Swedish oaths and seizing the end of the long tablecloth and pulling it towards him so that glasses and plates rained onto the ground. His guests had already departed – at the first sign of trouble they had run off as if the walnut trees had caught fire. In five minutes the garden was deserted except for myself and the Swedes. Dejectedly we made our way back to the house at Shahri Naw where the Swedes found themselves under house arrest.

The most widely believed rumour among the foreign community held that Hoffman was not just a shady businessman but the leader of a drugs ring involving countless people in high places. Not to mention me. Friends – especially from the Hotel – were full of I told you so's and warnings that I was damned lucky, old boy, not to be implicated as anything more than a spectator in the whole affair. I was given several accounts of the horrible Afghan penal system.

However anything, even a Kabul dungeon, was better than returning to the Hotel. I stayed on in Shahri Naw where the Swedes spent their time quarrelling and drinking whisky, ample new supplies having been brought in during happier days, except for Carl who retired to bed once again. Urgent telegrams were sent to Sweden. Even if the plane was allowed to leave, it would be without its original cargo. The consignment of karakul skins was no longer available, and the only alternative available was sheep intestines for use as casings for sausages.

Time passed, and then, when things seemed at their worst, Carl suddenly received a message that the plane could leave on condition that damages were paid for all the infringements of government regulations. What these were remained unspecified – only the amount to be paid was clear.

In Afghanistan events had a way of being resolved with explosive speed. Fruitless weeks had gone by without any action at all. Now, within an hour of getting the go-ahead, we were driving along the dusty road that led to the airport.

The airport consisted of a few sheds in a big barren field without the luxury of a runway. This expanse where the elegant little Lodestar sat and twinkled was the place that in years to come would appear on endless newsreels showing bombers, supply planes and helicopter gunships casting out magnesium flares to distract the Mujaheddin. Now we had it to ourselves.

It did not take long for the two pilots to load up the twin engined silver plane with sheep casings and a few carpets that Carl had managed to assemble hastily. Because no passengers were allowed to be carried on a freight plane, I had been appointed auxiliary crew. The engines were started and, looking out through the whirl of dust I could see Carl wearing his polka-dot bow tie, smoking his usual cigarette, waving goodbye as we were off with a roar into the empty sky.

I looked across at the biscuit-brown hills, the dried corrugated lines of the river, and the gleaming white cube of the British Embassy. I picked out landmarks – the Hotel, the long avenue leading to Darul Aman and the empty palace, the green circle of trees near Babur's tomb where I had often sipped tea, the Military College and the poplars under which I had defaecated. Then we turned south away from the haze of the Paghman and Takhut i Turkoman mountains topped in snow, rising in waves behind us.

The Lodestar took an hour to fly to Kandahar where the mountains which descended from the main range of the Hindu Kush became low foothills and trailed off into ripples of golden sand. A jeep was waiting to take us to Morrison Knudsen where we hoped to acquire some petrol.

Driven by an Afghan in jeans, tartan shirt and pith helmet, we bounced along the dusty road from the airport towards the high wire fence and security gates that guarded a piece of America. Inside air-conditioned creature comforts included a well-stocked canteen and a cinema showing the latest movies.

Morrison Knudsen was providing the cosseted conditions of the engineering expatriate. With the development of the oil fields this sort of inward-looking luxury which appeared so remarkable to me would soon become commonplace.

As I drank cold beer, sitting beside the kingfisher-blue swimming pool, I was observing a sad little piece of history.

MK had come to Afghanistan with the best of intentions – to make the desert bloom. The Hilmand Valley project had begun in the post-war years when the government of Shah Mamoud sought for means to revive Afghanistan's ancient reputation as 'the granary of Central Asia'. The Hilmand, the longest river in Afghanistan, was to be tamed to restore fertility to a huge desert area south of Kandahar. MK made a contract to build roads, two dams and an extensive canal system which would include intakes, waterways, laterals and sublaterals. The project, blithely undertaken, would change the lives of between two and three million people, about a fifth of the country's population.

The nineteen-fifties were pioneering times for the distribution of foreign aid, and there were many failures. The long, slow disaster of the Hilmand Valley project was unfolding by the time I visited Kandahar. Costs had mushroomed; all equipment had to be shipped from America through Pakistan where rumbling hostility provoked by the Paktunistan question meant endless delays. The human difficulties of settling new people in vast newly-created areas of irrigation to mingle with the original peasants who had farmed beside the Hilmand for years were never tackled properly. Problems arose for a myriad of reasons ranging from breakdown in communications; salinity problems; ethnic differences and the conflict between American bureaucracy and Afghan xenophobia.

Over the decade the Americans became increasingly unpopular. The differences between a rich patron and an underdeveloped aspiring state, where incompetence and lack of decision confronted impatient New World technology, contributed to the decline of American influence in Afghanistan and the domination of the Soviet Union. The desert did not bloom. The grandiose, ever more costly plans and projects became a mocking mirror of Amanullah's failures.

MK would not accept blame for imposing its engineering skills on an underdeveloped society without negotiation or explanation. Such delicacies were not the responsibility of rednecks. It was up to confused Afghan government officials to explain changing circumstances to several million peasants, including a million or two nomads who, it was piously hoped, would be persuaded to settle down.

When the Lodestar flew into Kandahar, MK was just past the peak of its achievement. It had completed ahead of schedule the 145-foot-high Arghandab Dam eighteen miles from Kandahar, and was well on target for the Kajaki Dam which it was rushing to complete in the face of gigantic rising costs. An ambitious and worthy idea – not a new one, since the deserts of Afghanistan are littered with the ruins of projects to tame its rivers – was rapidly turning disastrous. Meanwhile the enclosed world behind MK's perimeter wire was taken as a symbol of American disdain for Afghan values. Americans within ignored the poverty outside the compound and refused to feel shame.

So MK's employees enjoyed high tax-free salaries, air conditioning provided by oil generators which cost a fortune to run, Australian powdered milk, new cars and other perks.

In the main office the duty officer was expecting us. 'The petrol's here, but you'll have to pay for it.'

Mr Hoffman muttered something about credit.

'Are you crazy? What the hell do you think this place is? Yes, sure, go right ahead and phone Kabul.' And Mr Hoffman made the first of scores of telephone calls to Carl.

We settled in fairly easily, and as the days passed enjoyed the monster fry ups in the cafeteria, the doughnuts, the comfortable beds, the Coke, and above all the iced beer. The camp was an early example of the instant cities that were beginning to spring up around the world wherever American engineers worked. Everyone in the camp seemed to be on first-name terms.

'Hi, Pete, when are those goddam Swedes going to release you?'

'Don't let those guys fool you, they haven't a dime between them.'

We were living on lavish charity. MK put up with us and let us eat their hamburgers and look at their movies. Its people may have seen in the Swedish company a reflection of their own failure. They must have seen in Carl's sheep casings a little imitation of their own great schemes for dams and roadways where the signs of failure were already imminent. At least Carl's crowd belonged to the free world – anything to do down the increasing Afghan dependence on the Soviet Union.

Days passed pleasantly until the money came. As always after a period of lassitude, things moved very rapidly. One morning I was sunbathing by the pool when a flustered Mr Hoffman came running up. He could have forgotten about me, and I could have spent another decade lounging about MK. We had ten minutes to dress and get out to the airport.

In later years a lavish airport would be built at Kandahar, but now it was an even simpler layout of huts and scraped sand than the airport at Kabul. Around the Lodestar Sven was arranging a line of men with buckets to relay the precious petrol up to the wing tanks and slop it in.

'The place is full of police. Let's get away fast.'

Better not to ask where the money for the petrol had come from. The refuelling did not take long. As soon as the last bucket was carried up the two engines burst into life and in a moment we were over green fields that had benefited from irrigation.

As we flew higher the tins which contained the sheep casings began to pop with the pressure and the interior of the plane was splattered with blobs of sheep gut.

We flew over the harsh desert lands of Registan, crossing the knifelike ridges of hills. The land was every shade of brown. Very occasionally a startling sliver or patch of green would gleam somewhere in the complex folds and plains and ridges of the landscape, and the ancient passion to make the desert fertile could be understood.

The shadow of our little plane made the only movement across the wrinkled brown hills. Then it moved over a fringe of white onto the blue sea and we were crossing the Persian gulf.

We spent the night at Sharja, in those days a little place in the desert used by the RAF as a refuelling station. I remember a small Arab fort with a pair of old cannon outside the main gate, golden beaches and palm trees. The rest house was furnished with sagging wickerwork chairs and copies of *Punch* whose covers still bore Richard Doyle's caricatures. All night long came the 'fut-fut' of a small diesel engine trying in vain to blow wafts of cool air into our rooms. For breakfast we had bacon and eggs and toast with coarse cut marmalade served by an attentive Arab boy.

The remainder of the flight was punctuated by alarms and troubles and the increasing odours of rotting sheep intestines. From the moment Mr Hoffman entered the plane at Kandahar he did not speak to me, but sat in silence among the popping cans. Sometimes above the noise of the engines I could hear him mumbling to himself in Swedish.

We came to Nicosia, which English occupation had turned dismal – a Mediterranean Ramsgate with a fatal whiff of suburban values. The place was full of English soldiers and Greek nightclubs, a magnet for the two Swedish pilots who appeared the next morning clutching their heads after debauchery and Greek brandy.

The brave little plane flew over the Alps; the door to the cockpit was open and I could see Sven in dark glasses, his hat as usual at a rakish angle, bent over the controls. As we went higher over the mountains the tins of sheep casings reached a crescendo of popping. Then we were over Germany, and a long time later, amazingly, we landed safely at Gothenburg. It was midnight; before taxiing to the main terminal the crew stopped the plane by a perimeter fence at the far end of the runway and threw over the Afghan carpets in order to avoid paying Customs duty. Then at last we could leave the abattoir smells of the plane's interior to face Gothenburg in the darkness – shop windows furnished with luxury goods, sleek Swedish cars, and inebriated business men in smart suits swaying and falling in the snow in the middle of a fine red brick square.

9

NINETEEN FIFTY-FOUR

I SPENT the autumn in Ireland without hearing anything more about the Swedish plane and the regular service to Kabul. The Military Academy's vacation was long over and soon I was several months overdue. As Christmas approached I realised reluctantly that I would have to buy a ticket on a conventional airline to Afghanistan.

I contacted my friend Michael, and we arranged to join forces next year for an extended journey through Central Asia. Michael had a first-class degree in philosophy from Trinity College Dublin, which entitled him to a job as brewer in Guinness's brewery.

We planned journeys deep into the heart of Central Asia, following in the footsteps of the great travellers. It has been noted how in the nineteenth century everyone seemed to be dressing up and going to places like Kashgar. Those journeys had been forbidden and dangerous, and travellers met unpleasant ends, like Moorcroft who disappeared and was probably poisoned, and poor Stoddart and Connolly, taken up from the snake pit and beheaded, and Hayward who fell among thieves. Surely, in spite of communism's cold efficiency, things could be no more dangerous now.

Like Robert Byron we were obsessed with Central Asia. 'The name Turkestan has hyptonised me,' Byron wrote, comparing it to how the word 'Guermantes' had much the same effect on Proust. In addition to the early explorers, we read Sven Hedin, Auriel Stein, Mildred Cable and Francesca French, and Peter Fleming and Ella Maillart. We, too, would like to visit the singing sands of the Taklamaken, the Caves of Thisu and the Buddhas, the jade-coloured lakes, the Turfan depression, the Wakhan and the Pamirs. We refused to believe that the warlords, brigands, thieves and local uprisings of yesterday provided more formidable barriers to travel than the rings of steel shutting in China and Russia did now.

We would go further – perhaps to Siberia and across the Bering Strait to America. New names would appear in our letters – Yakutsk, the River Lena, the peninsula of Kamshaka. We attempted a cool and rational assessment of problems. 'Crossing the Bering Strait will be difficult as most of the year there are fogs and gales.'

Michael would join me the following summer. I left him to study the *Admiralty Handbook to Siberia and Arctic Russia* and *Army Survival Techniques* and set out once more for Kabul by commercial airline. The return journey ended abruptly at Peshawar since snow prevented planes landing in Kabul. Here I came upon the familiar figure of Mr Hoffman in his stetson on his way to inspect the progress of the company.

'Everything continues to go wrong. You remember those sheep casings? They stink in the plane. Why? Because everyone of them is rotten. Even those which have not escaped bursting from their cans. All rotten. God knows what that lunatic Carl is further mismanaging in Kabul.'

We managed to hitch a lift in a lorry. Soon the road was a river of ice banked on both sides by great drifts of snow where a bulldozer had cleared a way. We crept slowly forward over the Lataband. I thought of the retreat in 1840 and Lady Sale reading Hohenlinden before she set out:

> Few, few shall part, while many meet,
> The snow shall be their winding sheet,
> And every turf beneath their feet
> Shall be a soldier's sepulchre.

The Kabul plain stretched ahead, white and silent, a few bare trees visible under the frosty sky. When I had left in summer the streets had been crowded, the bazaars ablaze with life and colour. Now it was snowing hard when the lorry stopped at the corner of the lane leading down to Carl's house. We stumbled blindly through snowdrifts to where a security policeman stood huddled up in his coat and blowing through his fingers. He gazed at us curiously as we kicked and hammered at the garden door and thick snowflakes continued to fall. Many minutes passed before we heard the soft crunch of footsteps and Nabi's nervous voice asking who we were.

In the sample room Carl, wearing a collection of old coats and mufflers, was bending over a metal stove. Dense clouds of smoke were escaping through the rusted piping, while the heat given off seemed to be minimal.

'You did not get my letter?' In his excitement at seeing the two snow-encrusted figures standing at the door, the words tumbled out in a torrent. 'My God, what difficulties I have had . . . you remember the second agent? He was also a disaster . . . well, I had to pay him off, he was useless. Then I had two other men and they disappeared . . . then the plane . . .'

Hoffman groaned.

'But you, Peter. Why are you not in Kandahar under arrest?'

'Why should I be?'

'Didn't you land there with the other company?'

'What other company?'

'Wait, I tell you . . . but first we must have some coffee.'

No bourbon.

Huddled over the smoking fire, curling our fingers around lukewarm cups, we listened to another tale of misfortune. After Hoffman had left Sweden to return to Kabul, a rival firm had hired the plane with Sven as Captain and tried to appropriate for itself all Carl's schemes for the development of Afghanistan.

Meanwhile the International Trading Company, which for the last few weeks had consisted of Hoffman stranded in Delhi and Carl freezing in Kabul, had remained paralysed without money, support, and worse, without the plane.

Because of the snow, Sven's plane, now run on behalf of the rival company, had been diverted to Kandahar where everyone was promptly placed under arrest. In their confidence the company's directors had neglected the tedious spadework of hiring influential Afghan agents and making friends with ministers. Such precautions might seldom be of positive help, but to neglect them was fatal. The plane was now grounded, and three members of the company, Sven, Lars, the co-pilot and one passenger whom Carl had assumed to be me, had been lodged for the past fortnight in Kandahar jail in conditions that rivalled the snakepit at Bokhara.

Carl told his story with glee. Throughout the recital Hoffman said nothing, but suddenly his face became purple. Waving a pudgy fist, he rose trembling from his seat. I had never seen a man so angry.

'Is it not enough that first you discredit me in the eyes of the Afghan government with two dishonest agents who try and bankrupt me!'

'But, boss . . .' the astonished Carl smiled and put a restraining hand on Hoffman's shoulder. 'Everything will be all right, sure.'

'You tell me everything will be all right when another company has arrived to steal all our trade. And there is no money in the bank.' Like a ham actor he clasped his head in his hands and appeared to be about to burst into tears.

As usual Carl was optimistic and I retired to bed, leaving him hoarsely chuckling at the thought that Sven's plane would be permanently confiscated, a move that would undoubtedly finish off the new company.

I was welcomed back to the Military College with a few good-natured jokes about my long absence. Although I was three months overdue, there were no recriminations or hints that I should be sacked. The Wolf continued to come to my classes where there were scores of new Abdullahs, Rahmins, Azifs and Mohammeds to be sorted out and identified in their disguise of heavy winter coats and shaven heads pinky-grey with cold. In each classroom a small stove stood in a corner throwing out a suggestion of warmth, but it was far too cold for the cadets to take off their overcoats. They sat huddled against each other, breathing out white clouds into the frosty air. In the corridors the new Austrian coach and his athletes rushed up and down trying to keep warm.

The snow lay thick, covering the hills and blocking up the roads, replenished each morning by a fresh downfall. Few lorries could reach the capital and food was beginning to get scarce. Kabul was quiet, the silence broken only by regular slaps and plop-plops as snow was shovelled from flat roofs onto the heads of passers-by. Down below it piled up in huge coffee-coloured drifts which were crossed by narrow catwalks. The telegraph poles were down and life had come to a standstill. There were no buses or cars, no tongas, no horses, no women wearing chadris. There was no music shrieking out of teahouses. Most of the bazaar shops had closed down. A few people hurried, wrapped in heavy posteen coats, but the only real activity and noise came from the lane where blacksmiths hammered out new metal stoves from piles of discarded kerosene cans.

Under the snow life in Kabul took on a different emphasis in the daily struggle to keep warm. Some of the older houses had Russian style *kursi* stoves built inside the walls with cubicles placed above where a man could hibernate comfortably. Outside, piedogs died of cold in the streets, their corpses frozen until the thaw.

One afternoon I joined a party from the British Embassy which typically had managed to assemble some ancient homemade skis. Above Amanullah's palace at Darul Aman and the dreaming white city and its frozen river ringed by pointed hills, I skied down an icy slope and noticed three dark shapes looking across at me. I knew what they were. Stories about wolves were legion: how a child had been killed, or some old woman had been badly mauled by the starving packs of animals which came down to the city looking for food and tore through the silent streets. It was said that a particular target for wolves were the unfortunate night watchmen and soldiers guarding the embassies and foreigners' houses. At night I often saw these solitary figures wrapped in thick coats shuffling their feet in an effort to keep warm as they stood outside a studded door waiting for the dawn. They reminded me of those old coachmen in Tsarist Russia who waited in the snow for the ball to end.

Life at the International Trading Company continued to be a series of crises punctuated by long periods of inertia. The rival Swedish firm was released and arrived up from Kandahar, its members battered, but determined to take over the foreign trade in karakul. For the next two weeks the rivals watched each other warily, but Carl, used to sitting and waiting for developments, outlasted his opponents. In due course, dispirited and bankrupt, they abandoned the market. Hoffman returned to Europe, leaving Carl to restart trade with a new agent who had a gratifying number of relations in high government positions.

Meanwhile there was the cold to contend with. During the summer Carl had neglected to buy any fuel and now it was almost impossible to obtain. At street corners a few sticks weighed on a handscale would be fought over by chilled customers. When electricity was restored I went to bed with a small electric fire between the sheets. Carl never got up at all.

When two Danish anthropologists who were travelling to Nuristan to collect ethnographical specimens offered me a third share in their house, I decided to move. It was the lack of adequate heating that made me anxious to depart, even though I was to find that my new home offered me very little more. In fact the square building of mud bricks, lacking electricity, with its privy in a shed down at the bottom of the desolate snowy garden, perhaps within reach of wolves, was not nearly so luxurious as the house at Shahri Naw. But life there was a lot less hectic.

I had felt apprehensive in telling Carl I was leaving, but he was too busy to notice. Suddenly the International Trading Company showed a resurgence with an order for western-style clothing which had been arranged by the new agent. New servants were engaged and clothed in the American army surplus uniforms which were flooding the Kabul bazaar at the conclusion of the Korean war.

When I returned to Shahri Naw in spring for a brief visit I found the house had been redecorated in Asian style with bead curtains across the hallway, plenty of small carved tables inlaid with mother-of-pearl, and gaudy Egyptian rugs. Framed certificates now lined the walls, and all the trade samples, including the Swedish army boots, had vanished.

Carl brought out the whiskey and reported that he was busy, and although the Swedish plane service had not yet materialised, the company was at last showing a profit. He introduced me to new house-guests whom he had acquired during a short business trip to Pakistan, a German mother and her sixteen-year-old daughter.

'So much Carl has told us about you, Herr Peter,' said the mother, who wore an iridescent gold sari with an embroidered edge. 'Such troubles! No money! Such cold!'

'Such changes!' Carl said, clapping his hands loudly. Nabi appeared, immaculate in white dustcoat and new turban. 'Show your watch brought all the way from Switzerland.' Nabi grimaced and extended his wrist.

'You must come and see us often. We are not a big family.'
He winked at the two women.

'Such changes . . . no more starvation and Nescafé. Do you
like the way the house is? It is not bad for a beginning, but wait
until next year. I am bringing in complete new furnishing. New
carpets, new modern Swedish kitchen . . .'

Before I said goodbye, he made me promise to accept the
position of captain of the guard when he became Swedish consul
in Kabul.

Hans, a blond Viking giant, and Klaus (who later died tragically
in Nuristan) were kept busy collecting musical instruments for
a Danish museum. Every night the mice played them and I
would be woken by the drumming of little feet running up and
down the tables, sounding the strings of the long-necked rebab,
and making pinging sounds on the sarandas and the ancient
Nuristani harp strung across an inflated gourd.

The snow melted, spring came and we could dine out on the
terrace under the brilliant stars. The Danes talked of lonely
mountain passes and remote villages far from roads, of Kuchi
caravans, musicians, marches at night, of poetry. Sven would
recite Khushhal Khan Khattack at the top of his voice; I had
encountered him in Major Raverty:

Although every drop of dew should be the seed of a rose,
The nightingales' hearts would not be satiated with
    beholding it.

Their cook, who travelled with them on their various expeditions, was even more inefficient than Nabi had been. A
white-bearded patriarch, he spent hours on the mud floor of the
kitchen searching his body for fleas, his wrinkled fingers deftly
synchronised.

Klaus or Hans would shout, 'Abdul . . . a pair of chickens . . .
choak . . . zut . . . plenty of rice and nan!'

Six hours later something different would emerge from the
kitchen.

'I told you *choak*!' The New Zealand spam would be carefully
sliced and arranged with garnishing.

We struggled to get used to Abdul's grumbling efforts to produce a good meal, which were usually dignified and comical. If the rice was cold, if the chicken still had half its feathers and was only half-cooked, if the eggs tasted of gasoline, there was always an explanation.

'Eh . . . eh . . .' the old man would groan, shaking his head at the disappointment. The shopkeeper had swindled him, or he had been given no money for buying charcoal, or the evil-smelling ghee which he kept in an old tin had been eaten by mice.

Every foreigner knew that you did not employ Afghan servants, particularly cooks, unless there was no alternative. It was not that they could not cook, but they did not want to. Above all, being of independent spirit, they did not want to cook for *ferenghi*. Every foreigner sought instead to have in his employ one of the god-like creatures from Pakistan who had been trained by the English. Tall, dignified and silent, dressed in starched tunics, glittering cummerbunds and turbans wound hard as clay, topped by great frills, they were like extra-terrestial beings. Not only could they cook, but they lent distinction and a touch of mystery to diplomatic dinner parties, silently serving the roast beef and Yorkshire pudding.

'It will be wonderful having Mohammed after you leave.'

'I'm afraid I've promised him to the Wrights.'

'But you said we were first on the list!' Across the linen-covered table and the carefully arranged flowers two women would glare at each other.

I continued to correspond with Michael back in Ireland, exchanging messages in code. Tashkent became Wicklow 'Army authority intends to Feyzabad.' 'What plants can we safely eat?' 'The best protection for Arctic winters is second-hand silk underwear from the RAF. I have contacted a specialised store dealing in ex-army equipment . . .' Needless to say, I did not consult Carl.

Everywhere we wished to travel was forbidden.

Spring passed too soon, the roses faded and the dust returned. Every day there were dust storms so thick that you could not see down a street. Men wound their turbans like veils round their faces; women in their chadris were to be envied.

Prince Peter of Greece, who was an anthropologist, was coming to stay with my Danish friends and I had to look round for

somewhere else to live. After intricate negotiations I was introduced to an immaculately dressed young dandy who was prepared to disregard the strictures against foreigners.

'Why do you have no wife? That is bad,' he said, taking my
hand with a caress and a flutter of eyelashes. 'Do you like my
tie, Mr Peter?' he waved the gaudy stripes. 'Please, you must
have it.' In the same way I acquired his shoes which he pulled
off his feet before I could ask him about a house that he knew
was available for rent.

'Oh please, Mr Peter! My cousin is abroad and leaves his
second wife and family here.' It seemed that the house had an
empty room to spare. What about rent? He looked aggrieved.
Oh no rent from Mr Peter, no, no! He looked deeply saddened.
'Rent does not matter, Mr Peter.' His eyes appeared to fill with
tears, but then he gave me a brave coquettish smile. 'Of course
we are friends.'

Through the smiles and the hand-holding I managed to hammer out an agreement to pay him a small amount of money each
month for which I lived in a very large house with a superb
garden, far bigger than the garden at Shahri Naw. Its huge trees,
offering shade that was almost a darkness, were full of singing
birds; at night I would listen to the nightingale.

I appeared to have it to myself. No one was ever visible. On
opening the garden door I would be greeted by the sharp banging
of doors and windows being closed. The place seemed deserted
except for my rooms in the wing, where I would find delicacies
carefully arranged on the table, little kolcha cakes, thin crispy
elephant's ears, salads and fruit. Every evening unseen hands
would place them there.

The etiquette was easy to acquire. When I returned from the
Military Academy before I entered my part of the house I would
knock loudly on the door and wait a few minutes for the beings
inside to vanish. From time to time I would hear women's voices,
someone singing or laughing.

At my end of the house I acquired a gardener and a cook.
Ahmed, who had managed to get invalided out of the army, was
just like every other Afghan cook, spending his day curled up in
the kitchen fast asleep. When he cooked he performed his duties
as if he found them horrible, and it was melancholy and humiliat-
ing to watch his disdain as he stood and squatted before the

stove. A spirited and brave Afghan warrior was not destined for this menial duty. My new pressure cooker blew up in my face. When I asked Warren and his wife to dine, the chicken was still alive when we sat down. After that I told him that from now on I would stoop to women's work while he could behave like a man and act as runner for me to the bazaar. Immediately he became a different person as if he had stepped out of a ragged disguise. From then on I lived mostly on tinned porridge and the food provided by invisible hands.

Time was passing. The British Ambassador retired, a Soviet delegation appeared, some Americans were accused of corruption, the first Afghan woman since Queen Soraya discarded her veil and was seen publicly in a street. A new prime minister was elected, destined to be assassinated with more than usual brutality.

At the Military Academy Ramadan had come and another visit of the foreign military attachés was arranged. Every single detail of last year's schedule was repeated: the cadets sprinkled with DDT waiting hour after hour at their desks; the brisk inspection and the official lunch with the Commandant.

Michael was on his way. 'Tuesday 10 July. Just embarking from Southampton. Fabulous food. Met an attractive girl also travelling to Pakistan.' 'Monday 16 July. Port Said. Affair going well. Looking forward to seeing you soon. Hope everything is fixed.'

Warren guessed that I planned to go on my travels, leaving him in the lurch. He disapproved of my lukewarm approach to teaching and my long absence in Europe.

'But no one seemed to mind.'

'How do you know? I wouldn't say too much about your friend Michael if I were you.'

There were just the two Irish teachers in Kabul and the behaviour of one would affect the other. Warren reminded me again that he had a wife and child to support.

'Xenophobia is as natural to Afghans as breathing. It's understandable in a country that has suffered endless wars and invasions.'

'But Michael's just a visitor. A tourist. What about the new tourist board?'

'All foreigners are spies or worse.'

Why the tourist board had been established was a complete mystery. Foreigners did not come merely for a visit. Those who were not archaeologists, anthropologists, experts in some field or other, diplomats, connected with Morrison Knudsen or employed by an international agency immediately aroused suspicion. The hippies, then the Russians were yet to invade. 'Why does your friend wish to come all the way to see Afghanistan? There is nothing to see.' This was always said with a smile and a shrug of the shoulders.

Michael had a familiar introduction to Kabul. He wrote home: 'I arrived at 5 a.m. in the morning and slept in the lounge of the one hotel in Kabul, a really depressing tomb of a place with ghastly oriental music on gramophones coming from the tea-houses and bazaars in the street outside. In the morning I found Peter's house with some difficulty, a very charming place with a lovely garden. To sit out at night with that superb sky is wonderful.'

Before he departed from England he had shopped at the Army and Navy, and had the good luck to escape the attentions of the Pakistan Customs. So we had a waterproof tent, medical supplies, torches for use as gifts, a large flying suit filled with kapok, tins of fortified A-rations used by the army (one tablet carefully sucked would keep a man alive for a day), Swiss knives, a compass, maps, and insect repellent. Because of its weight and the fact that Nabi had burned it so often, we decided against taking my pressure cooker.

I sought permission to go to the Wakhan, land of snows, yak and Bactrian camels. This was turned down. Then I put in another application for us to visit Badakshan, and this time there was no objection. We could go to the provincial capital of Feyzabad and then on through Jurm to Iskashim, which led directly into the Wakhan and the Pamirs, and perhaps we could make some headway in spite of not having official permission. Our plans of crossing iron and bamboo curtains into the middle of Asia were vague.

10

T HE Post Office, which also acted as the bus terminal, was strewn with dead lorries and cars where groups of passengers squatted in the dust among the heaps of broken machinery. We arrived at nine in the morning on a hot cloudless day, and already Kabul sweltered in the sun. We were weighed down with our supplies and had added to our discomfiture by wearing silky blue and white turbans inexpertly wound so that we looked like extras in a B-movie about the north-west frontier. A uniformed cadet from the Military College walked past and, recognising me, saluted

Inside the Post Office the clerk scrutinised our official per-mission to travel and gave us our tickets, tearing them off a roll and punching each one with his teeth. He said that transport would soon be leaving for Katigan on the first stage of our journey. Soon meant instantly, straight away; with the usual explosiveness that followed lethargy, everything happened at once. Our rucksacks and bags were thrown in the back of a new postal jeep, a boy dusted down the bonnet and we squeezed into the front seat beside the driver whose name was Amin.

'Very good jeep, it came from Peshawar last night,' he shouted as we skidded round a corner, missing a string of camels that had the bad sense to be coming the other way. In a moment we had left Kabul and, trailing yellow dust, were speeding through the Koh-i-Daman valley that supplies the city with fruit and veg-etables. On either side of the road crumbling mud walls hid the orchards, while piles of wooden boxes filled with grapes lay be-neath them waiting to be picked up by lorries. Beyond the valley the brown hills leading to the main range of the Paghman Mountains were dotted with black tents of Kuchi nomads.

At Charikar Amin discovered that he had forgotten to deliver mail in a village miles back, and left us to swelter in the heat. Prone figures were lying asleep under the trees oblivious to the loudspeaker erected at the crossroads which erupted with the

usual screech of Indian music. Two hours later the jeep returned
with three more passengers piled in the back, a fat Uzbeg and his
two wives in chadris – not the shining pleated sort you mostly saw
in Kabul, but the stifling homespun variety of baggy cotton. We
felt hotter just looking at them – turning round to glimpse little
hands stained brown with betelnut passing objects to each other,
to listen to the whispered exchanges through the stifling mesh.
Once settled, their husband took no more notice of them than if
they were indeed sacks. They spoke no more after the jeep started,
never uttering a sound except when they were sick. Then they were
given tufts of grass to wipe themselves down with.

The road turned off and followed the fertile Ghorband Valley
over the Shibar Pass to the gorge of the Darra-i-Shikari which cut
dramatically through the main gorge of the Hindu Kush. Today a
similar journey would follow another route and use the Salang
Highway. The great highway, constructed by Soviet engineers
with Soviet finance, had not yet started, and the amazing three-
kilometre-long tunnel through the Salang Pass was not completed
until 1964. The tunnel, a magnificent engineering feat, at eleven
thousand feet above sea level, just about the world's highest, cuts
through the Hindu Kush, greatly shortening the time needed to
cross the country. Before the Soviet tanks rolled down, a passenger
car following the Salang could travel from the Soviet border
through Kabul to the Pakistan border in a day.

The traditional ancient route from central Asia is the Kotal I
Khawak, through which Alexander's troops made their way in
379 BC, frost-bitten and snow-blinded, eating raw sheep and
mules. Up until modern times all heavy traffic had to go by the
Khawak to the north, or take the long way round by Herat.
Amanullah made two attempts to construct the new road, ironi-
cally entrusting the task to Soviet engineers who failed to trans-
form two old pilgrim routes across the Aq Ribat and Nil Kotal
passes. It was Nadir Shah who fulfilled the old dream of connecting the Oxus and the central Afghan plain by constructing the
first motorable road through the Hindu Kush by way of the
Shibar Pass, a scheme completed in 1933. This was the route we
were now following.

We drove through the rich Ghorband valley until dusk when
we reached the opening of the great gorge. The road spiralled
upwards following a small stream through walls of rock. Higher

up the colours became diffused by the setting sun, golden or pink, other dazzling reflections of darkened blue, and occasionally a snow peak shone high above us.

In the darkness we passed the turnoff for Bamiyan with its two sandstone statues of the Buddha built in the third and fifth centuries, over the years a destination for countless Chinese and even Korean pilgrims. The signature of the early English traveller, William Moorcroft, is supposed to have been scratched on the wall of one of Bamiyan's caves; in the early days of the Great Game the Bamiyan pass was considered a feasible way for Soviets to reach India.

The famous statues have been considered one of the unsung wonders of the world, although Robert Byron found them hideous, mentioning their 'flaccid bulk . . . even their material is unbeautiful for the cliff is made, not of stone, but of compressed gravel.' After Amanullah's time this was designated a tourist area, whose amenities even included a hotel. Tourists were supposed to go there, and nowhere else.

'You must go to Bamyian. It is much better,' petulant officials advised us when we had tried to obtain permission to go further afield. Now the Royal Afghan Mail had no time for such a diversion; we speeded past the turnoff and were swallowed up by mountains and darkness until the jeep stopped abruptly because it had run out of petrol. We sat and shivered under the stars while Amin, who regarded the misfortune as a great joke, handed round cigarettes and sang, stopping to blow his nose and spit into the night. Hour after hour we shivered until at last we heard the beautiful sound of another lorry approaching. Amin jumped into the road, there was a murmured exchange and we were saved.

A few miles further on a fox was caught in the headlights as it ran into a bed of reeds. Amin screeched to a halt, produced an old rifle from under the front seat and stalked it, a lonely figure creeping along without result. Then the Uzbeg, who for many miles had been sitting bolt upright whistling through his teeth, made a sudden movement and was sick over his wives. Amin jumped down again to gather grass for the squeaking women. Just before dawn we drove into the colonnaded square of Pul-i-Khumri on the northern side of the Hindu Kush fifteen hours after leaving Kabul.

In the morning in bright sunshine we awoke to a circle of

slant-eyed Mongols fingering our clothes and bags of property.
We were on the road by ten o'clock, having deposited the Uzbeg
and his wives, and replaced them by three men travelling to
Kunduz, the cotton capital.

At last we were in Turkestan and nothing about it seemed
interesting. Thirty years ago Katigan province had been swamp
and jungle grass where malaria flourished – 'if you want to die,
go to Katigan' was a proverb. It was drained largely through
the exertions of a remarkable karakul merchant Abdul Aziz
Londoni, whose ancestors came from Kashmir to Afghanistan
in the eighteenth century. After making his fortune by building
up the karakul trade and introducing skins to the London market
which gave a boost to the lasting international fashion in 'Persian
lamb' coats, he earned the name Londoni. His subsequent
business dealings involved going into partnership with another
pioneering businessman, Abdul Majid Zabuli, and persuading the
Bank-i-Melli to grant a loan in order to plant cotton fields, and
build a ginning plant and pressing mill in Kunduz. When these
were being developed during the nineteen-thirties, machinery and
materials were bought from Great Britain, Germany and the
USSR. A few years after our visit in the mid-nineteen fifties, industrial development would spread all over the plain as the Soviet
Union and America vied with each other to provide economic
(and military) aid in order to gain Afghanistan as a friend.

Writing about a similar situation a century before, Louis
Dupree quoted Kipling's *The Ballad of the King's Mercy*:

> Abdur Rahman, the Durani Chief,
> of him is the story told.
> He has opened his mouth to the North
> and the South, they have stuffed
> his mouth with gold.

But the same emperor Abdur Rahman thought differently. In
his autobiography he wrote: 'I dream of nothing but the backward state of my country – a goat torn by a lion on one side and
a bear on the other.'

Meanwhile as far as we were concerned Turkestan was nothing but cotton stretching to the horizon, interspersed by drab
little new towns. The cotton plants were in bloom or seed or

whatever made them look like vast white cabbage roses stretching for mile upon mile northward to the far distant Oxus which the Afghans call Amu Darya. Afghan Turkestan is effectively part of Central Asia. The people south of the river are mainly Uzbegs, speaking their own Turkic, whose racial affinities are with those living north of the Oxus rather than with the southern races of Afghanistan.

We drove through Baghlan, a small tree-lined bazaar and a sugar factory. After three hot hours we reached Kunduz, only thirty miles from the frontier with Russia. Here was the centre of the Cotton Syndicate with its mill, grinding shed, oil refinery and a small factory for producing soap. Central Asia travel offered a club for foreign engineers and technicians where we were deposited for the night.

Conscious of our dishevelled appearance, we dined with two Indian businessmen, immaculate in white, who told us they were investigating the market for pistachio nuts which grow wild in Badakshan. While they were talking, I noted a European sitting by himself on the veranda staring intently at us through the window. The minute we had finished eating, he joined us.

'Come and have a snifter,' he murmured in a low conspiratorial voice, and safe in his bedroom he produced a bottle of Haig.

'Chambers, George Chambers. From Lancashire.'

'Something to do with cotton?'

'How did you know? I'm installing machinery at the factory.' One of the lads had told him we were English . . . oh, Irish. Anyway it was nice to see a white face. 'What a hole!' He offered us cigarettes. 'The Bolshies are only thirty miles away Thirty bloody miles!' He began to tell us about his work with the air of a man besieged on all sides by enemies. He had never seen conditions like this – not even during his previous job in the Argentine. What were we doing in this hellhole?

'Travelling? Just visiting? You must be barmy. You'll be lucky to get through alive.' He glared as a servant passed the door. 'They spy on me,' he whispered.

'Surely not?'

'Last night a head was thrown over the garden wall.' He pointed through the wide picture window.

'A head?'

'Yes, a head. A bloke's head.'

'Have they found out who did it?'

'Not bloody likely.' He puckered his face in derision. 'This sort of thing happens all the time.' Had we not heard about the man they found hacked in pieces in Baghlan, or why the German engineer had to be sent home? 'I'd clear out quickly if I were you.'

We were given a mauve-coloured room with two iron-framed beds, a bucket and a broken chair that smelt of overripe water-melons, which at this time of year was the predominant smell throughout Turkestan. Everyone was eating them. Even the latrines smelt of melons.

The young explorer John Woods came here in the winter of 1826 to search a route to the Wakhan. We were hoping to travel in the same direction. Unlike most of his contemporaries, Woods travelled simply, without even a tent. 'We adopted the costume of the country.' The land around Kunduz would not be drained for a century, and meanwhile it was 'only fit to be the residence of acquatic birds'. He had plenty of the usual sort of traveller's comments. 'To ask an Uzbeg to sell his wife would be no affront, but to ask him to sell his dog would be an unpardonable insult . . . The Kunduz breed of horses is very inferior to the Turkoman.' He described 'the gallants of Kunduz strutting around the small town. They love to show themselves off clad in scarlet or some equally bright and glaring colour, while the ladies on the contrary wear dark clothes, or dress in pure white . . .'

I thought of Woods setting out across the wintry marshes for the distant Pamirs, facing feuding Turcomen and wild animals. Today the club was soporific and the heat was without respite. The only cool place was the large walled garden and today it was full of policemen in grey uniforms and peaked red hats enquiring into the ownership of the head.

Mr Chambers appeared. 'Told you so,' he said with glee. 'They won't find the body. Most likely it's been washed up on the Russian side of the Oxus. The Russians are always dragging them out with nets, and nothing is ever proved.'

When we departed he said, 'Tell the Embassy in Kabul that I'm still alive.'

The jeep was going no further than Khanabad, the old provin-cial capital on the edge of the Oxus plain, a shimmering expanse of cotton with ancient *tepes*, funeral mounds, thousands of years old rising in scorched brown bumps over its surface. Many of the small earthen bridges over the irrigation channels had collapsed with the weight of lorries, and the jeep had to dive and climb steeply to get across them. On the horizon I could make out clouds and high above them, traced against the sky, the faint outline of mountains, their lower half cut off by the summer haze. The fact that we were at last approaching the Pamirs elated us. I could imagine cool nights and high pastures with wandering nomads; I had read about the Kirghiz with their flocks of sheep and yak who lived so differently from the wretches of the fiery cultivated plain.

Khanabad was another cotton town grilling under the hot sun. Here was another public park, more whitewashed arcades and squatting men selling water melons. Here was another club where we got out stiffly and said goodbye to Amin who was returning to Kabul by way of Mazar-i-Sharif. The mail had to be delivered.

We would never get any closer to the Oxus. Thirty years later I had a pang of recognition watching the defeated Soviet army crossing over to Termez across the ugly metal bridge, and the last Soviet general following, and never looking back.

Outside the clubhouse the town dignitaries were being photographed clustered around the Afghan flag, torn between posing for the photographer and staring at us. An elderly man – whether he was Uzbeg, Turcoman or Tajik was difficult to say – rushed down the steps to greet us. Like the others in the group he was dressed in a grey pleated mackintosh which prosperous Afghans wore as a protection against the dust. Behind his tripod the photographer emerged from under the towel wrapped round his head and delayed the photographic session so that formal introductions could be made. But before we had to shake hands with every important man in Khanabad, a servant took our bags and, watched by the spellbound dignitaries, we were led inside.

Here was another bedroom whose walls were painted deep violet and where, overcome by heat and weariness, we fell asleep.

We were awoken, it seemed minutes later, our eyes watering at the purple haze around us. A man was bending over the bed, prodding me with a finger.

'You are very beautiful,' he said in English.

For a moment I thought he was Mr Chambers with another dire warning. Then I recognised one of the men we had seen posing, who had taken off the mackintosh to reveal a dusty uniform.

'I am police chief of Khanabad.'

For a second his face took on a listless expression as he gazed out of the narrow window towards a sound of sharp tapping from the metal bazaar across the street. Then, pulling himself together, he asked for our visas.

'Do you like women?' he said, taking my hand and holding it tightly. He did not wait for an answer. 'Because you are here I will be happy. I will show you Khanabad.'

He had spent many years in this place, years of exile deprived of the delights of Kabul. Now he took it upon himself to show us the minor provincial pleasures of the town, beginning with a visit to the public park, which this evening resembled the location of a paseo in a Spanish village, except, of course, there were only men. I watched them parade in their best clothes under the chenar trees, bearded and scented, hand in hand, meeting and exchanging elaborate compliments. My hand was held too as we were introduced to the judge, the school teacher, and other important people.

Where was Ireland?

There was the usual confusion between Irlanda and Hollanda. In future years there wouldn't be anywhere remote enough on the globe for someone not to break into a grin of recognition at the name of Ireland and say 'Bang-bang' or 'Bobby Sands'.

In Khanabad we were fêted and dined. There was none of the suspicion of foreigners to conflict with the traditional code of hospitality. Every morning the police chief would appear at our bedroom door for some fresh sortie. Any refusal was mutiny.

'You must come. Today we go swimming.'

He would take my hand and lead us through the public park and the various bazaars to the fast flowing river where he would watch with concentration as we undressed and threw ourselves into the brown muddy flood. Walking down the dusty streets and through the park arm in arm I noticed that after those first introductions the other officials of Khanabad kept a safe distance.

There seemed to be no escape. For most people Khanabad was the end of the road, and no traffic seemed to be going further into Badakshan.

'Today we go to the circus.' This was a travelling Russian outfit with clowns on stilts, dancing dogs and boys dressed as female trapeze artists. The numbing effect of heat and virtual imprisonment induced inertia. By midday the town was fast asleep. Nothing stirred or moved, not even the leaves of the trees, limp in the stifling air. We drank bottles of sherbet, doused ourselves with buckets of cold water, went swimming, sucked grapes and sank our teeth into the warm pink flesh of water-melons. Nothing could dispel an overwhelming sense of torpor.

We might have stayed for the rest of the summer in Khanabad, but at last the police chief got tired of us.

'You wish to go to Feyzabad? I will see.'

Straight away a lorry was stopped at the sandy cross-section of the main square, and two unfortunate passengers sitting in the cab were thrown out. With profuse apologies for the state of the road and any inconvenience we had suffered during our stay at Khanabad, he installed us in their places. I have a last memory of him standing pensively in his crumpled grey uniform beside the municipal flowerbed, the evicted passengers slinking away. The new road stretched across the Oxus plain. For the first time since reaching Turkestan we began to pass flocks of sheep and the occasional horseman, while instead of flat cotton fields we drove among green hills, and rivers crossed by stone bridges that stood above them in a curving arc. The roar of the water rushing down from the snowfields to the fiery plain drowned out the noise of the engine.

Badakshan stretches from the Wakhan corridor at an altitude of twelve thousand feet down to almost sea level around the Oxus plain. It is cut in half from south-east to north-west by the river Kokcha, along whose banks ran the old trade route used by Marco Polo and other early travellers journeying to China by way of Wakhan. The Moghuls conquered the territory, but were driven out in the seventeenth century when the last reigning Mir was expelled. Some kings of Badakshan claimed descent from Alexander whose horse, Bucephalus, was supposedly bred here. Marco Polo describes the magnificent ponies, the rubies and lapis lazuli which are still found in the mountains, like the sheep named after him.

The rest of the day passed in a squashed moving metal can filled with Koranic texts, artificial flowers, dust, paintings of birds and garlands, and tassels. The velvet fringe of tassels was stretched across the cab window through which the driver peered at the winding track. Slowly we left the sweltering plain of the Oxus and as we climbed into the crumpled brown hills, the air had a suggestion of a breeze. Sometimes a lonely child, attracted by our trail of dust, hurled a stone at us, sometimes the road was blocked by cattle or herds of karakul sheep and shepherds in tattered coats stared in amazement at the struggling vehicle.

We stopped at a small hill village where the teahouse made of caked mud was vibrating to the sounds of an orchestra consisting of tablas, rebabs and other instruments competing with Radio Kabul. The arrival of two foreigners added to the tumult in that small overcrowded room. We dumped our rucksacks among the steaming pots and samovars before sitting cross-legged on the floor to answer questions. Who were we? Where had we come from? One of the drummers came over and examined us minutely, inch by inch. The questions were briefly interrupted by a child emerging from the kitchen with a plate of rice and singing in a high voice with such intensity that the room trembled and Radio Kabul was turned right down.

Who were we? We were taken for Americans, or worse, English spies. Russians, perhaps? No, not Russians. When you have crossed the main mountain block of the Hindu Kush distrust of foreigners reaches a crescendo.

While the argument continued, we ducked out of the smoky room and strolled along by the banks of the small stream which girded the village and through silent cobbled streets. Not a light gleamed; we could just make out the outlines of the shuttered houses as we made our way in the darkness back to the inn.

Suddenly there was a 'Pisht!' behind us, and a man came running out of the shadows.

'Bring the light here!'

Another figure emerged with a lantern swinging on the end of a pole. Now we could see that the first man was an officer who stood in front of us waving a drawn sword; behind him with the light was a soldier with a rough cloth cap pushed over his forehead.

The lantern was brought close to our faces, and the officer peered at us. 'Foreigners' he muttered. He added, 'Did you not know there were bandits in the town?'

'Bandits?'

'You are fortunate.' He poked at a heap of rubbish with the tip of his sword while his deputy banged on the shutters of the inn. There was a commotion inside, and a frightened face appeared. The officer shouted, the head nodded, and there was a sound of bolts being drawn to let us in. It was pitch dark inside except for the innkeeper's candle, as he guided us over the sleeping forms of his guests to where our rucksacks lay.

We heard no more about bandits, those elusive figures of menace found worldwide. Next morning everything seemed to have returned to normal, the same group of people gathering to watch us dress, the same man with the gangrenous leg lying beside the smoking samovar, the same chickens running around the floor.

The lorry took us on to Kishm, a small village of thatched houses lining a bazaar, where he left us to return to Khanabad. Here the first thing we did was to bathe in the Kokcha, the principal river in Badakshan, a mountain torrent white with foam, spanned by another curved stone bridge. Even at the height of summer the roaring water was glacial cold. Beyond the banks were meadows filled with wild flowers, and a rustling wind flecked a line of poplars silver.

A pony fair was being held. Groups of Uzbegs in striped padded coats, leather boots that reached to the knee, every man carrying a short thonged whip, haggled over the animals tethered to wooden posts a few yards from each other, each with an embroidered rug thrown over its high wooden saddle. Badakshan ponies are noted for strength and beauty, they are used for playing *buzkashi* and they are all descended from Bucephalus. The main street was crowded with loud bargain-hunters like a fair at home. Afterwards I watched the groups of riders making their way home across the rolling green hills, an old man with his wife in a white sack clinging behind him, a line of galloping horsemen kicking up a trail of dust, distant shadows.

In this village too there was fear of 'bandits'. In the evening we were locked in the walled serai, guarded by two soldiers who stood outside the massive gates with cocked rifles.

We were three days in Kishm waiting for another lorry, spending our time sitting beside the river surrounded by ragged children fingering our belongings. There was little transport going to the provincial capital of Feyzabad. In a country where cars and lorries were so few, a haphazard method of hitch-hiking was the only way of getting about. Intending passengers showed the bravery of their ancestors in the way they stood in the middle of the road and dared the oncoming driver to run them down. In this Afghan game of chicken, I have seen several very near-misses, the man standing his ground until the wheels were almost over him, then with the grace of a bullfighter, making a quick movement as the thundering beast with revving engine and blaring horn swept by.

The spectacle of two foreigners standing at the edge of the road was enough to make the driver put on full speed, and only a fortunate burst tyre outside Kishm stopped him. After much haggling we were given a position perched over the cab. Behind us and the bales of cotton and the bleating sheep were the main body of passengers, a packed crowd including a fierce man carrying a gun, some soldiers in thick winter coats who were being posted to Iskashim – a town bordering the entrance to the Wakhan corridor, exactly where we wanted to go – and plenty of veiled women behind a sheet.

We were off, shivering in the cold mountain air, the ends of our turbans wrapped around our mouths to keep out dust. Dawn came up suddenly over the steep black ridges, buttering the valley with golden light. For most of the day we bumped and slithered our way through the hills following the course of the Kokcha river. In places terraced fields descended to bluffs almost at the river's edge, dark shadow alternating with the glare of sunlight, as the country became more mountainous with every turn.

Feyzabad was at the end of a huge rose-coloured gorge of craggy cliffs over which the track spiralled up and down in dizzy twists. Scattered along the route were wrecks of other lorries, some overturned with their wheels in the air, others abandoned on the wayside, one in particular a twisted metal hulk squeezed between rocks with the river poured over it. Our progress was slow and fitful. The driver's *bacho*, the hardworked boy in attend-ance, hung over the back wheel, and at the least hesitation of brakes or engine jumped down with a block of wood to stop the lorry rolling out of control. From time to time we stopped at a frail wooden bridge and everyone except the women had to dismount and join up on the other side.

The lorry sagged as if struck by a bullet, and we came to a halt, the engine billowing out smoke. The front spring had broken. With the nonchalance conditioned by hundreds of such occurrences, the male passengers descended and sat under the shade of a rock while the *bacho* handed round slices of melon. The women remained on board, hidden behind their curtain, rustling like cats in a basket.

The driver took out a set of spanners and disappeared under the chassis, occasionally throwing out buckled pieces of steel to the *bacho*. In a country where mechanical skills were virtually unknown, lorry drivers were noted exceptions, able to perform miracles with the flimsiest of aids. The gorge was cool; we settled down for a peaceful rest listening to the hum of the river below. No one seemed the least unsettled or annoyed, and with an infinite capacity for making the best of things, some passengers brewed up cups of tea, while others even cooked tasty dishes of rice which they handed round. Even under these circumstances they managed to suggest the leisured atmosphere of a Moghul *fête champêtre*. An Afghan picnic is always a delayed feast where food is to be enjoyed in the expectation that somewhere nearby there are birds and blossoms and time is of no consequence.

By late afternoon, when the driver, collecting tools and bits of metal, emerged and told us that if Allah willed it we should reach Feyzabad before dusk, we were all the best of friends.

At dusk we emerged from the gorge into a wide valley full of fields of ripening corn fringed by little terraces climbing up low hills. We followed a line of sprawling telephone posts, then another escarpment, and deep in the shadows on the far side of the Kokcha was a large town falling down a bank in a series of rocky terraces, stone walls, cascading water, trees and mud. The roar of the river drowned out all other sounds.

11

A STONE bridge curved across the Kokcha, now an icy blue torrent fed by melting snows. The roar of water as it squeezed its way through a channel of rocks drowned out every other noise, even the loudspeaker in the square. On the far side of the river a steep lane ended up in this little square which was the centre of Feyzabad and here the lorry stopped and deposited us. A cold mountain wind blew through the labyrinth of little lanes over a number of people warmly wrapped and huddled over baskets of fruit. Instead of melons and grapes, they were selling apples, pears and walnuts; outside a teahouse a line of donkeys loaded with lumps of rock salt waited patiently for their masters. The loudspeaker clamoured for attention.

After being bumped all day in the petrol-scented cab we found the fresh mountain air was an intoxicant. As soon as we had struggled free from the lorry a policeman appeared with a message of welcome from the governor. The line of drunken telegraph poles we had passed had carried a warning of the imminent arrival of rare and alarming visitors. Accommodation had been arranged for us further up the hill in an empty house surrounded by its own large orchard. Outside on a terrace a servant was putting the finishing touches to a massive meal.

We had barely stowed away our baggage when a smartly dressed man in white trousers and navy blue blazer came into the garden followed by a servant carrying a jug and a plate of English biscuits. He introduced himself as manager of the local bank and told us that he knew how much foreigners liked coffee and biscuits, as hc had once been abroad.

'I was in Berlin in 1936.' He pointed to the crest on his blazer pocket which was that of the Royal Afghan Olympic Team. What was his sport? My Persian was not up to understanding the term he used, but he mimed. He had been a weight-lifter.

We sat down together at the wooden table on the terrace with the lights of Feyzabad shining below and ate our banquet. We picked over plates of different styled pilau and yoghurt, goat and sheep cheese, fruit, nuts, crusty nan and other delicacies. The pieces of grilled lamb hidden in the pyramid of garnished rice had been soaked in honey. The bowls of freshly picked fruit mixed with almonds, walnuts and pistachios only needed a glass of wine or brandy for perfection. All the time we ate the bank manager was pressing us in the Afghan way to take more, picking out the best handfuls and delicately pushing the food into our mouths until we were bursting. When we could eat no more the best part of the various dishes still remained.

Next morning we paid a visit to his bank, a white cottage built on a ledge of rock overlooking the river whose roar made speaking difficult.

'Come in, my friends,' he shouted. 'How do you like Feyzabad? What did you say?' He pointed to his ears. 'All my customers must have strong voices.'

We drank more coffee and told him of our intention of seeing more of Badakshan. Perhaps we would continue northwards into the little known province of Darwaz? We did not mention the Wakhan. Michael had developed a surprising interest in wild flowers, bird and insect life; my plans not only included a wish to see various archeological sites, but also the lapis lazuli mines for which Badakshan is famous. I had learnt that these mines were in the vicinity of the route we wished to travel.

Our plans did not impress the bank manager, who looked at us sharply as if he could read our thoughts.

'My friends, let me give you some advice. It is much better to stay here in Feyzabad. Don't worry your heads about any further travel. Here you can fish and swim and there will be no difficulties.'

That afternoon his servant brought fishing rods up to the house where we were staying and more English biscuits. For the next two days we fished and lived on a mixture of fruit, nuts, fish, cheese and lamb which the servant prepared in endless varieties. There was little else to do in this overgrown alpine village where the sound of gushing water replaced human voices, where even the beggars looked happy. The only sign of distress came from packs of prowling emaciated dogs creeping around the lanes and whining all night.

The local society consisted of five Kabuli officials who included the doctor, the governor of Badakshan and his emissary, the bank manager, who all regarded life in this charming place as a pernicious form of exile. On our third day in Feyzabad we visited the governor's official residence, a square flat-roofed house situated in a commanding position above the town. Dressed in a silky grey European suit with a tie that suggested membership of some very exclusive society or club, the governor received us in his study where he sat behind a large desk with a wonderful view behind him.

In later years whenever I saw President Nixon on television, shifty, untrustworthy, just about to have a shave, I was reminded of the governor of Feyzabad. In spite of the European accessories, there was an air of a robber baron about him. As virtual ruler of Badakshan, his authority was supreme; he was head of the secret police, chief of the army hereabouts, chief judge – and a sentence from him might well be a tough one – and a man who, it was rumoured, controlled the wealth of the lapis lazuli mines. Like others in authority, like the Commandant of the Military School, he reduced his subordinates to shivering obsequiousness. He hated us.

'How can I help you?' he asked after the usual round of polite introductions and tea had been followed by a strained silence. 'Do you like your food and accommodation? I have given orders that all food and anything you wish will be provided while you stay here.'

When we told him that we wanted to hire ponies and travel around Badakshan he looked very angry. There was nothing he could do to help us in this matter. Did we not know that the roads were impassible because of floods and many of the bridges had been destroyed?

'I have a permit.' Fumbling in my pocket I produced the precious document that we had been given in Kabul which he examined, looking as if he was inwardly cursing and condemning to death every official south of the Hindu Kush.

The scowl on his features changed to a grimace of disdain.

'This is no good.'

'Why?'

He twiddled with a gold ring on his finger, then, after three more cups of tea, some Chesterfields, various sighs and grimaces, and continuous minute examinations of the permit, he relented. Suddenly we found we had permission to travel as far as Jurm, a village about twenty miles from Feyzabad, where we could see what the conditions of the road were like before continuing on our way.

We had to be satisfied with this ambiguous phrasing, especially when he began to cheer up and become almost affable. We gave him information as to whether Ireland was part of England, the price in Europe of a good car, and how often Christians went to church. We offered compliments on the beauty of Feyzabad and the bountiful hospitality we had received. But that evening the food of our house was drastically reduced, and instead of rich platters of pilau we were served with greasy half-cold rice and rancid pastry cakes.

Next morning we had barely got out of bed and lit our primus, when there was a violent banging on the door. Outside in the street stood two ponies and a group of arguing men, among them the policeman who had met us when we arrived.

'For you!' whereupon one of the men threw up his hands and began wailing. The ponies were his only means of livelihood without which he would starve. We promised that they would return safely and we would pay him well. With the mention of money, much money, the atmosphere lightened as the owner, suddenly smiling, showed off his animals, pacing them up and down. They were far from representing the best of their breed, the famous Badakshan pony. These creatures with the ominous dogged long-suffering air which is the prelude to struggle between rider and horse would never be called upon to play *buzkushi*. However, since we were anxious to go, we did not want to complain or delay too long in case the governor changed his mind. A price was named, which we accepted at once, to the owner's astonishment, and his features took on a theatrical look of amazement at the ways of *ferenghi*.

Another man, a wizened old creature, whose anguished cries had been ignored by the crowd around the ponies, was now pushed forward. It appeared that he was our guide. He had come to Feyzabad only a few days ago from his remote village bringing some donkey loads of rock salt, and now he had been impressed into a job that caused him deep distress. When we suggested that we had no need for him, he looked more miserable still, and made it clear that he had no choice except to obey orders. In the days to come the poor man would endlessly exhibit a sense of dejection. At every small stop we would find him stroking his beard and wailing to himself in a quiet little moan. The packets of Russian cigarettes, fruit and sticky bars of Kabuli chocolate that we gave him had no effect.

That was in the future. Now he merely looked at us mournfully, waved his hand and, turning round, began to run off down the road leaving us to strap on our sleeping bags and go after him. We mounted, and followed by a crowd, passed slowly through the bazaar down to the river. We rode along by the side of the Kokcha until the last small boy who had run from the town gave up, and stood gazing after us, holding his side and panting. Then for the first time since leaving Kabul we were alone.

I had forgotten the many subtle ways a horse can dictate its whims and display its opposition to the wishes of its rider. With a succession of shouts and kicks we encouraged the ponies to continue at a walking pace, but their hides were tough. My pony ambled along, stumbling occasionally, stopping every few yards to graze, while Michael's, used to narrow mountain tracks, had a habit of walking just ahead. Between this enforced single file and the roar of the river, conversation was impossible. Our slow pace meant that it took us over an hour to catch up with our guide whom we found a few miles ahead chewing an apple. For just an instant his deeply lined, weatherbeaten features, fringed by a sparse and fluffy beard that was tinged with white, lost their look of despair and creased into a smile as he watched us dismount and ease our aching muscles.

Safely out of Feyzabad he began to tell us his troubles. He was a Darwazi from the country directly northeast of Feyzabad, an area, alas, heavily garrisoned with troops whom the administration and the governor imposed on peaceful people and forced them to feed and house them. And now, when he should be travelling back to Darwaz with his grandsons, he had been forced to stay and become our guide. What would happen to the boys? What would happen to him? When would he ever see them again?

Once again we suggested that we were not in need of a guide at all, and that we would be only too delighted if he set off for

Darwaz right away. He shook his head; he had his orders and as long as we pursued our foolish idea of exploring this country, he was obliged to remain with us.

He ran ahead out of sight, leaving us to cajole our ponies into wild scenery that suggested the surroundings of a robber's lair in an operetta. The further we travelled through a long desolate gorge, the more dramatic and grand the place became. The narrow sandy track skirted the river full of boulders, while above on the jagged bluffs were balanced clusters of walnut trees whose leaves would catch the sun with their particular luminous jewel-green. There was nothing living to be seen, the only movement coming with one huge roar succeeding another, the crash of water echoing and multiplied by the cliffs, as we rode by a succession of waterfalls.

All day we prodded our ponies towards our objective, the distant Pamirs, passing these cascades. There was a turn, and a change of angle as one gorge was succeeded by another, equally scattered with sparse vegetation, topped with stunted walnut trees and striped with waterfalls. We beat and kicked the ponies along this savage and romantic trail until late in the afternoon we emerged into more open country. The sun had gone into a bank of cloud, but now it suddenly came out, glistening on far snow-peaks framing a U-shaped valley. Here we found a little mud settlement named Barack, situated at the confluence of four rivers so that the roar of water, loud enough to make you have to shout, crashed interminably against the ears of the inhabitants. Above the noise we heard the piercing shout of our guide. A door creaked open, a dog barked and someone led us to a place where we could sleep to the sound of four angry rivers.

At cock-crow the wan light of dawn drifted into the serai. Near us our guide snored, his breath rising and falling in whistles. The battered funnel of a samovar belched smoke, and seeing we were awake, the landlord supplied a dish of hard-boiled eggs and a bowl of apples.

By daylight we could see Barack, a nest of ancient mud- and stone-walled houses, shaded in by orchards of apple, walnut and mulberry trees, where the noise of water drowned out birdsong and human speech. Near here the road, or rather the track, divided, one arm leading in the direction we wanted to go

towards Iskashim and the Wakhan, the other to Jurm towards
which the governor of Feyzabad had directed us. Beyond Jurm
was Nuristan.

After protracted negotiations with our guide we suggested that
it would be easier to follow the track to Iskashim rather than go
the governor's way. Michael slipped him a handful of money
which he tucked away in the small leather bag worn on a piece
of string round his neck, and for a few moments it seemed that
we would have our way.

The ponies with their mountain of baggage followed by the
guide had begun to negotiate a slippery path that led down to
one of the rivers, when an agitated Baracki came running up,
grabbed the rope halter of Michael's pony and turned it firmly
in the direction of Jurm. No one must go to Iskashim. Very well,
Jurm it would be; perhaps beyond that Nuristan where, safe
from bureaucratic control, we might be able to backtrack and
slip unobserved into the Wakhan.

The guide ran ahead, and we pushed the ponies on through
orchards and gardens divided by mud walls. Vines grew here
which would never be made into wine. (But strangely, the basic
rootstock for Californian wines originated in Afghanistan.)
A cluster of orchards would be succeeded by a stretch of
brown desert land and followed again by lush fertile groves and
gardens.

The journey from Barack to Jurm, once the chief town in
Badakshan, the gateway to Nuristan, and the threshold of the
Pamirs, took just under three hours. We trotted through another
little bazaar with rows of booths piled with melons where turbanned figures trailing long coats moved slowly in the warm
mountain sunshine. A steep lane, a rising avenue of scented
mulberry trees, led up to the governor's house which character-
istically overlooked the village. In front a circle of men were
squatting on a mud terrace.

Before I had time to gain more than a brief impression of rows
of jet black eyes frowning beneath shaggy turbans, an unexpected
figure got up from the centre of the group and came forward to
meet us. He was wearing the uniform of the New York Metropoli-
tan police, boots, blue trousers, khaki shirt, blue tie and a cap
with a silver badge.

'I speak good English.' From his trouser pocket he produced

a paper which declared that Mohammed Rahim had voluntarily left the service of Morrison Knudsen at Kandahar.

We read the paper and shook hands. Then he introduced us to a small turbanned Turkic with a pointed black beard who from the moment we showed up had begun asking questions which I couldn't understand.

'He is governor.' This one looked even more unwelcoming than the last. 'He wish to know where you go.'

'We want to see more of Badakshan.'

The response from this governor was immediate and furious. Spitting out a wad of betelnut, he talked angrily for some minutes, but the things he said were beyond Mohammed Rahim's powers of translation. We produced our permission, which was like tipping over a beehive, as all the others added their voices to the governor's disapproval. The shouts got brisker and they argued among themselves, until the governor got up and strode away. The others all followed him, except for Mohammed Rahim who could not hide his distress and disappointment at our shabby clothes and meagre equipment. No doubt he had given his friends an impressive account of the lavish lifestyle of the foreigners he had encountered at Kandahar.

He took us to the small room which had been given us for the night, stamping along in his black boots, examining the camera which swung from Michael's shoulders. He departed for his midday sleep, while the governor also had retired to his house, and the town settled in the shade. The only signs of life came from women slapping clothes in the river and a group of naked children who were hurling stones at some donkeys that had got into one of the walled vegetable gardens. Everywhere else figures in their long striped *kat* coats curled up under the walnut trees for the long afternoon.

That evening we decided to make a dash for the Pamirs, only taking what we could carry in our rucksacks. The rest would be jettisoned. Our renewed encounter with authority had reinforced our wish to escape. Beyond Iskashim there would be no proper villages or towns, and we hoped that we would be free men. For the first time it seemed that if we made a determined push we might be able to achieve something of what we had planned for so long.

After a meal made up of Michael's army rations and local

fruit, we divided our possessions into two piles on the floor –
the things we would carry with us, and those that we would give
to our guide. With these gifts and a little more money, he
accepted our plans and agreed that in the morning he would go
back to Feyzabad with the ponies before making his way home
to Darwaz. How he would square his disobedience with the
governor we did not ask; although his features were as miserable
as ever, with the aid of our money, he seemed to be prepared to
face possible danger.

At dawn a slight mist curled upwards from the river and the
air was heavy with the scent of mulberry. Already the guide had
the two ponies saddled, ready to take our surplus gear; like us
he wanted to get away safely and return to Feyzabad before
questions were asked.

When we put on our rucksacks and walked out it seemed an
easy start. We could see the track that curled down to the river
in the way we wished to go, and Michael was already impatiently
striding ahead when a strap of my rucksack broke. Only a couple
of hundred yards and we would have been free of the village,
and now there was nothing to do but wait for the cobbler to put
in a few stitches.

He was an old man, shortsighted from many years of mending
harness and stitching boots and chaplis for the people of Jurm.
First the correct thread had to be found, then the right needle,
and by the time he had started to put in a few stitches, a crowd
had gathered round, in the midst of which was the blue uniform
of Mohammed Rahim.

'Where you off to, Mister?' He tapped my arm authoritatively
as I heaved the mended rucksack on my back. Behind him I
recognised the governor's elders, the mullah, the schoolmaster
and his servant, a surly man with a wispy moustache who kept
reaching out to grab my arm.

'Just keep going,' I told Michael.

Followed by the male population of Jurm, we made our way
to the small stream that marked the town's boundary. Here
we would certainly have been prevented from going further if
Michael hadn't thought of taking a photograph. At the sight of
the camera the scattered group stopped and struck up poses,
grinning with delight, making a picturesque assembly, Mohammed Rahim in his policeman's uniform standing to attention,

the stately bearded mullah, the schoolmaster, various saluting children, a young man carrying a gun. While they were frozen in this way, we were sprinting down the lane. Nobody followed us, and soon Jurm had vanished around a sharp bend, and we were by ourselves in an empty beautiful landscape whose bare cliffs, stunted twisted trees, flowers scattered here and there, and distant mountains were the background stuff for Persian and Moghul paintings.

It was a good moment in our lives. Distances here were deceptive so that the range of mountains which loomed beyond the valley seemed to be near enough. Once we reached them, we told ourselves, we would be safe from interference. Ahead, no more than a few days away, was the Rangul Pass somewhere in the white blur that melted into the sky. We walked all morning, stopping several times for a rest and cigarette or a splash in the ice-cold river. How wonderful it was to be free of our guide, on his way back to Feyzabad, and anyone at Jurm who wanted to stop us. At last there seemed no reason why if we continued walking we could not reach China and anywhere else. What a simple purpose it was to set out and see the world, and why should anyone want to stop us?

Riding the ponies had been uncomfortable enough, but walking with a full load was worse. We had been lax about putting ourselves in training for travelling, and perhaps we would have been better prepared to carry out our plans if we had given up smoking. But everyone was smoking then – in those days the worst thing that could happen to a smoker was smoker's cough. The weight of our packs, still lovingly crammed with explorer's extras, and the fierce heat – in this valley between bare rocks there wasn't a bit of shade – was overwhelming, and every now and again we would collapse in a sweaty heap on the ground. The shimmering white mountains ahead continued to beckon.

We were about three hours out of Jurm and had stopped yet again when, looking back, we noticed a cloud of dust in the distance. At first we didn't pay it much notice in that country of dust, where the land was constantly erupting in little dust devils, spouts of golden particles like genies' lamps, and wind-carried clouds that might or might not subside in accordance with the wind's caprices. But this cloud grew bigger and nearer and soon we could make out the shapes of three galloping horses.

The horses – ponies, rather – passed us, wheeled round and took up a stand-and-deliver position across the little dusty road. We recognised two of the riders, the schoolmaster and the governor's servant. We recognised two of the ponies; they were our own. It was a tribute to Badakshani horsemanship that these men could coax the wretched animals to a performance that had the urgency of those who brought good news from Ghent to Aix.

We made an absurd attempt to push past and continue on. In particular, the governor's servant was determined that we should not pass, and fastened onto my arm like a hungry dog. The more I struggled, the more he clung on.

A sad procession wound its way back to Jurm, the schoolmaster riding in front, the governor's servant in the rear, ourselves and our packs between them. Our arrival in the town was watched by the male population as we were brought up through the walnut trees to the governor's house. For the last stage of the journey they tried to make us ride, but we refused, preferring to show our displeasure in this way. Not that it made any difference at all in a country where every foreigner was a spy.

Under the gaze of the solemn jostling crowd we were joined by Mohammed Rahim, late of Morrison Knudsen and led inside the governor's house. We were taken to a long empty room whose furniture was a small table on which was a telephone. We had followed the straddling poles across the mountains of the Hindu Kush, into the flat plains of Turkestan and up again into Badakshan; and here in Jurm the line ended. I wondered what new disaster threatened as Mohammed Rahim, still resplendent as a cop, handed me the receiver. Over the wires came a scream.

'No, no, no,' a voice wailed and was cut off.

'Telephone okay, governor not okay.' Mohammed Rahim gave the receiver a few knocks against the window ledge and replaced it. A few moments later there was a jangle of bells, and over crackles an unmistakable voice boomed out.

'I am governor of Feyzabad and I order you to return at once.'

'But our permits . . .'

'I order you . . . I order you . . .'

The voice trailed away with a squeak followed by silence. Mohammed Rahim replaced the receiver with the veneration of someone who had been in touch with God.

I asked if we could spent the night here, but Mohammed

Rahim shook his head. He was smiling. Outside, the Darwazi, who had been waiting for the ponies, suddenly appeared, and immediately began running back towards Feyzabad. We said goodbye to the city fathers of Jurm, receiving the warm embraces of the governor's servant. 'You must come back again – okay.' Mohammed Rahim waved after us.

We mounted the ponies, who scented home and galloped out of town. Soon we had caught up with the Darwazi and swept past him towards Barack which we reached at dusk. We set up camp in an orchard overlooking the river. We hadn't eaten all day. The lights played through the long shadows, occasionally sparkling on a bough weighed down with bright red apples, or glinting on the Kokcha swirling around the hill back to Feyzabad.

Just as we lit the primus and began to cook, a small delegation came into the orchard. One of them was the owner of the house where we had previously stayed, another a bushy bearded individual armed with a stick, the third a stern-faced man who seemed to be praying to himself with exaggerated postures.

'You must leave at once.' The man with the stick kicked over the primus.

Michael unrolled his sleeping bag and lit a cigarette. We were not going further today. There was no real camping site between here and Feyzabad and it was getting dark. The delegates wavered, torn between their innate sense of hospitality and the spectre of officialdom in Feyzabad. The innkeeper of Barack suggested that it was a fine night for walking.

We might have been left in peace if the Darwazi had not walked up. He was immediately recognised as a figure of fun. He was not only a Shia Moslem, but came from some remote part of Badakshan that no one had heard of. The more he called down the judgment of God, cursing the day that he had joined our expedition, the more he complained in his high wavering voice, the more people laughed.

I tried to interrupt, explaining that we had come thousands of miles to this beautiful country to find the people of Barack lacking in the famed Afghan hospitality. More cheerful than ever, the crowd took no notice of what I was saying, but began to steal the ponies which were tethered to a tree. Two men seized them by their bridles, two more grabbed the saddles that lay on the grass, and in a few minutes our transport and our tormentors had vanished through the orchard gates, leaving no trace except trampled grass and the noise of distant laughter.

Furious and helpless, we packed our sleeping bags and walked away from the village out on the Feyzabad road. We had not gone far when there was the soft patter of feet behind us.

'Where are you going?'

'To Feyzabad.'

'But you cannot; now we have decided that you can spend the night here.'

We continued walking. It was now almost dark. A few miles on the Darwazi trotted up with the ponies and the rest of our equipment that the villagers had decided to return.

We camped in a deserted building on the edge of the Barack plain. After Michael managed to cook a stew with the remains of some rice and one of our precious tins, we ate our evening meal to the background of noise where the usual sounds of rushing water were combined with plaintive squeaks. Since rejoining us the Darwazi had never stopped his complaints for a moment, and now he sat on a high rock in his woollen coat and pillbox hat silhouetted against the stars, making renewed calls upon Allah as his witness.

We woke to find that our company had increased by the addition of two soldiers whose job was to escort us back to Feyzabad. At least that little we could understand from the truculent manner with which they started to organise our bags and ponies. Ruffled by the usual bad night's sleep, empty stomachs and disappointment, we were in no mood to take this final insult. We tied our hands together with a piece of rope and handed the end to them. They fingered it and looked at us blankly. Fresh trouble started when our guide tried to intervene and hostile villagers refused to allow us to pass through them. Our sarcasm was wasted, and only after we had untied the rope were we allowed to go.

One of the soldiers shouted an order as we formed up in a straggling line and started walking. Another curious little procession wound all the way back to Feyzabad that late August afternoon, Michael and I sandwiched between two marching soldiers, the Darwazi riding one pony and leading the other.

We hoped for a sensational entry into the town, but received no more than a few curious stares. In our absence Feyzabad had undergone a transformation for the celebration of National Independence Day. Now the shops and houses were covered with flags and bunting, while people from all over Badakshan crowded the narrow streets of the province's capital.

The guards vanished and then at last the Darwazi departed for his distant homeland about which we had heard so much. We left it to him to return the ponies to their owner, as we wrote out a long testimonial, leaning a crumpled piece of paper against one of the saddles, each writing shaky praises as the animal moved and stumbled and flicked its tail at flies. Then he went off with a last little complaint to the effect that he never wanted to see a foreigner again.

Wobbling with heat, we picked up our rucksacks as people rushed by, cheering, shouting and waving flags.

An old man emerged from the moving crowd and tapped me on the shoulder. He announced himself as chief clerk to the governor, adding that his master eagerly awaited us at the club before the celebrations began. Did we not realise that the governor had been most anxious during the past few days in case we might miss the festivities? The sports were about to begin very shortly and only our presence was needed to open the games officially. Would we please come this way?

We could not help being impressed by the governor's strategy in getting us back to Feyzabad. But we declined his invitation.

We found a path twisting high over the town, and twenty minutes later we had reached a rocky ledge where a cliff fell to the river. Below us was a small beach jammed with booths, bonfires and hundreds of moving chattering people surrounding the clubhouse which was perched on a rock above them and decorated in the Afghan national colours, black, green and red. Officials dressed in morning suits swarmed over the rock, and among them we could see the governor wearing a panama hat, a distinctive piece of headgear among all the turbans.

A swimming race was just beginning. A gun went off behind us and faces turned upwards to watch some men hurl themselves off the bridge into the rapids. A score of heads bobbed past, their owners struggling to keep from being submerged. The onlookers cheered the swimmers as they were swept rapidly downstream, but just as they were approaching the club and the dignitaries, another gun went off. For a few seconds those in authority watched them float past helplessly on their way to the Oxus; then their attention was captured by a long delayed netball game.

While all this was happening we were composing an official letter of complaint to the governor. It would not have changed anything; now that we were safely back our little misdemeanour would be overlooked. It was unfortunate that we had insisted on taking the wrong road, just the sort of thing suspicious and cunning foreigners would do. Spy mania was rife.

We heard a noise behind us; the old clerk was slowly climbing up to our rock above the river with a letter from the bank manager written in English. 'My friends, the governor has found that your visas have expired and tomorrow you will have to return to Kabul. He tells me that you can stay for the night, and has generously offered you accommodation.'

We did not reply.

Could things have turned out differently? Could we have crossed Central Asia? Years later I met numerous determined people who managed to travel in Central Asia, China, Mongolia and Tibet without the aid of official permission. In the mid-nineteen eighties there was even an unofficial competition among travellers as to who could travel to the places furthest away from the backpacker routes and the hippy trail.

The netball game continued and, in a space cleared from the midst of the spectators, preparations were being made for a tug of war which proceeded with a degree of heaving and hoing that would have done credit to the Volga boatmen. The swimmers appeared to have vanished for ever. Beyond the town and the plain over which we had come back that day the outlines of the mountains became clearer as the sun moved towards the western clouds. A snow-peak caught in a flash of light floated in the sky, cut off from the earth; it was like our hopes. We thought of the things we had tried to see, the Kirghiz with their herds of yak and camels, the source of the Oxus, moon-shaped lakes, lost cities and burning wind. Michael opened his last packet of American cigarettes and we sat gazing at the deepening shadows.

12

AT the end of August we arrived back in Kabul, dishevelled and weary, and went straight away to the new Tourist Department to complain about our treatment by the governor of Badakshan.

'Why did you not visit Bamian?' sighed the languid official in charge of troublesome people, who spent his time steering foreigners towards the towering mutilated statues and the good hotel. As far as the Tourist Department was concerned, there was nowhere else to go. Most of those who attempted to go off the beaten track in the way we had done were disappointed, and the sight of bruised foreigners returning to the Afghan capital was a common one. For our benefit the official listed a number of frustrated travellers so that we would not consider ourselves unique. There was the English archaeologist who was discovered map making, the American archaeologist who worked for the CIA, the German who wished to study bees and had been found testing minerals, not to forget the American professor who wished to record tribal music and turned out to be a Mormon missionary.

Kabul still showed its fiery summer face, always half-veiled with dust, the sky above the dust storms cobalt blue. By midday all the shops and government offices closed. The Bank-i-Melli had run out of money. Foreigners retured to their houses and gardens to drink cold beer and nibble nuts and discuss the latest scandals involving people in their tiny private world. The head of the latest Soviet delegation had been arrested for drunkenness in a Kabul street; a nude bathing party had taken place by moonlight at the British Embassy pool; an Ambassador had decamped with his secretary for a holiday in the Lebanon – in those last torpid weeks of summer news of such goings-on helped to relieve the annihilating exhaustion and boredom.

We returned to the house in the walled garden which I

shared with the Afghan ladies. In the evening, while the sunset smouldered for hours over the western hills, we made alternative plans. Summer was ending, a new term at the Military College was approaching, and I faced the nightmare of teaching Milton to another batch of students for a third year. If I wished to leave I would have to go abroad and send back my written resignation. I could not return to Afghanistan again. I must make a decision quickly.

Gilgit appeared to be another route through which, as we knew from our reading, numerous travellers had crossed into Central Asia. We thought that Pakistani officials could only be easier to deal with than Afghans.

I bought an ancient jeep that belonged to the American military attaché; it cost twenty pounds, which seemed to be a tremendous bargain. We evolved a plan to drive it towards Gilgit and sell it for a profit when the road ran out.

The jeep had the appearance of a battle-scarred warrior, lacking a hood or any extras apart from MA painted in large white letters across its olive-green bonnet. Unfortunately the very week that I took possession, the Afghan government brought in a driving test. I had an Irish driving licence issued back home long before a test had been brought in – up until 1960 anyone in Ireland could legally drive for the sum of three pounds, providing they did not admit to be suffering from mental instability. In Afghanistan it was now decided that driving licences issued elsewhere were unacceptable. A stringent test, a new development in the country's progress into the modern world, must be passed by all foreigners wishing to drive.

It was my misfortune to be the first to have to take this test. Two days before the event I got sick, with something that seemed a little more severe than the usual KT. I insisted on ignoring the general shakiness which may have been aggravated by the hot weather; if I postponed the test, it might be weeks or months before I could get another date.

On the appointed day a group of officials, wearing similar belted mackintoshes and karakul hats and all carrying briefcases, assembled on a little sandy hill a few miles outside Kabul. I drove up very fast, pulling up in a dusty cloud and squealing brakes. I had a temperature which made me dizzy. It required an effort to notice the official in the gabardine coat who was taking a number of little wooden pegs out of a canvas bag and pushing them into the sand making a long narrow serpentine testing ground like a series of chicanes.

'You must drive down that route until you reach the end. Then you must reverse. None of the pegs must be moved.'

'None?'

'You will be allowed to hit three at the most.'

The officials watched closely as I lined up the front wheels of the jeep. There were as yet only a handful of cars in the city, and I was conscious that I was a privileged innovator.

I revved up the engine, pushed down the clutch and approached the twisting route in near-delirium. Somehow I advanced and completed the S-shapes without mishap and there were smiles under the karakul hats. Reversing was a different matter. Twisting backwards through billowing oily exhaust fumes, I ran over every single peg and rammed each one into the sand.

'You make big mistake.'

Perhaps I would have run over the pegs even if I was not feverish. I got out of the car and stood in the sun. The officials had gathered in a huddle except for the man in the gabardine coat who was painstakingly wresting the pegs out of the ground and putting them back in the bag. The sun blasted down.

The officials were all smiling. 'Many congratulations. You have passed.'

I looked at the crazy wheel marks in the sand and we exchanged more smiles. For years I kept this very first Afghan driving licence, a scrap of Farsi writing almost entirely covered by a large red seal. I was instrumental in bringing Kabul into the age of the motor car.

Michael left Kabul and I planned to join him with the jeep and our baggage in Peshawar. First I wrote a peevish letter of resignation to the Defence Ministry in which I made a number of suggestions for improvements: '. . . one of the most depressing aspects of school life for the foreign teacher is the large proportion of students who are sick. In one of my classes – 6C – it became almost impossible to teach because there were so many students either going to the doctor or coming from him. As sickness appears to be such a regular feature of school life, I draw your attention to it . . .

'The morale of any army institution largely depends on smartness and cleanliness. During the winter months I could not fail to notice that the standard of dress for an officer's training school was deplorably low. The thick and untidy winter coat is not discarded until midsummer . . .

'I have complained many times about the textbooks. The stencilled copies of text which my English classes are obliged to use are a disgrace. They should have been burnt years ago . . .

'I suggest that there should be a twenty minutes break every morning for students and teachers and that tea and bread should be provided . . . I suggest that the standard of intake should be raised and if possible the numbers should be reduced . . . The Military School must make up its mind whether it wants a large number of badly educated cadets to pass each year or a smaller number of well-educated students capable of forming an army elite . . .'

I do not think I hoped to accomplish anything by this priggish document, apart from enraging the Commandant. I took the precaution of sending it from Pakistan. Perhaps he rubbed his hands in glee at the realisation that I had finally absconded. He and all his unfortunate underlings were victims of the system. At least I was able to escape. How could new textbooks and uniforms be ordered when there was no money? Our salaries, so grossly inflated in comparison to the pitiable amount that even a senior Afghan officer earned, must have taken a substantial part of the annual school budget.

Something else reprehensible: I did not tell Warren that I was leaving, and I abandoned him to face whatever displeasure my behaviour might provoke. Perhaps I could excuse that behaviour by remembering that all the time I was making preparations to leave I continued to have a high fever.

At the last moment the Afghan authorities refused to allow me to drive my beloved jeep out of the country. They may have thought that I was intending to donate this elderly vehicle, which from the mileage on the clock appeared to have had a wartime history, to the Pakistan army. Instead it had to be sold off in Kabul at a small loss.

I packed my bags and saw old friends. I didn't tell anyone of my plans. I did not want my departure to become another rumour in a tiny community where rumour and secrecy flourished together.

The time was fast approaching when the Military School would be reopening. My limbs were shaking and trembling as I took my leave. I packed and paid up my remaining rent – I never met my two infinitely kind landladies. It was another hot day. I swallowed half a dozen aspirins and took a tonga looking for the last time on familiar scenes.

> Kabul town is sun and dust
> Blow the bugle, blow the sword.

Thirty-five years later, looking at television and the departing Russians, I tried to recognise the city I remembered in the flickering images of the heavily guarded airport and the hungry people queuing for bread, and to estimate how much the old pride and gaiety and charm and ease of life had been blasted away.

Sitting on the back of the tonga with a throbbing head, filmed in sticky beads of perspiration, seeing the last of the city in a dust storm, I had a final glimpse of the hotel and the surrounding bazaars and the *jueys*. The same policeman who had been there the first morning I arrived was standing on his little brick stand, whistle in mouth, trying to direct the camels, horses, sheep, bicycles, lorries, buses and pedestrians surging across the bridge. I saw the small traffic intersection with its few tattered trees where we waited for the military bus, the mud-brown houses and shops, the bright red rugs by the river, the same boy carrying his coloured bottles of sherbet down to the stinking *juey* to immerse them and keep them cool.

> Kabul town'll go to hell . . .

In the serai where the great decorated lorries were being loaded up people were busy, Hazara porters bent to ninety degrees under the weight of the bales of cotton they were heaving into a shed, a boy balancing a tin of heart-shaped nan loaves on his head, dogs, hens, a blind beggar. I found a lorry loaded with fruit from the Logar valley which was going to Peshawar. Someone pushed me inside the driver's cab squeezed between two burly men whose woollen clothes defied the heat, and we were away towards the mountains. I had a last look at the strip of new road that was being built out to the royal palace. It was a source of wonder, and in the evening crowds would gather to watch the bulldozers at work mingling the chips and the trickle of black asphalt. Time was running out.

Because I was sick I can remember very little of the journey along the pitted road over the Lataband through to Jalalabad. I can remember smells mostly – engine oil, tobacco, dirty clothes. All the time the driver was smoking and singing as the lorry with its cargo of grapes and melons roared and twisted its way east over the narrow stretch of dried mud. I remember stopping at several chaikhanas and a wild-looking tribesman jumping out into the road waving a gun because he wanted a lift. The final bump leaving the potholes of Afghanistan for the silky-smooth Pakistani road that led over the Kyber to Peshawar was the entry into another world.

I found Michael in the military club where we prepared to enjoy ourselves and order tiffin, English breakfasts, play billiards and down Murree beer under the gaze of Masters of the Peshawar Vale Hunt. But we were too ill.

In due course we felt so seedy that a doctor was summoned who diagnosed hepatitis and ordered us to drink fruit juice and stay in bed. I lay under a slow-moving fan and listened to the Sunday chimes coming from St John's Anglican church. For weeks we were nursed by the anxious management of the military club as our fruit juice was brought in to us by relays of stately bearers. It is good to be able to express my gratitude once again.

Hepatitis is a debilitating sickness leaving the sufferer drained of will and energy. I lost a stone, so did Mickey; watching our dried-up, yellowed, skinny figures stagger about under the moving fan we did not feel much confidence about plans to cross the nearest chain of mountains into China.

It was autumn and our permits from Gilgit had come through. Soon there would be heavy falls of snow closing off the Pamirs. We pared down our equipment to essential items, a tent, Chinese dictionary, sleeping bags, clothing and K rations. The day before we left we practised carrying our loads around the garden, much to the amusement of members of the club, mostly young Pakistani army officers.

The doctor recommended a strict diet of mashed food and more fruit juice. When he heard we were going to Gilgit he congratulated us on our wise choice, reminding us that Baltitis and Hunzacuts lived for a sensationally long time on fruit, milk, cheese, apricots and mulberries. We could do the same.

There was a weekly flight from Rawalpindi to Gilgit which was considered particularly hairy. The mountain weather could change in minutes from clear blue skies to cloud and raging storms. The Dakotas which were universally the workhorses of the aviation world were elderly and unpressurised; they had to fly between a terrifying corridor of mountains. The pilots were known for their skills; in years to come those who flew the Gilgit run in those old Dakotas came to be regarded as heroes.

At the little airport at Rawalpindi, a small grass strip at the edge of the hills, we found half a dozen passengers waiting for the Gilgit plane, small dark men wearing thick sheepskin coats and rolled up caps, and their women who didn't wear veils. Their baggage consisted mainly of sacks and crates full of chickens. A toothless old man handed us a plate of dried apricots with a courtly gesture. When I clutched my stomach and refused he nodded understandingly. Had he been offering us the chance to live for ever?

Together with all the chickens we crowded into an empty cargo hold with a few bucket seats. Flying this way was a relative innovation; just a few years before the way to Gilgit included crossing rivers on blown-up oxen. We were at fifteen thousand feet, but the Karakorams were that much higher. Soon after the foothills around Rawalpindi they closed in and hung about us, glaciers running down their sides, a floating menace of rock and snow, dominated by the jagged peak of K2. Banks of clouds rolled around its summit. When I looked down I could see the closed valleys which would soon be hammered by the Chinese into a three-lane highway. The old historical barrier of mountains, so important in the subtle rules of the Great Game, would be breached. Then the lorries would thunder through and the hippies would travel in droves in Shangri-La.

After an hour flying along a corridor through the Karakorams – years later a sequence in *Star Wars* reminded me of that flight – very suddenly we came out of the mountains and their perils into a green valley full of fields and trees. I could see a foaming river and a bridge, some scattered flat-roofed houses with mud platforms, and the fields edged with narrow stonewalled lanes. Our plane, which had escaped out of the perils of rock and snow, cast a small shadow on this sunlit Eden. The roar of the two engines changed to a higher pitch as the nose dipped and we came in to land; we followed the shadow running before us and then it suddenly veered away. A flock of sheep had wandered across the field below and the pilot aborted the landing. While we circled around waiting for the animals to be cleared away, one of the passengers wrapped in a brown wool cloak began to sing, in a high pitched note that reached again and again around the squalor of our confined metal box.

Although it was only early September, we had arrived in mid-autumn. The air was crisp and cool and in the little fields around the town pairs of oxen were ploughing up the land after harvest.

'Hullo, can I help you fellows?' As we staggered off the plane with our baggage we were greeted by a cheery middle-aged man dressed in tweed jacket, cavalry twill and silk choker round his neck. He introduced himself as Azif Khan, the DC of the Gilgit area; he had heard that foreigners were coming.

We were bundled into his jeep and his uniformed driver drove past orchards and stone walls, through a small bazaar with a clock like a small Big Ben at one end, which was full of the same sort of dark little men with rolled-up woollen hats who had travelled with us on the Dakota. The appearance of the DC's jeep was a signal for them all to stand to attention. We crossed a stream and headed up one of the many shady lanes that led up from the Gilgit river to the old Agency House built by the Public Works Department for the first Resident of Gilgit in the eighteen-nineties. It was still surrounded by the trees and shrubs which Sir George Robertson described, and when I returned thirty years later when all else had been defiled by progress, Biddulph's Bower had survived relatively intact. Here was the location of Paradise which old Empire servants, lucky enough to be posted there, remembered in their retirement as they remembered the good life of hunting, fishing, shooting and governing. From here, among other joys, they could go off at their leisure and shoot the poor old *ovis poli* as big as donkeys with horns frequently measuring sixty inches – every man who could shoot wanted a sheep with flaring horns to put up as a trophy.

Behind the residence, separated from it by an old-fashioned garden with a large herbaceous border full of fading autumn trees, was a small cottage.

'I thought you fellows might like to stay here,' said the DC. 'We still don't have many civilised amenities, but I hope you find it comfortable.' The good man left us while a servant brought in our bags. The cottage was chintzy and welcoming with blazing log fire, old copies of *Punch* and the *Illustrated London News*, a houseboy and a cook.

For a few days we continued to convalesce in luxurious comfort. In its mountainous isolation Gilgit was virtually unchanged since Lieutenant Manners-Smith established the Agency in 1897. No hotels yet, no cars apart from the DC's jeep, no visitors.

We went with the DC to watch an important polo match between the Gilgit Scouts and a local team. The sun shone warmly as he threw on the ball for the opening chukka before settling down in his deckchair. He sat up once to cheer a Scout in baggy white jodhpurs, white topee and red waistcoat who scored a goal. 'Yahir's a good player. So is his horse. The best horses come from Yasin. Those in Gilgit are no good.' During the intervals between chukkas, a turbanned servant handed round plates of nuts and apricots. The teams galloped up and down, watched by hundreds of spectators squatting on the surrounding low stone wall. At the time a band played, exactly the same sort as the one observed by Curzon, 'a big drum, a couple of kettledrums, and two or three clarinets with a note very much like a bagpipe'. In his day the losing team had been forced to wear women's clothes after its defeat.

Three days after watching polo, we packed our bags and headed north. Once again we had sought permission to travel and had been refused – we had wanted to go to Hunza which was still almost inaccessible. But the DC had allowed us to travel as far as Nilt, and we had vague ideas of continuing.

After crossing a fragile little suspension bridge we were confronted with two routes leading in the direction of Nilt and Hunza, one following the direction of the river, the other a wild contour over hills and rocks. Before the Karakoram Highway it was still as Younghusband described it, 'sixty-five miles of most execrable roads, bye paths climbing high up the mountain sides, around cliffs or passes, over rocks and galleries, along the faces of precipices . . .'

But since the spring floods had long receded, we could follow the flat sandy riverbed directly into the heart of the mountains where the shining white peak of Rakaposhi directly ahead dwarfed all its neighbours. We met very few people, the occasional shepherd or a solitary horseman travelling on his way down to Gilgit through wonderful steep valleys shadowed by immense mountains where, according to Lord Curzon, 'nature seems to exert her supremest energy and in one chord to exhaust almost every note in her vast and majestic diapason of sound'. I remembered how Curzon boasted of accomplishing 'a daily average march of over twenty-one miles for fifty-four days, excluding halts'. After half a day we were struggling; the jaundice still had us in its grip. By the time we reached Kishm late in the day we were both in a state of collapse.

At Kishm there was a small Dak bungalow offering the weary spartan comfort and charpois on which we collapsed. At this pace the short journey to Hunza would take a week, and we knew very well that we could travel no further. Once again we would have to turn our back on a tantalising vista of mountains.

'I thought you fellows intended to make a trip of it,' said the DC after we had limped back to Gilgit and joined him for drinks. 'A German mountaineering team has just arrived. Why don't you join them?' But we had no strength except to convalesce in his cottage reading back numbers of *Punch*. We would never get to Yarkand, Kashgar, the Turfan Depression or the Gobi desert.

13

NINETEEN FIFTY-FIVE

AFTER our failure to travel beyond Gilgit, we realised that we would have to abandon our plans; we would modify our ambitions of being explorers and become mere tourists instead. But we could still go to countries that were unvisited and unknown to Westerners – like the secret mysterious kingdom of Nepal.

After the conquest of Everest Nepal had been in the news. But Westerners did not go there, apart from a few mountaineers painstakingly making their way through the foothills which were still covered with forest, towards snow-peaks which were still unclimbed. The country preserved its rich and diverse cultural heritage unchallenged by the demands of mass tourism.

The first half of the nineteen-fifties was the very best time to be a tourist, as opposed to a traveller, in the east. For one thing, there were so few of us. The wonderful Dakota, a John the Baptist to the jet, had taken the edge off true hardship. Just a year before our visit the accepted way of reaching Kathmandu was on foot or by elephant.

We took a train to Patna in north India from where we could fly to Kathmandu. At the little airport the Customs officer raised his head from a desk littered with papers and cigarette butts, stamped our passports and began a discussion on philosophy. Learning that we were Irish, he expressed his ideas about Bishop Berkeley. The good bishop, he reminded us, had denied any reality to matter by showing that information received via the senses was not to be trusted. The great Hindu thinkers and philosophers had also denied any reality to the soul. It was an illusory concept, and we must destroy the whole idea of the ego. He settled back behind his desk, a small wispy voluble man whose appearance suggested that years of dehydration in harsh sunlight had shrunk his head into a wrinkled leather gourd. He continued to express ideas so much more absorbing than his duties. 'Karma is the idea you must get hold of. We all have karmas, which are our propensities and inheribted tendencies that change and are modified with each condition that comes for experience. You follow?'

Michael, at least, knew what he was talking about.

'There is no permanent immortal soul. Your Bishop Berkeley should have applied his great logic to this truth in the same way that he did with matter . . .'

The monologue was interrupted by the breezy arrival of another passenger, a plump young man wearing a European jacket over a traditional Nepalese costume of thin cotton jodhpur trousers and vest. He waved his hand at the Customs man, who subsided behind his desk once more, picked up a book and never spoke to us again.

The Nepalese removed his dark glasses to greet us. 'May I introduce myself? My name is Mohan Shum Sher Rana.'

We realised that he must be a Rana, a member of the former ruling class in Nepal. It was through accidentally meeting a Rana student in Delhi that we had been able to obtain visas to visit Kathmandu. Apart from diplomats and mountaineers, few foreigners sought or were granted permission to visit Nepal, and we had been extremely lucky.

Mohan was a younger, more rotund version of our obliging Rana friend in Delhi. They had the same slightly petulant expression, high impatient voices and a rattling hurried command of English learned from years of contact with English governesses and high-school teachers in Darjeeling.

'Would you please step into the lounge and have a cup of tea? This plane service is very inefficient and we may have a long wait.' He informed us that he was returning from a holiday in Calcutta. 'There is a city. Horse racing, night clubs, good food, and such pretty girls. Everything is there, and I can tell you that I have had a jolly good time.'

He poured out second cups and called for more hot water. 'You are coming to Nepal at a very interesting, even dangerous moment. The country has no real government at all, lawlessness is widespread, murder is rife.'

He leaned forward confidentially. 'It is expected that the government will collapse at any moment, there will be demonstrations.' He stopped talking and sat back in his chair with an innocent look on his face as a small man in tight-fitting linen trousers and an embroidered pixie cap came in, looked round and went out again.

'You do not know with these Nepalis – it is well not to talk about the country's difficulties in public.'

Our departure was announced and in a few minutes we were airborne, flying in a sturdy little Dakota over interminable Indian villages, their water tanks glistening in the sun and the great brown rope that was the muddy Ganges. Soon the light colour and detailed patterns of cultivated fields changed to dark forest which we knew to be the Terai, the jungle area full of tigers and other game, which stretched along Nepal's southern border. Foothills appeared ahead and became higher, until far away on the horizon they broke against the great snow mountains.

For about fifteen minutes the foothills rolled beneath us, then suddenly we skimmed over the last sharp green hill into the Kathmandu valley. I caught a glimpse of thatched houses and carefully terraced slopes stretching downwards into the wide oval valley which is the heart of Nepal. Golden temple tops gleamed in the sun.

One of the few vehicles in Kathmandu, an old station wagon with curtained windows, was waiting for us. As we said goodbye to Mohan, he asked us to visit him.

'I will be expecting you tomorrow. Just ask for the Jumla Durbar in the Durbar compound, and I can assure you that anyone will know it.'

Since the only way a foreigner could visit Nepal was as a guest, there were no hotels, just the government guesthouse situated outside the main square of the Tunde Khel. We stayed in a comfortable two-storey house with its own staff just for us. I remember large airy rooms, a dining room full of wicker chairs and tables with crisp linen covers, where we sat alone, and in due course, the two of us would be served a solitary and sumptuous Christmas dinner. The food was invariably good, and we were spared semi-European dishes or two-way Indian menus with their mulligatawny and creamed chicken. Instead we were feasted on new delights, golden wafers of bread, bowls of sugared rice, pastries, curries and fiery rainbow-coloured sauces.

Kathmandu was a delicate, crumbling, squalid little town

fallen to decay, never quite recovered from the earthquake of
1932. The sun glinted on curved temple roofs, filigree pagodas,
and other delightful battered buildings, not all of them ancient;
even the curious tower beside the guesthouse known as Bim's
Folly had a lacy charm. So much of Kabul had been destroyed
that there had been relatively little in the Afghan capital that
could be considered beautiful – the place had other charms. But
like Kabul, Kathmandu absorbed a medley of different races,
Magars, Gurungs, Kirats, Sherpas and Tibetans in wide-
brimmed hats trimmed with fur, high felt boots and huge turquoise earrings.

Not a European in sight.

The Tibetans were shopping in large groups, buying cameras,
black umbrellas and western fedoras such as are worn by gang-
sters or businessmen on Wall Street. This was the season
they came down to trade, and they would not be returning
until the mountain passes opened in spring. Some, though
racially Tibetan, came from the Nepalese side of the frontier
and were known in the valley as mountain people or Bhotias.
But many were true Tibetans, coming from as far as Lhasa,
since intercourse between Tibet and Nepal had continued in
spite of the Chinese occupation. The flight of the Dalai Lama,
the repression of Tibetan culture and the descent of the ice
curtain, was four years ahead.

We walked through the cobbled streets of the old city where
the houses built of rose-coloured brick, generally three or four
storeys high, had doors so low they seemed made for dwarfs.
Dark rooms inside had no chimneys or staircases, but a series of
ladders linking floors.

The temples were mostly pagodas: the Nepalese believe that
the style originated here and the Chinese copied it. Almost
every inch of wood in these temples, the struts, beams, window
sills, surrounds, ledges, doorways and eaves, was carved
ferociously, into a fantastic world of mythology: gods and
goddesses intertwined with writhing demons, copulating
couples, while sedate Buddhas were wrapped in forests of
vines and leaves. So much was tumbledown and neglected;
tufts of grass grew under the golden tiles, curling eaves of the
temples had split open and bushes and plants had seeded
themselves in the cracked masonry.

Many of the lanes were so narrow that people could talk and even pass objects from window to window across the street. We passed figures framed by carved wood leaning out, shouting or quarrelling. A girl's head with a mane of shining black hair appeared at a window; a few doors away we were blasted with the whine of fifes and rattle of drums announcing a wedding party, and around glittering, golden, carved pagodas worshippers were praying and making their daily offerings of flowers and food.

We emerged from the medieval quarter to a section of the city that was not exactly modern, but Edwardian Imperial. First the stretch of grassland, the Tunde Khel, which divides the city, the heart of the Gurkha area, scene of military parades and great religious festivals, including the one where they chop off animals' heads. All over the acres of grass were scattered groups of Tibetans who were gambling – some of them had fluffy little dogs with them, whose long hair blew down their faces. In the centre stood four statues of Gurkha soldiers, commemorating those killed in foreign wars, and at various points around the perimeter pranced equestrian statues of Rana prime ministers. The horses rearing upwards with the vigour of the horses of Marlay and their bewhiskered riders, proudly erect gazing over the city, seemed more lifelike than the sleek black bulls lolling on the grass beside them. The Tunde Khel was used as a grazing ground for the herds of cattle and sheep brought down to the city from the mountains to be fattened before they were sold in the market. But the great bulls with their humped bison backs were sacred and wandered over the pastures disturbed only by Nepali cattlemen who led their cows here from all over the valley. Life was good; they were too lazy and contented to do more than snort occasionally and paw the ground at passers-by.

The buildings surrounding this maidan, consisting of the modern area of Kathmandu – and how those that survived looked endearingly old-fashioned when I returned thirty years later – included a large army barracks, Tri Chandra college and the Durbar square which contained most of the former Rana palaces. We found the entrance to Mohan's palace, the Jumla Durbar, down a narrow lane with high brick walls on either side, where a sentry sat dozing next to the entrance gate, his rifle

beside him on the grass. Two crumbling white pilasters flanked
by rusty iron gates opened onto an avenue choked with weeds
running past a little Hindu temple which had become a refuge
for cats and a nesting-place for stray hens.

The Jumla Durbar was a huge white three-storeyed building
designed by a Japanese architect in Graeco-Roman style. It
called to mind a watering place – Carlsbad, perhaps, or a very
respectable seaside resort; it might have been an old-fashioned
hotel in Biarritz or Monte Carlo or situated in Yalta with a lady
and her dog passing by. Colonnades of Corinthian columns
supported decorated plinths and along the Palladian front a line
of empty niches waited for statues.

A small army tent was pitched on a piece of waste ground in
front of the imposing façade. As we walked up the avenue the
tent flap lifted and a veiled woman fled towards the palace. Then
the flap lifted again and Mohan, accompanied by two children,
came out to greet us.

'Hullo. Welcome. Permit me to present my children. Here is
Trixie and may I introduce Ranji.' Ranji's solid build and
puckered mouth, clearly Rana traits, were already pronounced.
Mohan himself was wearing national costume, a tight fitting pair
of jodhpurs over which a tunic buttoned up diagonally to the
neck. On his head perched his homespun embroidered hat.

'Come inside. You see me here in my winter headquarters.'
He spoke in Nepali to the children who followed their mother
up to the palace. Like most Rana ladies Mohan's wife lived in
strictest purdah.

Inside the tent was very warm, furnished with a camp bed
and a trestle table on which was a copy of *How to Win Friends and
Influence People*. We sat on the edge of the bed, Mohan between
us.

'I retire here in winter to seek warmth because the palace is
chilly. Tell me your impressions of Kathmandu.'

We described the guesthouse and our morning walk.

'Splendid. Now since it is becoming unbearably warm in here,
permit me to take you over to my palace.'

We entered through an empty basement from where we
climbed a wide wooden staircase to a series of vast staterooms.
On the flaking walls were trophies and photographs of the hunt,
mostly tigers. Dusty snarling heads gazed across at windows

long empty of glass, and beneath them photographs showed their slayers grouped around their bodies.

Under the chandelier in the drawing room stood a silver equestrian statue presented to Mohan's grandfather by Edward the Seventh. Dust sheets that did not quite conceal gilt cabriolet legs covered a vast amount of furniture which had been imported from England at the turn of the century. Around the walls spaces between the tiger heads were crowded with portraits. Mohan pointed out with particular pride Bhin Sher, the maharajah, wearing white trousers embroidered with gold and a red jacket blazing with decorations, towering over the tiny figure of his wife dressed in Victorian black – she had worn no veil while sitting for the artist.

We were led past signed photographs and portraits of kings and tyrants and innumerable imposing dead relatives, grand uncles and cousins, scattered among the splayed tiger skins and elephant tusks. We went upstairs past attics crammed with trunks and displaced furniture to a small staircase leading onto the roof from where we were given an incomparable view of the Kathmandu valley. Around us spread the Durbar compound filled with other mothballed residences which were the homes of Mohan's cousins. Just beyond the king's palace was the austere flat-roofed bungalow belonging to the crown prince. The immense ornamented rococo front of an ex-maharajah's palace, now the secretariat, looked down on spouting dolphins and ornamental pools copied from the gardens of Versailles. ('I showed that to an American who said, "Makes the White House look like a country cottage."')

So recently the scene of great wealth, in the space of a few years these aristocratic buildings had an air of abandonment and galloping decay far more striking than the long-term neglect of old Kathmandu. It was as if their downfall – and in some cases the word could be used literally – had come with great suddenness. Indeed, some palaces had foundered in the earthquake of 1932, subsiding into the ground where they still lay, their ruins covered in pink weeds. Around them derelict gardens led to more derelict gardens where the formal terracing had crumbled and broken down before being dumped with the remains of old decency. From the rooftop of the Jumla Durbar we noted how these gardens had become repositories of Greek pillars, broken gas-lamp standards and broken statuary and noted the rubbish dumped in the ponds and artificial trout streams.

When I returned to Kathmandu thirty years later, of course all this florid decay had long been tidied up. The palaces had been pulled down or converted into something useful; in particular the King's palace, a monstrous dinosaur of a building, had been replaced by a slick Dallas-style modern palace. It was pleasant to see the Jumla Durbar had survived.

Back in the tent a servant brought glasses of lemonade while Mohan told us a little about his family. We had come to Kathmandu at a difficult time in Nepalese history and for the Ranas in particular. Their power had been swept away overnight, and now they had to adjust themselves to changed circumstances. The empty rooms shrouded in dust sheets and the new life passed in austere modern bungalows and army tents erected beside their palaces were a result of vast reductions in Rana incomes.

Revolution and change had come in 1951. Before that, to be born a Rana in Nepal meant a promise of excessive privilege. Though a young Rana might never use a gun, he would automatically become an officer in the army. He might build or inherit a palace in Kathmandu, and other grand residences in Bombay, Calcutta or Benares, while an estate in the Terai bordering India would supply both revenue and hunting grounds. In a country of perhaps ten million people the Ranas, a tiny minority, kept power and money to themselves.

However, there were curious differences in status in the Rana hierarchy which were the result of a combination of caste rules, admiration for European bureaucracy, and an abiding obsession with military rank, part-copied from British military law and tradition. When the Ranas reorganised their army ranks, they combined the worse aspects of the old English purchase system with the most blatant abuses of caste. Rana men were divided into A class, B class and C class. An A-class Rana, whose parents were of equal caste, would automatically become a major-general as soon as he reached manhood, and could rise to the highest rank. B-class Ranas – those whose mothers were not entitled to eat rice with their husbands – could rise no higher than the rank of lieutenant-colonel. The poor C-class Ranas, whose parents could not eat with each other at all, started off life as humble lieutenants and, however gifted as warriors, could only become majors.

Although in theory this was an admirable way of curbing the ambitions of relatives, these rules caused deep divisions in the Rana ranks, B- and C-class Ranas becoming bitterly hostile to the privileged A class. In 1934 certain dissatisfied C-class Ranas were banished from the Kathmandu valley and their subsequent activities contributed to the eventual downfall of the hundred-year-old Rana oligarchy and the revolution of 1951.

Mohan described the life his father and uncles used to lead. Most of them maintained houses in India's big cities to which they would travel from Nepal. In a few weeks' spree in Benares they might spend up to three lakhs of rupees – about twenty-five thousand pounds. The old field-marshal who was Mohan's grandfather still lived in an inordinately shabby palace beside the Jumla Durbar, while in the royal palace nearby, the king employed six hundred servants, most of whom were idle. Before the 1951 revolution all the great Rana families had large numbers of servants, a necessary indication of rank. Mohan now retained about sixty, and the numbers were constantly being reduced. The unburdening of hundreds of retainers by suddenly impoverished Rana families was causing prolonged domestic problems, since the majority of servants had no alternative way of earning a living. Mohan would have liked to dispense with nearly all of his, but feared that if he did, they would face starvation.

He was born in 1932 under an unlucky star. His father called in a soothsayer, who predicted that he would bring misfortune to his family. So his father dispossessed him and threw the baby out of the palace. For some time nobody would have anything to do with the ill-omened child, until an aunt, a brave old lady of considerable standing in the Rana hierarchy, agreed to adopt him.

Shortly afterwards there was a dispute among the Ranas, splitting them into two camps, with Mohan's family in the losing group. As a result most of his relations were thrown into exile and he was the only male member of the family left in Kathmandu. The old lady brought him up well, giving him a university education and making him heir to a fortune. He was far better off than his brothers, living in exile in the Terai, deliberately deprived of education by their old father in case they should become disloyal.

'I never see them now. It would be most unwise to jeopardise my political position.'

'What about the ordinary people? Surely they cannot like the Ranas?'

'That is very true.' We learned of some Rana excesses like the hall of the Seto Durbar, with its crystal staircase, pillars of cut glass, Italian marble tiles and Persian and Belgian carpets. Since there were no roads into the country, every tile and crystal had to be carried in on human backs, mostly by men and women conscripted to forced labour. There was the Nach Gar, the dancing hall in the Lal Durbar, illuminated with chandeliers and gas lamps where the girls from the harem danced, or else voluptuous Talimay girls played Indian musical instruments, and performed erotic dances. (Later the Lal Durbar became part of the Yak and Yeti Hotel.) There were the Ranas who drank, including one mukhtiyar or commander-in-chief who had to be lifted by two people to put on the head-dress of the mukhtiyar on the day of his appointment. There was a general air of excess among the Ranas, even among the most respectable like the prime minister who ate his lunch and dinner off heavy gold dishes, his diet consisting largely of grilled partridges and roast wild fowls since, as a particularly high-class Brahmin, he was prohibited from eating ordinary domesticated chickens. There were tales of harems, cruelties, revolts, executions, wealth amassed, wealth squandered and every reason to welcome the revolution of 1951 which had brought about the Ranas' downfall.

'Of course, immediately after the revolution we were all very nervous of what would happen. Some Ranas changed their names, but when nothing took place they became Ranas again. Now it seems we will be allowed to keep some of our possessions.'

How long could the Ranas hold on to their shrinking wealth and position? In 1955 they still commanded some respect from the people. The maharajah's scholarly brother, Kaisar Shum Sher Rana, had been made Minister of Defence, and other Ranas still held important government positions. But it was difficult for a clan so used to absolute power to have complete equality thrust upon them. Even Mohan, however hard he tried to be democratic, found it hard to forget the old priveleged life. Even as a C-class Rana he had been used to social superiority. Until recently people froze to attention as he passed in the street, and when he arrived at his palace servants would prostrate themselves at his feet.

Although most Ranas still owned their palaces in Kathmandu, their vast estates in the country were being taken away. Signs of financial strain were everywhere. Mohan no longer used the great black Packard with its ruby-eyed exhaust in the shape of a serpents' head (like so much else, carried up to Kathmandu from India on porters' backs) to travel round the city. Already there were plans to turn a Rana palace into a hotel, for soon the tourists would invade. Mohan himself had expectations of this inexhaustible source of revenue. Naturally he would put up guests. Would they require hot water? What about food? He would personally supervise the cooking. Were European women as immoral as he had been led to expect?

Taking us around the house, he sought our advice as to how to convert the large draughty rooms. This one with its rows of stuffed tiger heads (more than average – there must have been at least a hundred deceased tigers in the Jumla Durbar alone): would it be suitable for a bedroom? The billiard room – that could easily be changed into a reception lounge. In the drawing room he would put on a display of Rana relics, the sort of things likely to appeal to tourists – jewels and medals, ivory carvings. The hunting mementoes would have to be rehung so that the fangs of the largest tigers would appear to better advantage.

The evils of the deposed Ranas appeared lurid. I quote from *Whither Nepal*, written by Mr Regmi, the foreign secretary at the height of the movement against the Ranacracy.

'Nepal's aristocracy is a blood-sucking vampire and a lordling wolf! The Rana's is a condescending mood whenever the people are brought in touch; otherwise he sits on the pedestal, much like the sky-high mansion he occupies . . . The people are not permitted to use conveyances, rickshaws included, to use European musical instruments on festive occasions – they have to contend with the old conventional instruments – to keep closed the windows facing a mansion, and lastly, not to build a building of the size likely to compete with those of the aristocracy.'

This abuse, Mohan admitted, had existed. Like many of his contemporaries, he had felt that if Nepal was to advance or even survive, she must become a democracy. When the revolution came, he was full of high ideals to improve his country and decided to enter politics. It was a brave choice at a time when his relatives, considering themselves lucky to be alive, remained as inconspicuous as possible or made hasty plans to retire to their palaces in India.

Mohan joined the party in opposition to the Prime Minister, Mr M. P. Koirala, whose leader was confusingly the Prime Minister's brother, Mr B. P. Koirala. When we arrived at the end of 1955 the political position was still volatile, with members of the party in opposition making fiery speeches on the Tunde Khel or sending representatives flying through the narrow streets of Kathmandu in jeeps provided with loudspeakers.

Mr B. P. Koirala had given Mohan the unenviable job of organising a public protest, a demonstration based on the *satyagraha* ideal evolved by Gandhi by which everyone should seek arrest. This might continue for weeks, Mohan assured us, but eventually all the jails would be overflowing, and then the army could do nothing, so that without authority the government must collapse. The demonstration would be combined with a general strike. He himself would lead a group of peasants to the gates of the secretariat and there they would fling themselves down on the ground so that no one could enter.

We were alarmed that our new friend might be thrown into prison, remembering that during the Rana regime hundreds of people had vanished for years. He assured us with the bearing of a martyr that he would almost certainly be out of prison in twenty-four hours, and perhaps he would find himself a junior minister in a new government.

When the time came Mohan organised his little troop, arranged that an Indian representative of *The Times* should be present, and proceeded to invite punishment as dictated by the message of *satyagraha*, convinced that the government was doomed and Mr B. P. Koirala would rise to power. However Mr M. P. Koirala defeated his brother's strategy by simply declaring the day a public holiday. This was not quite democracy, Nepal-style. Often when the Ranas had faced political difficulties, they declared public holidays or days when gambling – normally illegal – would be permitted, an irresistible diversion for Nepalese, however politically inclined.

Although no one had been embarrassed by the prone bodies of Mohan and his rustics, he appeared quite cheerful in his disappointment.

'Nepalese jails are unpleasant places, and perhaps we can succeed by negotiation instead of by such desperate measures.'

The rest of this chapter is history, much of it derived from Mohan's admirable account of Rana society from the inside published in 1979.

The Ranas ruled for a century from 1847 to 1951. Their people, the Gurkhas, who moulded modern Nepal into one unit with its borders formed by Tibet, Kashmir, India and Sikhim, were a warrior race claiming descent from Udaipur Rajputs of India. Originally the term Gurkha applied only to people living in the vicinity of the town of Gurkha to which a group of Rajputs ejected from their homes fled about four hundred years ago.

Before the Gurkhas gained ascendancy in the valley, Nepal was a loose confederacy of independent kingdoms ruled by the Malla kings. It is the Mallas who have left Nepal her richest heritage, the hundreds of pagoda temples, and the monuments and tombs built by the Newars under their patronage, which we had seen crumbling side by side with the Rana palaces.

The first recorded Malla king was Devi Malla who reigned during the middle of the thirteenth century. His descendants ruled until the eighteenth century when a Gurkha general named Prithwi Narayan descended with his troops and broke a power already weakened by internal feuding. When the Gurkhas marched on Kathmandu they found the inhabitants happily engaged in the great Hindu festival of Kumari-Jatra when most of the Malla troops were drunk. Prithwi Narayan announced to the surprised populace that Kathmandu had been captured, but in the tradition of Nepalese politics, gave permission for the merry-making to continue. Later he followed the custom of the Malla kings by bowing before the living goddess Kumari, who placed a vermilion mark on the forehead of the new king of Nepal. (In the nineteen-nineties the current living Kumari goddess still plays an important part in politics.) So the Malla dynasty was overpowered and for the first time Nepal become a united kingdom. During the next hundred years Nepal pushed its frontiers right up to the borders of Kashmir. In the south, Nepali expansion roused the concern of the British, who stipulated in the treaty of 1816 that border raids must cease and that a British agent should be admitted to Kathmandu.

Jung Bahadur, the founder of the Rana dynasty, came into power in 1847 during an extraordinary palace revolt. He was an ambitious young Gurkha general growing in reputation as a courageous soldier; among his deeds of bravery was the single-handed slaughter of a mad elephant. During a period of political banishment in India he assessed the growing power of the East India Company and laid the foundations for friendly relations with the British.

Meanwhile the Gurkha king of Nepal, Rasjendra Bikram Shah, had surrendered his royal powers to his junior queen, Rajya Laxmi Devi, and appointed her regent. On the night of 14 September 1846 she learned that her lover, a young Gurkha officer named Gagan Singh, had been murdered. Having seen his corpse she rushed to the royal courtyard known as the kot on the Tunde Khel followed by four armed handmaidens, and summoned by bugle all the high ministers of state before her. By the light of flickering torches she waved the sword of office and demanded the identity of the murderer. Suspicion fell on a certain Kazi Bir Kishore, who was a rival of Gagan Singh, and the queen, having first ordered a general to cut off his head instantly, advanced with drawn sword towards the bound man threatening to do the deed herself. (The king had hastily withdrawn from the kot and sought refuge at the British Residency; diplomatically, on the grounds that it was past midnight, the gates did not open.)

While the queen was being forcibly restrained from killing Bir Kishore, one of her generals slipped away to fetch his soldiers. Fearing his intentions, the queen ordered Jung Bahadur to arrest him; Jung had already taken the precaution of having a troop of loyal soldiers around him. While he was attempting to detail the general, shots rang out, whether from his troops or elsewhere, is not clear. In the resulting fighting hundreds were killed before Jung Bahadur gained control.

The carnage, known as the Massacre of the Kot, resulted in the queen making Jung Bahadur her prime minister. A few years later, when he grew powerful enough, he overthrew her. Tiring of her repeated plots to assassinate either himself or the king, he succeeded in banishing her to Benares before making the office of prime minister hereditary and exclusive to his family and descendants. Together with the title of maharajah, the position of absolute ruler was inherited by the eldest male member of the family, although the reigning prime minister could appoint another member of his family to succeed him if he wished. The royal family lost all its power and the King became a figurehead. The true ruler of Nepal was the Rana maharajah and prime minister, recognised as such by other states and countries. When Jung Bahadur sided with the British during the Indian Mutiny, he gained his most powerful allies, who continued to support the Ranas until partition ninety years later. After the British left India a new political fervour swept Asia, which in Nepal took the form of revolt against the old undemocratic Ranacracy. In 1951 the last Rana prime minister, maharajah Mohan, resigned and in April of that year the king proclaimed the end of the hereditary office established by Jung Bahadur.

14

Mohan took us to meet some of his Rana cousins whose palace was larger and more derelict than his own, with the familiar flaking balustrades, fountains that did not work, and a private zoo empty of wild animals. The spirit of decay and past greatness filled the lofty freezing rooms whose walls were encrusted with tigers and ancestors. Huddled in overcoats, blowing on numbed fingers, we sat on deckchairs assembled in the middle of an enormous empty room beneath a Murano chandelier of pink and blue lilies.

'You wish to see my crown?' a young Rana interrupted the silence as we nibbled sugared rice and nuts. He went out and returned with a linen bag from which he unwrapped a jewelled hat which he placed casually on his head. It was a magnificent creation topped with long plumes of white bird of paradise feathers, studded with pearls and fringed with emeralds the size of lollipops. The contrast between this regal headpiece and the young man's jeans and open-necked shirt could not have been more striking. Everyone laughed.

'Do you ever wear it now?'

'Those days are over.'

The crown was placed in its bag and put away again. I was reminded of the Anglo-Irish.

Dilip, our host, got up and, striding around the huge room, began talking. He told us that his ambition was to visit Europe, making a journey through Russia, visiting Moscow en route. He wanted to fox-hunt, deep sea-fish, drive fast sportscars and to sail. But since the future of the Ranas and of his own family remained undecided, he was obliged to remain in Nepal. Here his favourite pursuit was big-game hunting in the Terai. That skin over there, and that head, and that one were his bag. It was terrific good sport.

Then Mohan suggested that Michael and I should be guests

at a tiger hunt. Since this was standard entertainment for visiting dignitaries, we were honoured to be considered worthy of such an invitation. Just a few years later, still in blithe pre-conservation days, a more distinguished visitor than ourselves, Prince Philip, caused an uproar by shooting a tiger which his hosts had anxiously arranged to be driven in his direction so that he could not possibly miss it. But perhaps these Ranas could foresee that this particular pastime was on the decline, and therefore our presence was justification for a spot of fun.

'It is too easy. Dilip owns plenty of land on the Terai.'

We would fly to Pokra and then take a train to his estate. A hunt would be arranged with a tiger apiece guaranteed, and perhaps a leopard, panther and crocodile thrown in for good measure. As background entertainment we could slaughter lesser game such as hog and deer.

Perhaps the surfeit of snarling heads all around us persuaded us that we would be taking part in a routine sport. It offered the opportunity of seeing more of Nepal in the company of these delightful Ranas. Killing big game had not yet become a disgraceful occupation; my family had shot quite a few wild animals whose heads were stuck on the walls at home – nothing like the Ranas, of course. Would I take home a tiger head to be mounted beside great-uncle Phil's sambur?

We all became very excited and Dilip in particular began telling us about big-game hunting. A Rana would be accustomed to hunting from childhood, taking part in the big shoots; a boy would enter a tiger hunt mounted on an elephant with as much nonchalance as we used to show when we went out after rabbits.

Formerly every Rana possessed scores of elephants, but their numbers had declined drastically. The king's stables, the largest in Nepal, had maintained over a thousand beasts, which had recently been reduced to three hundred. The disposal, often the slaughter of elephants which had been happening not only in Nepal, but in every ex-maharajah's palace in India, was a consequence of democracy. Elephants were symbols of power and pomp; they ate too much – six hundred pounds of fodder a day – and they were generally regarded as obsolete, no more to be seen swaying through Durbar processions with jewelled howdahs on their backs and ropes of pearls twined through their trunks. However, we were assured, there were still enough around, and a ten-elephant hunt on Dilip's estate could be organised without difficulty.

Dilip described the Terai with its thick luxurious growth of jungle and its inhbaitants, the Tharus, whose knowledge of game was such that they were reputed to talk to wild animals. We learned how a Nepali kills a wild boar by sitting on a log and waiting for it to charge; then, without changing his position, he will split it with one upward sweep of his kukri. We talked of tigers and were told how an ageing maneater would be driven from village to village by the entire male population until it might be hounded from one end of the Terai to the other, a distance of over six hundred miles. Dilip had met Major Corbett, whose name was still respected throughout the Terai for his efforts in ridding the place of maneaters. He told us about wild elephant hunts, and described how only last season he had been chased by a herd and had only escaped because their bulk prevented them from charging through impenetrable undergrowth. Sitting under the skins and the portraits of Rana generals, we received tips on how to deal with bears. The women who lived in the mountains above the Terai commonly stuck a fork into bears' necks just as they were about to be hugged.

'Do not ever run away from a wild animal. They can scent fear. The thing is to hold your ground and if possible walk up in a calm manner towards them as if you are greeting a friend.'

Dilip pointed out that we would have to start as soon as possible, since the malaria season would start in a few weeks. In order to reach the right area of the Terai where he and his family had always hunted, it would be necessary to leave Nepal south of Kathmandu, enter India and travel along the border to re-enter the country at the appropriate point in the west.

We could not seek direct permission to go on a hunt, for this would certainly be refused. From the first the new government's attitude towards hunting had wounded the Ranas' pride more than anything else. Hunting was now considered *déclassé* and feudal, quite out of keeping with modern times. The Ranas protested that tigers were increasing in numbers, becoming a growing menace in the villages in the Terai.

What other reason could there be for wanting to visit a hot mosquito-ridden jungle? Already the foreign experts, the anthropologists and advisers, were moving into Nepal; we could pretend to be among them. We decided that we would be folklore specialists, and mugged up a couple of travel books on the Tharus. Meanwhile we practised at a rifle range. The last time I had done any shooting had been in Dublin under the eye of the Colonel. Watching us, Dilip thought that we might hit a tiger at close range.

Then all our plans went wrong. Mohan's aunt, the one who had adopted him, became ill, and as far as he was concerned there was no question of a tiger hunt while her condition remained serious. Next day Dilip received a telegram from Almora in India where his sister lived. 'Leila broken leg, help needed, come at once.'

That seemed to bring our hunting expedition to a quick and sad conclusion. Suddenly Ranji, the fat background Rana, the one who had hardly spoken, the one with the emerald and bird of paradise head-dress, became articulate for the first time. What a pity that such calamities had taken place. Would we not please come hunting with him on his uncle's estate? It would give him so much pleasure. Mohan and Dilip joined the entreaties – it was an opportunity not to be missed – please to consider that they did not wish to let us down. By now we rather wanted to go hunting, and so we agreed to accompany Ranji to his uncle's place on the Terai.

A week passed during which plans were made, unmade, changed, reconsidered and revised. One day we were to go to Ranji's estate, then it was decided that we had better go with Mohan after all. Would we visit Dilip's stretch of territory, even though he had gone to India? Then the old lady became better and Mohan thought he might definitely be coming with us. Then Ranji protested. There were discussions about guns and ammunition; we would have to bring adequate food. Then the old lady had a relapse. The Ranas poured over maps – not that place, there are no crocodiles – this spot here is better.

It came as a surprise one evening when Ranji announced that we would be starting next morning.

We said goodbye to Mohan in his tent outside the Jumla Durbar. Once again he apologised that he was not coming with us. We must be careful with tigers; they were treacherous beasts and he himself had seen a man torn to pieces by one.

There were poisonous snakes of all kinds on the Terai, and we must beware of rhinos that charged at the sound of a breaking twig. We must remember never to travel without a gun and endeavour not to fall off elephants – if we did we would certainly break our legs.

'I am sure you are not sorry to be leaving Kathmandu. Next year I will go to Ireland to see you and perhaps we will be able to hunt there.'

Ranji's palace was yet another crumbling mansion with Corinthian pillars and flaking plaster. We sat fidgeting in the bare hall for about ten minutes before a figure dressed in pyjamas leaned over the broken balustrade.

'Coming soon,' Ranji shouted and disappeared. An hour later he came down attended by a crowd of anxious uncles, brothers and cousins, who had covered him in garlands of chrysanthemums. James, his Brahmin cook, followed, carrying his bag, a gaunt figure, meekly obedient, in flowing white dhoti.

Impatiently freeing himself of relatives Ranji took off the garlands and led us to the waiting car which took us to the airport. Here a detachment of the king's guard in scarlet uniforms and black pillbox hats was drawn up outside the little airport building to honour the crown prince who was flying to Switzerland. Ranji joined the spectators, greeting old friends with courtly gestures, very much the Rana. He pointed out a turncoat Rana who had to change his name after the revolution, and without embarrassment greeted a politician who had spent half his life in exile outside the country, and another man who had been in a Rana prison for twenty years.

A twenty-minute flight by a Dakota of the newly formed Nepalese Airways brought us to a small airfield cleared out of the Terai. After the alpine coolness of the Kathmandu valley the heat rose in sticky waves. A dense wall of trees surrounded the clearing, and a few scattered shanty-type buildings with grass roofs ran along the side of the airstrip. Here was a tiny railway station, where a solitary carriage was waiting on the narrow track which disappeared southwards into the jungle. We were at the terminus of Nepal's only railway, built in 1870 by Mohan Shum Sher, the ruling Rana maharajah, who had never completed it. Up until the year that we visited Nepal, 1955, all travellers had continued into Kathmandu on foot. Now that

India and Nepal were linked by air, a journey that formerly took several days was completed in less than an hour.

We made our way over to the carriage; even the few yards' walk made our shirts sticky with sweat. Inside were two old-fashioned parallel benches, and between them, perched high on a pile of luggage, sat a Rana general, a Nepalese Colonel Blimp, voluble and pop-eyed, who immediately began to dole out food from a tiffin basket. Hard-boiled eggs, curry puffs, little cakes covered with silver balls and curling pink icing that melted in the hand were dumped on the bedding rolls and wooden trunks in front of us, as the general and Ranji began an argument about timetables.

A small green engine arrived pushing two other carriages before it. It came to a stop, letting off steam, and a cloud of bright-coloured parakeets flew over the tall elephant grass. The clearing became alive with people emerging from the jungle and rushing for the new carriages ours, of course, was First-class. Much clanging, shouting and a jolt that threw us together in a heap on top of the bedding rolls meant that our carriage was being joined to the little train. Then there was a shrill whistle and we were off, chugging out of the station into the jungle.

The air was hot and sleepy, the dull green of trees alternating with the summer of rice cultivation. The general, sallow faced beneath his topee, launched into an account of how he had fought a tiger with his bare hands. His eyes gleamed, his hands fluttered in the sunlight, and he lifted up his shirt to display a long scar across his back. When I fell asleep he was talking about maneaters.

We changed trains at Birganj on the Nepalese border where gangs of coolies plucked at our luggage, piling it up into a great heap on the platform before weaving their way through the Tibetans who had journeyed down from the mountains to visit the holy places of India. The general wished us 'good shooting' and, bowed down with guns, we crossed the tracks to the Indian village of Raxaul on the other side.

Back in Kathmandu when we were making and remaking plans for this expedition, neither Michael nor I had fully grasped the lengths that Rana sportsmen would go for their recreation. We had not realised that the weary eighteen-hour journey we were now making to Benares would only get us halfway and we would have to cross the width of India in order to reach Ranji's patch of tigers.

From Benares station we took a pair of rickshaws to Ranji's grandmother, who like many members of the Nepalese aristocracy chose to live in the holy city. Her palace on the bank of the Ganges was a big brooding dark building with steps leading down to the water, and on the land side an entrance through a tiny cobbled alleyway. We stopped in a dark courtyard, discouraged by two notices in Hindi and English which said 'NO ENTRY', and also by Ranji's solemn warning that on no account were we to go further. We were too disgusting. His grandmother, we must understand, was very orthodox. If we ventured inside the whole place would be defiled and would have to be scrubbed out, a job that might take anything up to a month's hard work.

We agreed to spend the night in a hotel and meet Ranji the next day. We could hardly have planned a more unsuitable way of touring the holy city, ignoring the great rose-coloured palaces and temples along the great brown river, keeping away from the ghats and pilgrims and instead going round shops and bazaars in a tearing hurry to buy cartridges. Only by a last-minute rush did we get to the station to catch a train at eleven o'clock and face an all-day journey to Lucknow. And still at Lucknow we were nowhere near our destination; from here we would begin the overnight stage that would take us back to a point of re-entry into Nepal.

On the brink of exhaustion we began our last eight hours' train travel before we reached tiger territory. Ranji was in expansive form, singing army songs, and striking up a conversation with a man in the corner of the carriage, another hunter who sat with a rifle between his legs. The hunter passed around a bottle of brandy and sat discussing elephants and their uselessness compared with tractors and bulldozers. As a landowner in Chittagong, he had had to get rid of ninety of his elephants since Indian independence with little or no compensation – at best they could be sold for about five hundred rupees on a glutted market. He and Ranji exchanged addresses, pressing each other with open invitations to hunt each other's land, illustrating the merits of their properties with many tall hunting stories. Once again we had to change trains – this time in the early hours of the morning. When we were installed in the new carriage Ranji informed us that we could not unwind the bedding rolls – he had an unlicensed gun concealed in one of them and he was not sure which. If it was discovered we would all have to pay a heavy fine. Michael and I climbed up into opposite luggage racks where we settled down, not too uncomfortably for what was left of the night.

I slept soundly for an hour or so, when I was abruptly woken by Ranji whose voice was quivering with agitation.

'Something really most unfortunate has happened – most inadvertently . . .'

As the early dawn lit the carriage I could make out Michael's unconscious body where it had fallen out of the luggage rack onto the floor. We lifted him up, his face deathly white, his hair thickly clotted with blood.

'Hold on just one sec,' Ranji said. The train had pulled up at a station, our final stop, and he leaped out onto the platform, returning a few minutes later with James, the engine driver and a brass bowl full of boiling water from the engine. From a small handbag he took out a bottle of Dettol and some lint and, with the engine driver's help, washed Michael's wound and gave him a neat crown bandage.

'I often have to do this. It is only a scalp wound, nothing I can assure you.' Ranji sighed, overcome by unpleasant memories. 'I have seen with my own eyes a man's skull ripped in two by a tiger. It seemed impossible that he would live.'

At last Michael recovered consciousness.

'Apart from loss of blood there is no serious injury.'

We decided that the hunt should go on.

We sat beside our pile of baggage watching the train rattle out of sight. The sun beat down; around us were stretches of elephant grass, and in the distance a line of trees showing the beginning of the forest.

An hour later, with a slow shriek of creaking wood, two painfully thin bullocks, ropes through their nostrils, their grey hides covering skinny ribcages, dragged along a cart with solid wooden wheels that did not seem to be absolutely round. The cart had been sent by Ranji's uncle whose village would be our base during the hunt. We climbed in with our luggage, settling Michael, still dazed, among straw-covered suitcases. James sat up very straight carrying a bunch of guns. I held another, which belonged to Ranji, who was already leaning out of the cart straining to catch the sight or scent of something to shoot.

The driver, who sat on a crossbar between the oxen, got them into motion with a sharp cry. We set off at walking pace towards the fringe of jungle, a wall of green spilling down from the Nepalese hills. The sun which had blasted us from an empty sky sank behind the trees as we entered the first wooden glades into a deepening green gloom. Michael said nothing, looking directly ahead. I fingered the .303 rifle which Ranji had given me. The creak of wooden wheels, the shriek of cicadas and the rustle of movement through the thick waist-high grass were the only sounds that broke the cathedral silence.

'Quick, the gun!'

Ranji had slapped his hand on my shoulder. He snatched the weapon and there was a bang and a flash of azure feathers as a peacock flew into the trees. I was reminded of our driver in Badakshan hunting the fox in the darkness as Ranji leapt down from the cart and followed the quarry where it had flown off into the trees. He was smiling sourly when he returned.

'Next time you must watch – that is why I gave you the gun. Please remember that we are no longer in Kathmandu.'

Any more game had vanished in the heat of the day. We passed a boundary mark that indicated the frontier between India and Nepal, a small white obelisk a little larger than a milestone nearly hidden in ferns and grasses. Giant trees enclosed us; shafts of light falling through the branches struck us like lasers. A few miles further on the canopy of the jungle was torn by a wide meandering river with sandbanks on either side that swept through the trees. Now there were more sounds, rattles, honks, quacks and shrieks of water birds. The cart sank to its axles as the driver twisted the tails of the bullocks splashing through the shallows. Then once again we were back in the gloom and the noises were reduced to cicadas, the creak of wooden wheels and the driver's occasional harangue of 'Hut! Hut!' addressed to his animals. No one else spoke. Ranji in his new guise as big game hunter took up a commanding position in front of the cart with James beside him, promoted to loader. But there was nothing to shoot.

Late in the day, dripping with heat, swaying with inertia, we emerged from the forest into a huge clearing several miles wide, part swamp and part cultivated fields where a few small villages, groups of straw and bamboo huts were dotted here and there; the largest of these, our destination, was two miles from the edge of the trees.

We approached it through an area that appeared to be a tropical knacker's yard. Scattered over the hard ground were corpses and skeletons of animals with groups of vultures ponderously leaping from corpse to corpse and plunging greasy snake-necks into stomachs and intestines. Some had eaten enough and clustered on the branches of dead trees, leering at us as we slowly passed them.

We came to the village which was protected by a bamboo palisade lying outside the gate. Some thin dogs got up from where they lay panting in the dust, and feebly barked as we drove up to a large grass hut which stood apart from the others. While Ranji and James disappeared inside, we were left in the cart to exchange grins with a group of villagers.

At last Ranji came out with his uncle, a fine-looking old man with a bushy moustache and a face the colour of mahogany who was dressed in cotton jodhpurs, a thick serge shirt, and a khaki balaclava folded and perched on the top of his head. He was gruff and shy; there was little to suggest the Rana about him, and in his habits and simple way of life he had become very much the village headman. His son, a young man of nineteen, referred to by Ranji as 'my cousin-brother', had smooth hair glossed back from a narrow oval face which made him more Indian than Nepali in appearance.

'They speak no English,' Ranji said. 'These people living in these miserable places have little opportunity for advancement.'

Their hut was by far the largest in the village, distinguished from the others by having a second floor used as a granary. The main room below was the only room; it was empty except for two low wooden beds. We squatted down on them while the old man spoke urgently to Ranji whose face had resumed its normal petulant expression.

'There has arisen a certain fundamental difficulty.'

He went on to explain that in the area surrounding the clearing there were plenty of deer, peacocks, wild fowl and perhaps some wild boar; back at the river there were crocodiles and in the swamp ducks galore. But to go after big game like tiger and panther it was necessary to penetrate deep into the jungle up to the foothills. Naturally to do this on a proper hunting basis elephants were necessary. He had hoped that the village would be able to supply at least five or six, but alas, the government had commandeered all elephants round about to carry out a land survey. He shrugged his shoulders. What could he do?

We assured him that duck and wild fowl and all the other game he had mentioned would be quite sufficient to satisfy our blood lust.

'Good. It is undoubtedly a pity. But even if we don't obtain big game, I will be able to show you a hunt.'

Meanwhile two straw walls had been strung together to make a room for us close to the uncle's hut, to which Ranji escorted us before dinner. Here there was no danger of our defiling anything. He would eat nothing that had not been carefully cleaned and protected from every source of contamination by James' pure Brahmin hands. We were making life very difficult for James. In his dealings with us, he had to be particularly careful, and on the train the rules had been strictly kept. Our plates and cutlery were carefully separated from Ranji's, and washed with extra thoroughness before they were wrapped in rags and put away in a bag he carried about with him, full of kitchen utensils. We were not allowed to go near any kitchen area, because if by bad luck our hands touched even a table, supper would have to be cooked all over again.

From where we sat in our grass tent we could see James crouched over pots of rice issuing streams of commands to the circle of men around him. A little later two of them came out and built a fire in front of us, followed shortly by two more carrying our carefully marked plates piled with boiled rice. Ranji had already retired inside his uncle's tent for his meal, but we did not dine alone; the entire village watched us eating, their eyes bright in the firelight. Only after we had unrolled our sleeping bags were we left to ourselves.

Ranji had told us to be up by five next morning ready for action, but at nine he was still asleep. Already the sun burnt down and the earth was cracked into a web of thin black lines; vultures wheeled overhead.

It was nearly ten before he emerged from the hut, dressed in pyjamas, attended by numerous hastily impressed servants.

'I feel terrible. The climate is too damned hot.'

'What about the hunt?'

'There is plenty of time. First I must have my bath.' He pointed to where James was directing a crowd to carry a galvanised tub from the kitchen into the open air and fill it up with two kerosene cans of tepid water off the kitchen fire.

For the next hour Ranji sat in his bath and splashed before an audience, his plump body protruding from the tub in contrast to the skeletal thinness of the spectators. At midday he donned a magenta-coloured dressing gown and at last we were off to hunt, followed by the retinue.

Our first engagement was to shoot duck in a huge swamp stretching away to the forest. 'This will enable you to get your eye in for bigger game,' said Ranji. The heavy green water lay between clusters of reed and large storks stepped elegantly in and out. Ranji discarded his dressing gown, handing it to a servant; rolling up his pyjama trousers, he began to approach the swamp in a low crouch while another servant followed close behind him. Other men were dispatched as beaters, and a moment later two shots rang out as a flight of birds crossed the sky. A few minutes later Ranji returned with a grimace of annoyance.

Michael, still wearing a bandage like a white crown, demanded a turn with the gun.

'It is no good. The duck are far too nervous.'

'I still wouldn't mind a shot.'

Ranji was silent for a moment before handing over the gun and two cartridges.

'Don't waste any.'

We watched Michael wade out into the reeds while the servant trod slowly through the marshes in the opposite direction from the way he had gone before. There was a great rustle of wings and shots followed by curses.

'Bad luck . . . what did I tell you?' Ranji said as Michael waded back.

'I was sure that I had a line on them.' Wet and crestfallen, Michael began to play about with the gun. He did a little investigation and discovered that he had been handed two cartridges for deer stalking.

We wandered back to the village convinced that our band was

not the stuff that produces big game hunters. The tigers were safe enough, and even the duck would find that any threat from us would be confined to a few missing feathers. This opinion seemed confirmed, when just as we were sitting down, to midday rice, firmly segregated, Ranji came rushing out of his uncle's hut holding up a fistful of bullets.

'They are all of the wrong calibre. They will not fit the rifle. You know what that means – no deer, no crocodile . . . That damn fool of a dealer in Benares has given me the wrong ammunition. What a tragedy!' He paused. 'I know; you shall have to go back to Benares and change them, it is the only thing to do.'

'What about yourself?'

'Oh that journey is too long. I do not like trains.'

He disappeared into the hut. Ten minutes later he reappeared to report that he had found twelve bullets of the right calibre, and departed with these into the forest, scores of people trailing after him.

We took the shotgun and the cartridges intended for deer and wandered around the swamp, chasing duck which had become elusive. After a time we gave up and took to bird-watching, a more rewarding pastime. We lay on the edge of the swamp listening to the sounds of birds magnified by the great silence and watching the pairs of grey stork sweeping across the dull glaze of water. There were smaller white herons perched on submerged logs, moorhens, dabchicks, a great snakebird plunging its beak into the water, and little unknown brown birds darting through the reeds. When we returned covered with leeches to where the vultures were flying, we found Ranji arguing with a police officer and four soldiers who had arrived in the village.

The officer had told Ranji that he had received a telegram from the secretariat in Kathmandu stating simply that two Christians were arriving in his district. Thinking that this sounded sinister, he had set forth from the district capital across the forest to the village; now he was willing to accept twenty rupees to leave us in peace and to overlook the matter of Ranji's unlicensed gun.

It took more than an hour's negotiation to decide who was going to pay and how much. Ranji mentioned that it was our fault that the soldiers had come along, and if we had left it to him instead of arriving as we did, quite possibly we might all have got away with paying five rupees or less. But now it was twenty rupees and we handed the money over; the soldiers squatted down and shared the villagers' evening meal while we completed our bargaining.

James had returned from an expedition in search of elephants. His news was bad; the government survey party had vanished with the elephants into the jungle and would not be back for at least a month, by which time the season would be over.

'Never mind, we will go by bullock cart.' The cousin-brother took us round to the back of a group of huts where two specially adapted carts were stabled, queer V-shaped vehicles, designed to push through long grass, their progress made easier by the fact that the bullocks drawing them would first of all have blazed a trail. We would crouch inside, keeping a sharp lookout; as a special favour Ranji would give us four of the precious twelve bullets that would fit the guns.

We set off next morning in two parties, James, the cook, the cousin-brother, Michael and myself in one cart, and Ranji surrounded by half a dozen chattering retainers in the other. The trees stood out in a grey profile against a swirling mist and dew glistened on the jungle grass. The two black bullocks pushed and stumbled through the thick undergrowth, and the cart followed with such a crunching, cackling and groaning, that it seemed doubtful if we could surprise any animal that was not stone deaf.

The sun rose and we were beginning to feel thirsty as we plunged through the long grass. The cousin-brother looked heart-broken when we suggested that perhaps the cart might turn back, and promised that in just five minutes we would see a deer. We were resigning ourselves to more fruitless bumbling about, when he stiffened like a pointer, and we saw our first deer flitting swiftly behind the trees. A few minutes later the cousin-brother pointed again at a magnificent stag standing out against the trees. A perfect target. Michael slowly raised his gun until the creature was aligned in the sights and pulled the trigger. There was a sharp click. As he broke the gun and found the barrels empty, all eyes turned and focussed on James who had forgotten to load.

We jolted on for another hour, during which Michael had one wild shot at a distant shadow. At last we persuaded our companions that we had had enough, and set off on the long slow journey back to the village.

In our absence Ranji had shot a crocodile and we found him calculating how much the skin would fetch on the open market at Lucknow. The crocodile, about seven foot long, together with a deer, lay stretched outside his uncle's hut, touched and stroked, measured and patted until James took them away to be skinned.

That evening we ate smoky hunks of venison with rice; we ate alone because the village had retired to eat its share.

Although one crocodile, one deer and some duck feathers were not too bad a mixed bag for the first day, with nine remaining bullets between us the future of the hunt looked bleak. When we told Ranji of our wish to leave he was disappointed.

'You must come again, and then we will have a real hunt. With elephants. I tell you there are plenty of tigers. Last year I shot four only a few miles from this very spot.' He spoke to the cousin-brother who nodded in agreement. But we had had enough.

The bullock cart was waiting. We said formal goodbyes to the village which lined up under Ranji's direction to watch us leave. The sky was a cloudless pale blue, the sun fired down over the trees, a pair of vultures were quarrelling over a thigh bone, and a row of dark brown faces was watching the driver putting our few pieces of luggage into the bullock cart. It was Michael who spotted the small tear in the bag containing our money. There was an ominous silence as he pulled out the contents which should have included over a hundred pounds in Indian rupees tucked up among our shaving things. A frantic search through our clothes and then around our hut proved fruitless.

The thief must have been among those who squatted and gazed at us each morning as we ate our breakfast; that little group which watched us with such concentration knew our habits and details of our hut. There were so many of them all of whose lives were made hideous by poverty. The money was a fortune to people who earned less than ten or fifteen pounds a year. Probably by now it would be buried in a field under some landmark, perhaps one of those leafless trees outside the village where the vultures sat around and waited. There it would remain untouched until the whole affair was forgotten, perhaps years later.

Ranji summoned the whole village to appear outside our hut. We spent the morning questioning suspects while James translated their energetic protestations of innocence. As the awful day progressed a certain atmosphere of suspicion seemed to centre on a thin bony man with a particularly large caste mark splashed on his forehead who had shown avid interest in our possessions. Michael and I had thought that perhaps he was a bit mad; there was something more vacant and wild about his staring eyes than those of his companions.

We told Ranji of our suspicions and he said that a show of force would be necessary; nothing but fear would make a man give himself away. He looked at us both for some time, and then perhaps remembering my distaste for using the rifle, indicated Michael. In order to reduce the man to a suitable state of terror, Michael should approach him in a threatening manner and beat him.

'Don't restrain yourself. Give him some good hefty clouts, the harder the better.' Ranji went up to the group and, catching the suspect by the car, dragged him over to us. Very nervous in a role that was hardly tailor-made Michael gave him a few taps.

'Harder! Harder!' cried Ranji. The man had dropped to his knees, the better to receive the sahib's wrath meekly, and was even helpfully indicating the precise spot on the nape of his neck where the blows should be aimed.

Looking like the young Nero at the Coliseum, Ranji continued to urge Michael to further efforts. The suspect seized the wisp of hair on his head by which he hoped to be pulled into heaven, and offered it as proof of his innocence.

'Cut that off, and let the deed be forgotten,' was James' unhelpful translation.

Neither by bullying nor by imprecations could the thief be discovered. In an atmosphere of mutual hostility we continued to walk around, peering into dark huts, questioning the villagers. But we realised it was useless; our money was safely hidden somewhere in the wild jungle beyond the village stockade. We must face up to the disaster and take our leave.

It was a most embarrassing goodbye. Ranji seemed to imagine that the loss was a mere trifle to us, and it seemed the kindest thing to leave him with this misconception. As we slowly jolted away in the same bullock car that had brought us in, we caught a glimpse of him setting out happily towards the river to hunt another crocodile.

Thirty years later when I returned to Nepal and the subject of the theft came up, I was assured that it was Ranji himself who had taken the money. Who can tell? I hope not; I hope it was a poor villager. In any case it served us right.

PART THREE

15

R ANJI offered to pay our train fare to Calcutta; even so we were nearly broke. At Calcutta we resisted the temptation to find a taxi and chose a bicycle rickshaw instead. We sat and clung to the sides of the wooden throne with its flapping canvas canopy that had been grafted on to a smoky old motorbike and set off towards a dusty part of the city full of cows and unpleasant dogs.

Here were picturesque aspects of India, a cow chewing vegetables off a stall while the owner looked on helpless, a set of colossal teeth advertising a dental mechanic, a colossal foot advertising a chiropodist, a colossal open hand advertising a palmist. Here were beggars, withered, maimed, leprous, with pink clubs instead of hands, at least two cut in half and confined in little boxes with wheels. There were blind men of every sort, like Breughel's painting, some with eyes tight shut, some with milky-blue pupils, some with no pupils at all, most with miserable small boys leading them around. Here was a line of squatting men in white dhotis adding to the smells.

Down a side alley we found a hotel run by a Mrs Wilson, a large lady with sleepy black eyes who wore carpet slippers and a sari of the colour you get when you press hard on your eyelids. The Windsor had a courtyard with a balcony running round it like an old English inn. At present it couldn't be used because of its dangerous condition; a week before one of the cleaning boys had fallen through the crumbling wooden slats and broken his leg.

Here were more smells. Round the courtyard ran a wide fetid drain, emitting odours that blended with those from the midden in the middle. Goats, cats and some hens ran up and down the little hillock searching for food. Occasionally a chokra picked over the garbage looking for the eggs which had escaped the rats which were gathered in a basket. It seemed that the omelettes prepared from these eggs had a reputation for excellence among the small loyal clientele which came here to gossip and play cards.

Our bedroom had two brass beds and a red tiled floor, while the adjoining washroom was provided with a shower, a bucket of water, and a stiff brush. When we complained about the cockroaches the boy who had led us up here, stepped on some with his hard bare foot, leaving blood stains.

We lay down on the beds below the fan, conscious of the other cockroaches gathered beneath us. Outside the traffic sounded tired, the tinkle of bells, the hoots of old cars, passing voices, mostly agitated and quarrelsome, and the faint trickle and thud of bare feet. Across the passage other heated bedrooms looked out onto the courtyard where the noises were different – creatures munching or scratching, the perpetual chatter of the chokras as they prepared food, pulled out chickens' intestines, and scrubbed brass pots with sand.

Later Mrs Wilson entertained us with sweet sherry and introduced us to her two sultry daughters, Alma, who had just come home from a good boarding school run by Irish nuns, and Rosie who favoured heavy make-up and was engaged to a roving English seaman.

The Windsor was an old-fashioned establishment which held a whist drive every Saturday afternoon and a sherry party on Sundays. However, the place had not prospered after partition, and Mrs Wilson was in two minds about going Home.

'But how in God's name could I manage without servants?' So home was confined to reminders, a picture in the parlour of Anne Hathaway's cottage, another of our lovely young queen.

Dinner was served by two old men who were addressed as boy. They wore dirty white jackets and red cummerbunds, and had served at table for as long as the elderly guests could remember. The two-way menu remained unchanged, European food on the left, Indian food on the right. Nearly everyone ate European food, mulligatawny soup, chicken curry, Irish stew (very strange), treacle tart and Camp coffee whitened with sachets of milk powder.

Later, lying naked in the heat watching the cockroaches scamper across the tiled floor, we conceived the idea of going to Bhutan. In Bhutan, we thought, the unknown could be breached with comparative ease – to reach it no mountains or deserts had to be crossed. It was utterly forbidden – no visas were issued to anyone at all, and foreigners and Indians alike were excluded from its borders.

In the nineteen-nineties Bhutan still keeps the hordes outside. It strives to remain the last of the inaccessible Himalayan kingdoms; others have undergone revolution and change, suffered the dictates of outside governments or let the tourists stream in. In particular Bhutan has resisted tourism and has persisted in a determination to keep outsiders from defiling its history and tradition. In spite of external pressures, the temptation of easy pickings, and the mere demands of curiosity, the Bhutanese have combated the presence of outsiders. Their continued reluctance to let them in must be justified when they look westward and see how the onslaught of strangers – not only tourists, but Indians as well – has changed Nepal irrevocably.

Bhutan has not quite excluded everybody. There are some foreign aid workers involved in health and education programmes, and two thousand visitors a year are allowed in and herded here and there to see archery contests and picturesque festivals. For the privilege of a ten-day stay a huge levy must be paid. As a result tourists are confined to the very rich and to Shirley MacLaine, while the country remains the world's last secret place.

In 1955 fewer than half a dozen Europeans had travelled in Bhutan during the century.

The buildings and landscapes depicted in the drawings made in 1783 by Samuel Davis, a member of Warren Hastings' mission, were wholly unchanged. Bhutan was still a medieval country, where the inhabitants lived placidly, unaware of progress and largely ignorant of wars fought outside their small world. The cycle of their lives followed a pattern of pageantry. Their strange enchanting world contained penlops, lamas and lopons; the king's bodyguard wore chain armour and helmets modelled on those worn by the warriors of Genghiz Khan.

There are roads now, but in those days Bhutan was wrapped within its borders of jungle and mountain. Geographically the country resembles Nepal varying from its northern snow barrier with Tibet to the southern border with India which is an extension of the Terai. We knew that throughout no wheeled traffic existed; communication consisted of rough tracks, often no more than a few feet wide, which in the south had to pass through thick rainforest. After that a traveller, climbing northwards, would reach deep clefted valleys covered with oak and scented pine and rhododendron where villages crouched under cliff faces beneath monasteries whose frowning outlines were softened by gaily striped prayer flags.

It sounded fine. Avoiding guards and sentries we would walk in illegally across the jungle border not far from Darjeeling. It would cost us very little, which was an important factor in our plans, since we had lost nearly all our money.

But the terrain was difficult. Michael discovered a copy of the Sikhim Gazetteer, dated 1896, which was fairly up to date in regard to literature about Bhutan. 'No one wishes to explore the tangle of jungle and fever-stricken hills, infested with leeches and the pipsa fly, and offering no compensating advantage to the most enterprising pioneer. Adventure looks beyond Bhutan, science passes it by as a region not sufficiently characteristic to merit exploration.'

We would leave Calcutta by train and travel to Silgurli, the junction for Darjeeling. There we would change trains for one that ran along the Indian frontier and seize the opportunity where we could to enter the jungle. A small railway terminus on the Indian side named Jainti was marked on our map near a track which seemed to lead directly into Bhutan.

We sold off everything we possessed. Michael took his signet ring to the smartest-looking jeweller in Calcutta who gave him thirty rupees, I sold my binoculars to the local fire chief who lived beside the hotel. Our posteen coats, camping equipment, several pairs of shoes and an ivory-backed hairbrush were auctioned off in the Calcutta flea market. We still had hardly any money.

We set a hundred rupees aside for expenses and for Third-class tickets to Darjeeling. It seemed better not to mention Jainti which was an odd sort of place for people like ourselves to be going to. We bought supplies of food, ten pounds of rice, two packets of quick-cooking porridge, saccharin tablets, tea and a bottle of chutney. We travelled Third class in circumstances unusual for sahibs – no water, no lavatory, every window heavily barred to keep thousands of struggling people inside, squashed brown bodies wrapped in white dhotis, every start and stop of the train sending showers of resigned and remarkably tranquil passengers tumbling off their seats with their trunks and bundles.

After Silgurli, the change for Darjeeling, we could see the hills which were thick in vegetation where they intercepted the moisture-laden winds from Bengal and received up to three hundred inches of monsoon a year. Outside our carriage window was a thick green curtain, giant ferns, banana trees, groves of giant bamboo, matted together by strings of lianas like netting. The little train rattled its way through a landscape designed to keep out intruders; among the tangled creepers there would be snakes and leopards and tigers to discourage us, not to mention the leeches and the pipsa fly.

The train pushed its way through the jungle towards Assam, stopping frequently at tiny stations crowded with hill tribesmen. Sometimes we crossed rivers which cut a swathe in the jungle; where gangs of men were at work bolstering them up with bags of stones before the next monsoon floods. In the late afternoon we came to Rajabal-Khawa from where a branch line went to Jainti. Like any of the other stations we had seen during the day Rajabal-Khawa was little more than a clearing in the jungle, a railway platform, a corrugated shed and a cluster of waiting passengers squatting in the sun. Apart from a fakir, his body smeared with ashes and face framed with greasy ringlets, we were the only travellers to get out. When we learned that the train for Jainti did not arrive until nine o'clock, we decided to hide rather than inviting suspicion by remaining on the platform for five hours.

It took a moment to walk the track to the jungle surrounding the station where, under the thick leafy branches, we settled down to wait. It was a decisive step. In Badakshan and again in north-west Pakistan, although we had conditioned ourselves to break laws, we had never actually done so. Now we had taken our first steps in illegal travel; they might not lead us across Central Asia, but they were in the direction of an unknown, forbidden world.

Michael found some greenish water in a pool, filled our one saucepan and presently, very hungry, since we had only eaten oranges for the last two days since we left Calcutta, we sat down to sticky rice dumpling seasoned with chutney. The flame of the kerosene stove made the rice stick to the saucepan bottom, and all our subsequent cooking was flavoured by the first meal of our journey.

Hidden in the bush a few yards away from the railway track, we settled down to wait and to examine our route. On our map the Bhutanese frontier post beyond Jainti at Buxa was marked by a small pimply dot; behind it was a large intimidating blank. Having seen the jungle, we realised that the likelihood of finding the trail marked on the map by a thin brown line was extremely remote, whether we searched for it by day or night.

We picked out a river called the Raidak coming down from the Bhutanese hills about sixteen miles from where we sat. We had seen rivers all day and noticed their sandy banks. Rather than attempt to find a trail through the jungle, would it not be far easier just to follow the banks of the Raidak northwards to the borders of Bhutan and beyond? We did not know then that the shifting boulder-strewn spits of sand and pebble scattered thinly along the shores of rivers like the Raidak provided trails that were far more difficult to follow than any slender mountain path. It would have been a lot easier to hack our way through the thickest of creepers.

'I suppose there are bridges higher up.' We remembered photographs in geographical magazines of rope ladders swinging over ravines.

'We could always swim.'

Hour after hour we sat under the trees waiting for the Jainti train. We could see the signalman checking the points and the large Brahmin bull which had gone to sleep in the middle of the tracks. As night fell the air became full of fireflies probing the jungle above our heads.

More sparks of light came from the funnel of the train coming clattering down the track. To our dismay the six carriages were filled with soldiers from the local Bengal militia whose very job was to man the frontier stations. Although it was a short twelve miles to Jainti, the journey was interminable. Nothing happened to us; no one took notice of our shabby clothes, as distinctive, it seemed to us, as convict uniforms. The soldiers, engrossed in their own pursuits, did not ask why two foreigners should be travelling this way. Sahibs were not unknown since there was still a sprinkling of European tea planters living in the area.

The train shunted into a small station, the beam of its searchlight picking out the wall of jungle beyond the dancing moths and flies. Knowing that the soldiers were also getting off the train at Jainti was an incentive for us to vanish as fast as we could. Outside the station we found a road skirting the little group of houses that formed the town, winding up north-eastwards, as far as we could make out, roughly in the direction we were going. According to our map, a sixteen-mile-to-the-inch edition which left most of Bhutan's topography unsketched, the river was marked some miles up the road – quite how far it was impossible to estimate.

For a time the road took us through country which was not jungle at all. We were in the Duars, the long fertile strip of land, once part of Bhutan, but annexed to India during a frontier quarrel in 1865 when the British sent an empire-expanding expedition one hundred and twenty miles into Bhutan 'to secure our valuable province of Assam from being disturbed by the incursions of Bhooteah marauders'. The punitive force consisted of seven thousand troops, a thousand of whom were European, the rest native infantry. The going for them, as it would be for us, was tough – 'the nature of the country . . . admits of only "single-file marching"'. A few forts were subdued with 'Armstrong guns and mortars bursting the shells most satisfactorily . . . committing considerable havoc . . . Forty-four dead bodies of Bhooteahs have already been found, but their loss must have been far heavier'. The 'Bhooteahs' resisted with matchlocks and 'showers of stones and arrows thrown . . . with great force and precision'. ('Let it be remarked that a heap of stones coming down the hill while you are going up is a particularly disagreeable greeting.')

The expedition finished successfully and British India acquired a lot more land for planting tea. We were travelling through territory where planters had taken over the slopes of the foothills and grew the finest of Darjeeling tea; instead of jungle we could make out neatly trimmed bushes on either side of the road, and the feathery outlines of jacaranda trees planted in rows above them, their roots holding the soil together to withstand monsoon landslides. Sometimes we glimpsed lights shining invitingly from planters' houses, evoking a comfortable picture of long wicker chairs and clinking whiskey glasses.

We walked for miles, occasionally diving off the road to avoid passing lorries. Midnight passed before we heard a faint sound of rushing water in the distance. The tarred road became a sandy track leading to the banks of the river where uprooted trees lay thrown around the flood plain, a wide band of sand and shingle. Along the dunes of sand was a ferry, and nearby a shanty village raised high on stilts.

The roar of water drowned out all other sounds. The moon was up, floating above the treetops and the sandbank gleamed silver as we scratched out hollows for our sleeping bags and lay down and slept.

By day the river looked huge, its main stream divided by islands of sand, fast-flowing currents, and eddies formed by the splayed branches of huge fallen trees. Around the edge of the forest the full force of water had pulverised the jungle in a wide arc of desolation, and tree stumps, rocks, brushwood and other debris had been hurled around as if the old Armstrong guns had been at work. Downstream we could just make out a village where the crooked bamboo struts of houses were nearly hidden by the curve of the river.

A fisherman was wandering slowly along the banks towards us flicking a fan-shaped net into the water. As we watched the graceful arc of the net and the symmetry of his movements, we realised that if we wanted to remain unobserved, we would have to fight our way through the jungle. We rolled up our sleeping bags, stuffed our rucksacks with our belongings, and plunged into the nearest patch of green right behind us.

It was our first experience of trying to make headway against the dark green wall we had seen the day before from the train. Every moment branches pulled at our rucksacks and swung back into our faces. Of the many vital pieces of equipment that we neglected to bring, perhaps the most essential were knives or kukris for each of us to hack a path; instead we had to peel aside the branches and knotted creepers with our hands, the person in front protecting his eyes from the pins and needles and daggers ahead, the person behind ducking the lash of the branches.

Our faces were scratched and bleeding, my shirt was ripped and Michael had torn the seat out of his trousers. The heat was foul and I had never been so repulsively hot, tired, thirsty and blind with rage as we struggled along inch by inch through sticky green netting.

The scent of burnt wood came as a relief. Suddenly we were free of briars and thorns as we stepped out into a patch of blackened ground swept clean by a recent forest fire. The fire could only have happened a few hours before our arrival, for in places stalks of grass still glowed at their tips like cigarette ends among the charred tree trunks and pools of ash that were all that was left of a huge area of thick green vegetation. As we picked our way over what we discovered were burning embers, the rubber soles of our shoes became sticky and started to melt, but we managed to avoid the worst of the burning patches by keeping to the edges; burnt feet would not have been a good preparation for a difficult journey.

We crossed the clearing, and too soon were back in the awful forest, our faces and hands blackened like commandos. Night came very suddenly and the light that filtered in through the branches was cut off by a switch. And still we struggled with infinite slowness until we reached the Raidak and greeted it like an old friend.

We stripped off our clothes and wallowed in the water as it soothed our cuts and bruises before we made camp along the banks of the river under another sandy shoal, dining under the moon on porridge mixed with leaves and wood ants. We thought that over the whole day we had travelled a couple of miles at the most – never would we leave the river again. Fireflies darted through the trees above us as we lay in our sleeping bags, smoking *bidis* the cheap Indian cigarettes which had been all we could afford, the acrid tang of tobacco and the low murmur of the river sent us to sleep.

Our second day's walk brought us close to the hills which rose in dark green waves ahead of us under a bright blue sky. We knew that the forest ahead was full of game. Immune from the guns of Ranas and other big-game hunters, it contained wildlife that was vanishing from so much of India. Today, thirty-five years later, the country remains to a large extent untouched by big-game slaughter and retains much of the jungle that is being destroyed elsewhere in the Himalayas.

Sometime during the morning we had come across a path running out of the trees down to the river into the sand. There was no warning. One moment we were among rocks and boulders, beside the foaming current and still pools and jungle trees, and the next we were standing on the outskirts of a little frontier village of bungalows with pointed gables and latticed verandas, typical of any planter's house in any hill station in India. Probably this was the last Indian frontier post before Bhutan, but after journeying and struggling for a day and a half, it was depressing not to have yet shaken off civilisation.

The sound of voices made us run for shelter across a lawn into a grove of matted grass. Hardly daring to breathe, we gazed out from our cover which appeared to be in the centre of village life. There were constant sounds of hammering and shouting. A few yards away some naked children played with a ball, a woman came out from a house and walked towards the river carrying a brass jar, and a group of men with spades and pickaxes over their shoulders passed a few yards from where we squatted.

We resigned ourselves to spending the rest of the day hidden. We had not chosen a comfortable perch. For one thing our cave of grass was barely big enough to contain both our bodies together with our rucksacks, so that the slightest movement would be visible to anyone standing outside. There was the danger of passing dogs and of a ball being kicked on top of us. Worse was the sun. Worst of all were the insects and flies. We covered our faces with handkerchiefs to keep off the flying poochies, but it was more difficult to discourage the beetles and the colony of red ants which crawled all over our arms and legs, secure in the knowledge that by flicking them away we might make a movement which would betray our position.

At the time we found nothing comical in the idea of two nervous Europeans hiding in a bush of long grass in the middle of an Indian village while the normal noisy life of its inhabitants continued all round us. Once during the sweltering afternoon danger threatened when Michael sneezed just as a villager happened to stroll nearby, an old man hobbling along with the aid of a large stick. As the sneeze rang out through the grass he stopped, and we thought he must find us. Michael cupped his mouth in a desperate effort not to make a repeat, while through the grassy curtain I could see bonelike withered legs sticking out from under a white dhoti. Then they slowly moved away.

Five blistering bad-tempered hours passed in torpor. How

eagerly we watched the sinking sun falling behind the dark line
of trees. Lights shone in houses as the cooking of rice and dhal
reached a crescendo and the men returned for their evening
meal. We watched smoky fires, heard a few hens and goats, and
then came the great silence as soon as darkness fell.

We waited a little longer. Michael stood up and peered out.
His stubble – neither of us had shaved since leaving Calcutta –
was like a dark rash under his mouth. He held up a hand, and
with a rustle of grass that magnified in our ears like the crackle
of thunder, we both ran towards the nearest trees.

The distance could not have been more than a hundred yards,
but just as we were passing the first house a dog heard us. Soon
others were barking, lights flickered, and it seemed that from
every house figures poured out, bumping against each other in
the darkness. We had a head start as they pushed under the
trees and bushes after us, stopping and chattering excitedly
before plunging through the creepers. A beam of a torch caught
Michael's startled face, and his rucksack bobbing up and down
on his back. But once we were in the jungle, it was impossible
for them to see us; the moonlight was no help to them and the
thorns and scratching twigs were our friends. There were more
shouts and screams, and finally a silence as they gave up and
returned home.

Now we plunged through the undergrowth and stumbled along
blindly until there came the wonderful moment when we rejoined
the Raidak gleaming silver under the moonlight where it curved
under the first hill, and it was clear that we would have to ford to
reach the sandbank on the other side. It never occurred to us that
crossing a river was a risky business. More as a gesture to safety
than from any sense of imminent danger Michael suggested that I
should take a rope, and just as casually I knotted it round my waist
and stepped in. At first there seemed no danger; the shoal of sand
led into the river, the sheen of water reflected in the moonlight
had a deceptively smooth appearance and the far bank seemed
a short enough distance away.

I did not hear Michael's shouts for me to come back, as
suddenly what had seemed a placid pool was transformed into
a powerful current tugging at my legs. Ford o' Kabul river in
the dark! The water reached my waist and lapped around my
rucksack; then the current lifted me and I was being carried

away helplessly downstream. I could hear the roar of the water that filled the whole forest in its escape from the mountains as I was whirled in the creamy torrent, a victim of the last cascade and flourish of a whirlpool before the Raidak reached the plain and turned lazy.

Michael, who had been standing on the shore, the rope lying loose in his hands, sprang to life and, bracing his feet in the loose shingle, held the rope so that my wild progress downstream was halted by a great tug. Then he hauled, fighting the current to drag me upstream inch by inch until at last my feet felt the shifting gravel beneath the current. How calm and beautiful everything seemed with the trees rising above our heads on either bank, and the river no longer a killer.

We awoke on a fresh cool morning with nothing to remind us of last night's near disaster except my wet clothes drying on the bank. We could see now that the swollen Raidak, café au lait in colour, was far too strong to attempt to cross where it swirled past the overhanging cliff. We had no alternative except to climb our way over the jungle-covered hill.

We finished our breakfast and sat in the sun, partly to let my clothes dry, and partly to delay the moment when we would have to plunge into the undergrowth again. At this moment two men appeared at the bottom of the cliff and, brushing aside the creepers, vanished without a sound. They hadn't seen us. Giving them time to get well on their way, we went over to where they had vanished and peered inside. Between the cliff wall and the curtain of creeper was an ingenious series of bamboo ladders hanging down from the ledge at the top of the cliff. Each led to the next in a series of dizzy falls – looking up we could make out the cliff-top and grey jungle light filtering through overhead branches.

Michael went up first; the ladders, made for smaller men, buckled under his weight and that of his rucksack, and for a time it looked fairly likely that something would snap and he would fall down at my feet. But the contraption held; I waited until he had reached the first platform before following him. There were four tiers, and at the top a narrow catwalk tied to projecting tree roots led us across to the other side of the cliff where another set of swinging ladders went down to the river bank again. We had gained a few yards around the first barrier, and better still, had found a path to follow. It led into the trees, a well kept route climbing upwards, weaving in and out of the trees. All that day we followed it, walking northwards through the foothills, until it suddenly turned at right angles and led us back to the river, where it disappeared into the sand.

But here the river was narrower and easier to cross. For the first time we tried a technique at which we would become quite expert over the next few days – wading, swimming and carrying our equipment over in plastic bags. There were occasions when the river, forced between boulders, produced rapids, and on one occasion it seemed that nothing could prevent us having to take another wide detour back through the forest. Faced with a gorge through whose precipitous sides the river ran white, we tackled it with bamboo poles to make a flimsy safety rail between the boulders. We waded into the icy water one at a time, the ends of rope tied securely round our waist, clutching at the bunches of bamboo which we had wedged between the rocks. They were shaky, and never tight enough in place to withstand the force of the current for long, and one by one they were swept away. But by this time we were confident at facing the torrent, although it took most of a day for us and our possessions to reach the safety of the other side.

The effort of slowly moving from stage to stage was exhausting us. Our clothes were shredded and torn into rags, and with all our delays and detours food had become a problem. Our chief topic of conversation was how much longer it would last. Five days had passed, the porridge was finished, and the rice was nearly gone; we rationed ourselves to a cup of tea in the morning and a small tin plateful of rice before we went to sleep, allaying our hunger the rest of the time by sucking saccharin tablets.

It wasn't much of a diet, and we were no good at woodcraft. We were totally unequipped to live off the land and take advantage of the occasional clawmarks and little bird's trails we saw in the sand, or the untidy remains of wild boar. Sometimes ahead of us there would be a flutter and squawk as a jungle fowl or perhaps a peacock flapped out of our way, but soured by our experiences of hunting in the Terai, we had brought no gun. Nor a fishing rod. And fish were leaping in the Raidak – occasionally we caught sight of large brown trout drifting in the shallows under the rocks. At one point Michael made a hook out of a sardine tin and baited it with worms and tied it with string which he dangled over the water fruitlessly for hours.

Butterflies hovered over the moist sand, giant swallowtails with patches of white and red on scalloped wings, clouds of velvet-black and brown, swarms of little brimstones and others displaying wings of scarlet and black and kingfisher blue.

Behind the river up here on the hills the jungle slowly ceased to be a menacing net of impenetrable creepers and turned into forest. Day after day, always within sound of the Raidak, we walked among big beautiful fat-trunked forest trees that made their own endless empty silence. Animals kept out of our way – there was not a trace of a human being except for the occasional trail that made our journey easier.

On the fifth day we came to a bridge. A flimsy latticed bamboo structure, tied together by creepers high above the Raidak, linked one boulder to another with the torrent rushing under it. Tower Bridge could not have seemed more solid and durable as we crossed to the far side and celebrated with rice topped by the last spoonful of chutney. As we ate we caught sight of a man, the first we had seen since the day after we had hidden in the Indian village. He was on the opposite bank advancing upstream by hopping from stone to stone.

Behind us another man appeared from the trees. He was young, short and stocky, wearing a blue tunic pulled up over his knees with a pouch from which protruded the handle of a knife. His bullet-shaped head was covered with brown hair cut in an urchin's bob, and we knew that we were meeting our first Bhutanese. Meeting was too strong a word for our short encounter – in an instant he had run off into the trees.

We ran after him. Here was another small forest path cut out of dense foliage leading into the hills. We left the river entirely and ran uphill leaving the river far behind. We went for miles at breakneck speed, the man running ahead without stopping, until we reached a clearing, in the centre of which was a small bamboo house with a bamboo platform, a thatched roof and a bamboo terrace.

The man bounded inside, Michael and myself hard on his heels, into a hut wreathed in a thick, acrid, blue wood-smoke where we made out a dead goat on the floor beside a fire that burnt between two stones; above the flames pieces of blackened meat hung from the slender rafters. There was an old man with a thin white beard and bulging eyes, his neck swollen by goitre.

We crouched under the low roof as our young guide began talking or rather shouting. They talked excitedly at length and then offered us food – a platter of rice sprinkled with leathery black meat which the old man fished out of a bowl. It was wonderful – we gobbled it up, our first real meal since leaving Calcutta. Our first contact with Bhutanese was one of unquestioning and immediate hospitality as we came blundering into their home.

After we had finished the old man pointed out another path leading into the hills. From here we passed more clearings burnt out of the forest, more bamboo huts, and a good many goats which seemed to be these people's only possessions. The river had vanished far behind us, and we missed its soothing voice and angry roar – and what was more important, water to drink. We met nobody.

At dusk, with the instinct of motorists who picnic as near to the road as possible, we built our small fire at the edge of the forest path. Our old host had insisted on filling up our bag with some of his precious chunks of dried goat, a compound of leather, string and smoke for which he refused to accept payment. Still hungry, we ate his gift with gratitude and slept until the fire was nearly out.

We were woken by traffic – sounds of voices and footsteps hurrying up the hill. It was a dark night with no moon and we could see nothing. I remember we were sitting upright in our sleeping bags when there was a sudden flash from a torch and five men leapt out of the darkness.

My first impression was that we had been waylaid by bandits. They dragged us out of our sleeping bags and we stood blinking at the knives and guns which they kept jabbing at our stomachs. I watched their thin-faced scowling leader search through our rucksacks, passing each object and each filthy garment as it appeared to the others to inspect. Only the camera raised a little interest. They were all shouting and chattering at the top of their voices as they waved their weapons in our direction. The leader had to shout to address us. 'Visas!'

Now we noticed that they were dressed in tousled khaki uniforms; round their legs were wound khaki puttees which were tucked into plimsolls. They all carried guns, the leader a sawn-off shotgun. It was a relief to learn that we were not surrounded by criminals, but disappointing to meet frontier guards so early in our journey. Later we learnt they had been searching for us up and down the country after the village we had blundered into on the lower waters of the Raidak reported our existence.

We stood half dressed in our shirts while the leader did a dance of impatience. For a few minutes more we stood transfixed while they turned our bags upside down and gave expressions of amazement at the state of our clothes. Now I remembered that back in Ireland I had got the passport office to write in the names of various countries that we might conceivably be visiting, though of course the authority of the Irish government, unsupported by proper visas, meant nothing. It had been an exercise in wishful thinking; we might have asked them to add Atlantis and Ruritania. But now, summoning up all the force of outraged dignity I could express, I showed him the page in my passport on which was written 'Valid for Tibet, Nepal, China, Bhutan and Russia'. There was the passage from the Minister for External Affairs asking that the bearer be allowed to pass without let or hindrance. Michael read this out slowly and handed round cigarettes. The result was satisfying. The leader was convinced and shouted to his troop to replace our things in the rucksacks. Then he saluted, and disappeared with his comrades into the night.

We listened happily to their vanishing footsteps, thinking that the patrol would have to report to some provincial governor. Then, in the uncertainty of communications, the matter might be passed over for weeks in case the king or some other high official had actually given us permission to travel. By which time we would have seen a lot more of Bhutan.

We had left the subtropical zone of vegetation behind at the Raidak, and now had entered the centre of Bhutan, the principal inhabited area of the country, consisting of a series of valleys about forty miles wide covered with trees. It was springtime, they were burgeoning with soft green and were scattered with white cherry blossom and among them were towering pink and white and scarlet rhododendrons in a haze of melting colour. Butterflies were everywhere.

All morning we climbed to the trees until we met our first

village, a collection of wooden and bamboo huts built on stilts pitched to the side of the hill. Each had its small platform with ladders reaching down over the sides. The men and women who greeted us wore similar bobbed hair and functional tunics, but in spite of the richness and beauty of their surroundings, they lived miserably. Their utensils were of the simplest kind; some bows and quivers of arrows stacked in the corner of a hut, braided bamboo lengths for carrying water, some cheap Indian knives. They looked ill, gaunt and pockmarked, while goitre, the scourge of mountain people, was very evident. They all seemed old, even the children, and it was difficult to tell their sexes apart. We hesitated to accept the plates of goat and saffron-coloured rice they offered with so many smiles and grunts. They watched us eat, fingering our clothes and bags.

We left them in the evening and camped in a gulley vibrating with cicadas. Next morning when we followed the upward path out into an open ridge we saw that the forest clad hills rolled away to the distant outline of snow mountains. Bhutan is about the size of Scotland, and we had walked through half of it.

Why shouldn't we go on until we reached Tibet?

Our perfunctory camping equipment had not included any water bottles, and our kettle had been punctured during a river crossing. This meant that we carried no water with us, which was fine as long as we were beside the Raidak, but was an increasing problem ever since we had left the river. Today was hot, and the higher we climbed, the chances of finding a stream became less. Several times the path wound out of the trees onto land which had been cleared, then deserted and left to be overgrown by a new wave of thick greenery. A patch of tall grass would denote an abandoned village where the land had been cleared; then we passed clusters of roofless huts and the shapes of a few terraced fields, from where people had moved on. They gave an impression of sudden disaster, but more likely the fertility of the land was deceptive and poverty had forced a difficult nomadic pattern of life. We saw a snake, passed a heap of dried animal bones, and picked out the goats' horns.

There was no shade and we walked in the full glare of sunlight. Now we were out on another low saucer-shaped piece of land, thickly matted with bamboo. No water here either apart from a stagnant pool choked with mud and green slime until there was nothing more than a wet patch of earth. Just beyond, the path vanished into another thick bamboo grove. It was getting dark, too late to retrace our steps to the point where we had branched off. We camped reluctantly and went to sleep thirsty.

For the second time since we left the Raidak we were woken at night by violent noise. The sound we heard now was the snarl of an animal coming out of the bamboo that stood out black and silky in the darkness. It seemed very near from where we sat quaking in the dark.

Another deep rumbling growl about ten times louder and an octave lower than a cat's purr sent us scuttling towards a nearby tree. It was so unexpected that not until we had heard it for a third time did we become afraid. We had never taken precautions against wild animals; our untrained eyes had found no signs of trails to indicate that we were travelling through one of the few untouched game preserves left in the world. The growls were followed by a sound of crackling sticks as something moved nearer very quickly. A tiger – or perhaps a panther. I remembered the trophies we had seen decorating the walls of Rana palaces, glass eyes copied from life, pasty pink jaws jacked wide open to show the cruel teeth.

Grasping sticks, we stood trembling, facing the clump from which the last growl had come. Then the next – it was fainter as the fastidious brute turned up its nose at the wretched meal we would have provided and walked stealthily away into the forest. For the rest of the night we patrolled up and down whirling our sticks and listening for noises until the dawn lit up our haggard faces and bloodshot eyes.

Late in the morning we emerged from the forest onto another area of cleared land. The town was a total surprise – there it was ahead, across a river, perched on a cliff face, substantial, dominated by a monastery, a sprawling whitewashed building on a razor edge of cliff. A steep flight of steps led up to a square where we could see some monks in russet robes.

It took the rest of the morning to reach the town, first going down into the valley, then climbing the steps to the square where a ceremony was taking place involving some metal cauldrons steaming over a fire. Our arrival caused consternation, as we were surrounded by gesticulating shouting shaven-headed monks.

'Chukha Dzong?' we asked, the name of a town on our map, but it brought no response. An elderly monk with a moustache no more substantial than a drooping whisker led us towards one of the houses, most of which were far more solid than those we had seen before, and built of stone. The lower floor was used for keeping animals; we were led upstairs to a large communal room whose windows were covered with sliding wooden panels carved in a fine trellis work to let in light. Nearly everything we could see seemed to be made of bamboo, the cooking utensils, the woven mats in which food was served, the hollowed-out stems used for carrying water. In one corner leaned several bamboo bows and arrows in a bamboo case.

A group of women in striped woollen dresses, wearing large quantities of heavy silver, coral and amber jewellery fed the fire in the middle, their arms and necks jangling as they moved. We squatted on the floor to be feasted on rice and scraps of chicken washed down with Tibetan tea and murwah, the native beer made from fermented millet. It was strong dizzy stuff, probably the brew which George Bogle, Warren Hasting's emissary, had come across when he reported: 'The coldness of the climate inclines the Bhutanese to an excessive use of spiritous liquor.'

Hours later, we staggered out of the village. The path had broken up into a number of small tracks leading more or less in the same direction. Choosing one at random we followed it until it ran into another burnt settlement where the stark frame of a wooden house rose from the nest of grass. By now the valley had reached a bottleneck where sides of tawny-coloured hills, bare of forest, fell steeply into a deep gorge. A spring of clear water sent a small stream tumbling hundreds of feet below. We followed the track back to its junction and took another which plunged down to a suspension bridge made from metal chains interwoven with a lattice of grass. Before the path left the river on the other side, climbing back into the hills, we camped in the shadow of a cliff, building a fire to ward off wild animals. We had settled down to wear off the effects of exhaustion and too much beer, when a man carrying a flintlock came panting up the path.

'Chukha Dzong? Paro Dzong?' we asked as he came to a stop in front of us. We had intoned these names of towns in southern Bhutan in each village we had reached, hoping to find out where we were. We knew from our map that Chukha Dzong was on the Raidak, but we had no idea if we had passed it or come within miles of it. We were not even quite sure whether the river we had followed for so many days from India was indeed the Raidak and not a tributary. We were no good at taking readings by the stars and our maps were no help, nor the fact that we had been unable to speak to anyone except by smiles and pantomime.

The man with the flintlock shook his head and pointed back the way we had come. As we rose to retrace our steps, he turned round and followed us. We didn't think too much of this since during the past days a number of people had felt a mild curiosity to see more of us. Coming round a corner, we ran into a group sprinting up the hill towards us, and it did not need the surprised exclamation of the small man carrying the sawn-off shotgun or the grunts of the men behind to realise that we had walked straight into the arms of our original posse.

The last time we had met these men was in total darkness, a confused medley of shapes and faces lit up by the beam of a torch. In the following days we had hardly thought about these people now rushing up and shouting, or the man behind us joining his flintlock to the circle of antiquated guns. By daylight we could see that the epaulettes of their khaki battledress were adorned with the words 'BHUTAN FRONTIER GUARD'.

There was a commander of the troop whom we did not recognise, a man in civilian clothes wearing a black silk forage cap and the same plimsolls as the rest, who pushed into my hand a scrap of paper and asked in English if I had anything similar. It was a forestry permit from the Bhutanese agent in Kalimpong given to Indian contractors, and probably the nearest thing to a visa that the government issued.

We could only say no. There was no time to argue the point as, surrounded by ancient guns, we were taken prisoner. A line was formed, with two soldiers in the rear carrying our rucksacks.

'We go! We go!' shouted the small man in the black cap and soon we were being rushed down hill towards the river at a fierce jog, separated from each other by two burly little soldiers. I concentrated on the man in front of me, watching his pistols in their holders bumping against his sides, and his legs moving effortlessly, his muscles hard as billiard balls. To keep up with these people, moving at constant breakneck speed, was impossible, but any sign of weakness invited a tirade from the leader and only a moment's rest before we were off again, pushed along by mountain men effortlessly gobbling up the steep miles.

By nightfall we had reached another small town where the whole excited population pushed and craned to get a look at us.

We were brought to a house where a meal was being prepared. While it was cooking the soldiers relaxed – now that we were safely in their hands they lost their aggressive posturing and ceased nudging us with their awful old guns. They took off their plimsolls, cleaned their weapons and produced a display of pills, combs and cosmetics to the fascination of the village. It appeared that they had never been to this part of Bhutan before and they aroused as much curiosity as we did. The villagers stood around in the darkness outside the circle of firelight, a few faces illuminated by the small butter lamps scattered round the room. Occasionally a soldier would hand them a nail-file or a comb which would be passed from hand to hand and tested against a finger, the owner watching carefully to see his property was returned.

The civilian, squatting on the floor making an inventory of our belongings, informed us that when he was not acting as a special constable, he was a civil servant. No, he could not tell us where we were being brought to. Why were we travelling to Tibet? The man with the pistols sang the words of 'Tipperary', learnt in the army in India. Cigarettes were handed around and a villager intoned a prayer in front of a small Buddhist shrine. Food appeared, scrambled eggs, chicken, rice and murwah. We ate, and yawned in the firelight until finally our guards rose and chased the audience away. Then even the fleas were unable to keep us awake.

Someone was shaking me by the arm. Opening my eyes I found the grinning youth with the flintlock standing over me; behind him Michael was climbing out of his sleeping bag. The fire was revived, butterlamps lit, and another meal prepared. Outside it was dark; the time was two in the morning.

The Bhutan Frontier Guard was making an early start. We

ate a hasty meal and left the village, travelling in single file by
the beams of two torches. The villagers were fast asleep; we
heard a dog bark, pigs scuttling under the bamboo floor of a
house, and then there was silence as we found the path in the
cold morning darkness. No one spoke apart from the odd muted
curse muttered by Michael or me as we collided with some
obstacle. The soldiers insisted on travelling at the same steady
fast trot, almost running through the trees. Slowly we travelled
through the night, diverging from the original trail which
we had followed up from the river. Now we took a path
which twisted up the side of the valley so steeply that only by
pulling ourselves up foot by foot could we reach the top.
Another short rest, and we went downwards through groves
of oak and rhododendron, then up again, climbing another
long hill.

It was like that for a week. There were few stops, perhaps a
pause to puff a cigarette, or doctor an aching muscle or sore foot.
My boots had rubbed blisters on my heels and Michael had
strained his ankle so that he had to hobble with the aid of a stick.
The spectacle of two foreigners limping along as rapidly as they
could was one that the soldiers found very funny. We continued
at the same killing pace, sandwiched between the line of soldiers
with little possibility for rest. The only remission was when a
soldier spotted possible game and the leader held up his hand.
Since we were docile, there was no reason to keep a close guard
on us, and it seemed a pity not to use up some of the ammunition
that each man carried in his pack. We would all sit down under
the trees while a man would stalk off into the bushes and shoot.
Nothing was ever hit.

We travelled between two in the morning and noon the following day when we would come to a village which would supply a
guide to the next. Then we would set off again in darkness,
running away from each sleeping village. We were travelling
southward, back towards India; each day it became perceptibly
hotter, and on the fourth morning, even by nine o'clock we
poured with perspiration as we ran along. The giant butterflies
reappeared, and now there were swarms of midges following us
unremittingly through the tepid air. My boots were in pieces, I
had not washed or shaved since we had left the Raidak; for
eight hours on twenty-four all my thoughts and efforts were

concentrated in trying to keep up with the man in front.

On the fifth or sixth evening after we had been caught – it had become difficult to count the days – we arrived at a village where a fresh detachment of soldiers belonging to the same Bhutan Frontier Guard was waiting for us. They all wore immaculate khaki drill and gave off an air of military authority, very different from our old familiar captors with whom we had built up an easy relationship.

Accompanied by our new escort we set off as usual in the small hours of the morning, clambering in pitch darkness down hillsides slippery with bamboo peelings which covered the ground.

At dawn the troop moved through a gulley leading towards a river; we were following a watercourse from which the jungle tracks would branch out onto the plains. While we rested in the sultry morning sunshine, a soldier produced a rusty cut-throat out of his pack. With some concern I watched him sharpen the blade against a rock and then turn towards me with an expectant smile.

'Today we meet governor. You must clean.'

Ignoring my protests he set to work, and fifteen painful minutes passed before he finally snapped the razor shut and produced a mirror. I examined an unfamiliar, long, sheep-like face turned piebald where the white patches of my denuded chin contrasted with the sunburn of my cheekbones and forehead. Michael had to be shaved as well before we were civilised to everyone's satisfaction.

We descended the last low foothills, and then suddenly, round a corner of the track, there was India. The plain to the horizon shimmered with a flat pasting of bright spinach-green on which the sun blazed unremittingly. For the first time in weeks we were standing on level ground, and already were missing the trees and coolness. The little we had seen of Bhutanese life had provoked a curiosity to see more; we had caught a glimpse before the door shut in our face.

Heavily guarded we were marched in single file through the luminous green fields of sprouting rice. We turned off cross country and passed huts where the increasing number of kerosene tins and photographs of Indian film stars pinned on the straw walls indicated the approach of civilisation.

Around three in the afternoon a galvanised roof broke the empty skyline, a signal for a tightening up of the ranks. In single file, ourselves sandwiched in the middle, they marched us through a tumbledown bazaar, their faces grimly composed like guardsmen. With a final 'Shun!' we stopped exhausted outside a wooden bungalow. Closely followed by our captors who appeared to think we might make a last bid to escape, we climbed onto a veranda.

A slightly built man in a crumpled flannel suit, his thin face wizened after years in the Terai, called off a poodle who was smelling our trousers.

'I am sorry about Ceasar. He was brought up in Kalimpong and Europeans are scarce here. He wants to make the most of the opportunity.'

A tray of sandwiches and a pot of coffee arrived. Not until they were consumed did he beckon the leader of our escort, who all the time was standing to attention, and told him to bring the bags containing our scraps.

A quick glance at these, and they were returned to us with a gentle apology.

'I can see that you had no attention of conquering Bhutan. What I want to know is how you got into the country and eluded our frontier guard?'

The map was produced and we pointed out the course of the Raidak.

'You just wanted to take a look? Well, I will have to get in touch with my lord, as you would say, boss in Kalimpong before making any decisions.'

He spoke like a housemaster. 'Make yourself comfortable. Ceasar and I are moving out for the time being – this house is too crowded for all of us.'

In the evening he took us for a walk through the village. There was very little more to the village of Kalguli beyond the bazaar set among the paddy fields where a weekly fair was held to enable the Bhutanese who came down from the hills to barter their goods across the Indian border. A few trees and clumps of wild banana backed into the jungle; and across the river we had been following which was called the Gadahar – the Raidak was some miles to the west – we could see a few European-type bungalows in Assam.

A thundercloud was rolling up from the Assam hills, growing blacker until its shadow loomed over the village.

'That is the beginning of the monsoon,' the governor said. 'It is lucky you arrived before it broke. Even if you withstood the force of the rain I think the mosquitoes would have got you. And leeches – the forest is so thick with them that when it is raining and a man passes under a tree the leaves bend towards him under their weight.'

A deafening crack of thunder followed by the heavy patter of rain brought images of ourselves being caught by the flooded waters of the Raidak with no other protection than our sleeping bags. How could we have been so remiss in our plans as to ignore the monsoon? We ran for the bungalow while the rain lashed at the frail bamboo and grass dwellings of the inhabitants of Kalguli who took shelter in the barracks and the governor's bungalow. The small living room was packed with people who huddled on the floor, praying in the darkness or moaning softly. Occasionally their prayers would turn into a loud gasp as a sheet of lightning lit up their frightened faces for a moment. It happened every year. Next morning most of the village was flattened as if it had been bombed. Pieces of roofing and broken sides of houses lay scattered in the mud.

Slowly life resumed, the huts were repaired, and although puffy white clouds had descended over the Bhutanese hills, for the time being there was no more rain. Day after day it got hotter and more oppressive.

For the week we stayed in Kalguli the governor was our constant companion. In our conversations with him held over tea and English biscuits, he told us that Bhutan was the only country he knew of which stationed its principal officials and its seat of government outside its borders.

'We are dependent on India.'

He had spent most of his life in Kalimpong, and although he was Bhutanese, had never been into the interior.

'Like you. If I had my way I would let you see more of my country and perhaps visit our capital at Paro.'

'Would that be possible?'

'We shall see.'

The thought of having official permission to travel in Bhutan was incredibly exciting. But it was not to be. The messenger who arrived from Kalimpong brought the news that we were to be handed over to the Indian government. India had inherited from the British control of Bhutan's external affairs and we came under this heading.

'I am sorry. It is out of my hands.' The nicest of men, and we too were sorry to say goodbye. A jeep arrived for us, driven by a tea planter called Tim Nicholson. Small world – he had sailed out with me on the *Strathnaver* two years before. Now we would spend the night at his bungalow and he would drive us to the police station at Kalimpong. The two Indian police-men who accompanied him in the jeep would officially hand us over.

The jeep made its way out of Kalguli, the policemen sitting in the back. There was no actual frontier between Kalguli and the tea estate beyond a few miles of tussocky golden grass. It took half an hour to travel from the last Bhutanese outpost to the velvet green lawn, herbaceous borders and white wooden balconied tea planter's house. Servants in white housecoats and cummerbunds greeted us. In our bedroom clothes had been laid out – white trousers with knife-like creases, shirts, socks, while from the hygienically clean bathroom came the sound of running water.

Our taste of a sahib's life was brief, and next morning, having changed back to our rags, we were handed over to a Bengal police officer and two soldiers. Another short journey took us to the courthouse, a solid Victorian building from which emerged a roar of voices. We were hustled into the main waiting room, one side of which consisted of a steel cage filled with prisoners, while everywhere members of the Bengal militia talked in loud voices. Occasionally a lawyer in a black silk jacket darted out of a room at the side, and an officer would wake a prisoner in a thunderous voice, handcuff him and lead him away. Our escort cleared a passage for us to a desk beside the cage.

'You must write a report. For what reason did you enter a forbidden territory?'

It was the beginning of a series of interrogations to which we did not give a satisfactory answer. A letter we had drafted to the ruler of Bhutan asking for a visa might have got us into trouble, but I had managed to pull it out of my passport. Since the governor of Kalguli had made no charges, no real case could be made against us. It was not for want of trying. Days passed, as we travelled up and down Bengal from court to court declaring that we had not gone to Bhutan to stir up a revolution, nor were we American or English spies.

Having consulted his books the District Commissioner at Alipur could find no precedent on which to act, and doubted if he had authority to try the case. He sent us to another court which ordered us to Jaipur, the main town in the province. Eventually justice tired of us and released us on condition that we reported to security control in Calcutta. We were back where we started.

16

Nineteen Eighty-Eight

I SAT in a restaurant under the Galatea bridge watching the ferryboats coming in with their usual drama. The SS *Sarayburer* from Prince's Island docked, and others from the mouth of the Bosphorus – Rumali, Kavag, Anadolu Kavagu and Trabizond – burped, whistled and made frothy wakes around Seraglio Point. A fisherman was frying mackerel on a brazier in an open rowing boat tied up to the pier and selling them to passers-by with rolls of bread.

Now it was 1988, more than thirty years since we made our forlorn exit from Bhutan. After we had landed back in Calcutta we gave up the old dreams and embarked on the prosaic sort of travel that thousands would soon be doing. There was Borneo to visit where Dyaks were still being ruled by white men in topees attended by Union Jacks. A spell of gold mining in Kalgoorlie, an impersonation of Santa Claus in a Sydney department store, a period working as a wharfee in Wellington, a month as purser on a White Star liner – those were the sort of occupations that scores of writers would be listing in their biographical notes. Then we settled down to marriage and middle age.

Today Michael tells me that he always felt a great sense of relief whenever we were prevented from continuing on our way to Tibet, Central Asia and beyond. But I had mourned my lost travels. Now, as I ate my fish and drank my beer in Istanbul, I reflected how fortunate I had been to encounter many places before they were polluted. The Afghanistan I saw had suffered the devastation of progress before the Soviets had a hand at flattening it altogether. I had known the things that Bruce Chatwin lamented: 'the high, clear days and the blue icecaps on the mountains; the lines of white poplars fluttering in the wind, and the long white prayer-flags; the fields of asphodels that followed the tulips . . . the fat-tailed sheep brindling the hills . . . the Buddha . . . at Bamyian upright in his niche like a whale in a dry-dock.' The loss would always be there, but so would the memory; everything that came later was an anti-climax.

I would not care to return to Afghanistan. In 1988 Bhutan still continued to sleep behind its thorn hedge, and a visit was still a luxury I could not afford. So Bhutan must remain an absurd and lovely adventure. I had seen the secret medieval kingdom of Nepal on the verge of radical change; when I returned three decades later I viewed with a mixture of dismay and admiration how the Nepalese faced the demands of mass tourism.

In 1982 I revisited north-east Pakistan to encounter the worst excesses that Western values could bestow on a grim conservative society. For the lonely visitor of 1955 the changes were nothing less than horrific; it was painful to view Gilgit bazaar in the heat, crowded with complaining hippies, the place that had run out of Pepsi-Cola.

During that disastrous trip I met Rahman Qul encamped with his tribe in their river bed. The Kirghiz whom he ruled as Khan had been among the first of the Afghan refugees, having left their homeland even before the Soviet invasion. In 1979 they abandoned their nomadic ways and ceased to wander among the Pamirs where the Soviet Union, China and Pakistan meet. Having been harassed for decades by Soviet border patrols, they fled to Pakistan and became part of one of the twentieth century's most miserable statistics – seventeen hundred among millions of refugees. But when I met them in 1982 they had been on the verge of rescue. The tribe had been about to embark for Turkey and a new life.

The Turkish government had drawn up a scheme for the resettlement of five thousand Afghan refugees of Central Asian origin, including this tribe. The plan was to settle them near Van in eastern Turkey, where among the high mountains they would be provided with livestock and have the opportunity to resume a vestige of their old nomadic life.

After I had talked with Rahman Qul in Gilgit sitting outside his tent, and wished him well on his journey, I returned to Europe and heard nothing more about the tribe apart from a brief newspaper report on the resettlement plans. Six years passed, and I continued to wonder about these Kirghiz. What had become of them? How had they settled? Had they become model Turkish citizens, or had they remained as dejected as I had seen them in Gilgit? Their fate haunted me. Refugees and wretchedness were synonymous in today's world; among the millions here was a group which seemed distinctive, which might possibly find some satisfaction from the enforced changes in their lives. In the summer of 1988 I thought I would go to Turkey and discover what had happened to them.

No one seemed to know their current whereabouts. I got in touch with the Irish Red Cross and learned that many Afghans of Central Asian origin had been settled near Sivas in Central Anatolia; other groups were scattered in different parts of Turkey. Then through the organisation Afghan Relief I wrote to Bob Darragh, an American businessman who had dealings with this particular tribe of Kirghiz and had bought carpets from them. He gave me the name of a friend who lived in Tokat, who might possibly help.

From Istanbul I took a bus to Ankara to find that my arrival coincided with Ramadan. For a week everything closed down. During Ramadan what else was there to do besides visit Hittite antiquities and the young People's Park where groups of sad-faced men and women watched television under the trees? I viewed cake shops and statues of Ataturk, and walked down wide streets filled with embassies and plush offices. One of them belonged to the United Nations Commission for Refugees, where I managed to speak to an official. He was polite but had never heard of the Kirghiz.

I took another bus, and embarked on an eight-hour journey across Ataturk's heartland, minuscule villages swallowed up in a landscape that had no end. Waves of mountains rose and fell. The bus was grand. In a country where cars are beyond the financial reach of most people, where trains are slow and aeroplanes expensive, Turkish buses are clean, fast and comfortable and go everywhere. They go to and fro over the endless plains and hills to the highest mountain-top villages, and the remotest hamlets in that vast country. The *otogar* has replaced the caravanserai. It is a place where people meet, a medley of restaurants, ticket offices and touts trying to sell you showy suitcases and bottles of scent. It is filled with a subdued hum of voices like a cathedral.

I arrived at the *otogar* at Sivas and sought out Mr Luften, the governor at the *vilayet* in the main square surrounded by ancient Seljuk monuments. The governor was a pleasant handsome man sitting in a large, wooden-panelled office, Ataturk in a dinner jacket and white bow tie staring down over his desk. I remembered other icons in Afghan chaikhanas, Kerry farmhouses, embassies and government offices – Jesus exposing his heart, one pope after another, John F. Kennedy, jaunty President Zia, white-bearded bespectacled Nadir Shah touching his sword, Queen Elizabeth strapped in her blue Garter or standing behind a puddle of Coronation robe.

All around me were friendly but inarticulate Turks.

'Can anyone speak English?'

'*Yok.*' They nodded their heads emphatically.

We sat drinking glasses of tea and eating cakes, occasionally grimacing to each other. I was introduced to the Director of Museums, the Police Chief and government colleagues. I was taken on a tour of the museum and the recently restored Sifahiye Madrasa just opened to welcome the foreign tourists who were expected to come in droves to this little provincial town. Would Sivas turn into Kathmandu? A teacher from the local high school entertained me for lunch with his family, and in the evening I met an Irish woman married for twenty years to a Turkish professor. For the first time since I had stepped off the bus at the *otogar*, I heard English spoken with fluency, in the accent of Cork.

I encountered nothing but goodwill, but I learned nothing about the Afghan Kirghiz. To find a small group of nomads appeared next to impossible in a country where refugees were pouring in, Iranians fleeing the Gulf War, and Kurds; a little later the Bulgarian Turks would begin to arrive. Mention of the Kirghiz drew some stares of incomprehension and so many '*Yoks*' that I began to wonder if their departure from Pakistan had not taken place. Perhaps after I had tea with Rahman Qul in the summer of 1982, just as he and his tribe had been on the point of leaving, the whole enterprise had been aborted. Perhaps the Kirghiz were still in their black refugee tents in Gilgit just as three million Pathans were encamped outside Peshawar.

But the American, Bob Darragh, had known about them, and he had given me the address of Mr Sharif Dogan, an Afghan who lived in neighbouring Tokat a hundred kilometres away (which in Turkey is a hop, step and jump). I set off from Sivas in another bus, a humble rural cousin to the glossy vehicle in which I had crossed the steppes of Anatolia. I sat among women draped in black shawls holding babies and men in baggy suits and flat hats spitting out husks of sunflower seeds. We drove through the hills behind Sivas which were bare and brown, baked by the sun, but although it was late May much of the ground we passed was covered with deep patches of snow.

Tokat, surrounded by mountains, had the usual shabby modern thoroughfare, some crumbling fortifications and a few ancient mosques. There was the Turquoise Madrasa which was not turquoise any more since it had been renovated and most of the blue tiles had been taken away. Not far outside the town at Zile, Julius Ceasar defeated some Pontic kings in a battle that lasted only four hours and said '*Veni, vidi, vici*'.

I asked about any Afghans living in Tokat.

'Afghan camp,' I was directed up the dreary main street. The camp turned out to be a line of high-rise flats built around a courtyard. By one of the happy coincidences that make the lives of travellers easier the first man I met coming out of an open door was Mr Sharif Dogan.

He was middle-aged with crispy white hair, a trimmed beard, slit eyes and a face as round as the moon. His family had come to Turkey in 1982, together with eighty other Turcoman refugee families, and he had been living in Tokat ever since. They were given a small monthly allowance by the Turkish government and had tried to supplement this by making carpets. That was how Bob Darragh had made their acquaintance. Unfortunately in the last couple of years increasing competition from cheap Pakistani carpets had broken up the business altogether. Now Sharif and his family and other Afghan families living in Tokat had turned to making leather jackets. He had five children to support and life was not easy.

Lunch was Afghan, a great dish of pilau studded with nuts and raisins. Sharif could speak stuttering English, far more fluently than the Turks I had met. He had learned it in Kabul, like his friend, Mohammed Sarwr Akbari who joined us. Mohammed Akbari had been in the Kabul parliamentary assembly before the 1979 coup, after which he was in prison. Later he lived in New York for a time. Unlike the other Afghans in Tokat, he was a Pathan.

I found out at once that they both knew Rahman Qul and his tribe whom they had met in a village called Kara Kunduz close to Van over in the far east of Turkey.

Mohammed Akbari said, 'Sharif, why do you not take our Irish friend here over to see them? Without your help it might be impossible to find them.'

'Why not?' Sharif smiled and nodded his head, as if the idea of leaving his family and throwing up leather jacket-making was of no consequence.

'What about your work?'

He shrugged his shoulders. His sons would continue with the jackets and he would enjoy keeping me company. This was his *duty*. How well I remembered the words with which an Afghan brushes aside any argument which impinged on hospitality and kindness. Here was the duty to be a host and to give rather than to receive, to put your friend first before any personal consideration.

He may have liked the idea of taking a week's holiday.

In a few minutes everything was agreed. Sharif would come with me to find Rahman Qul and then return home. No payment whatsoever.

Next morning he arrived at my hotel carrying a rolled-up prayer mat and a small leather suitcase containing pyjamas, a tin of snuff, a cuspidor and an English dictionary. For the days we travelled together this last item was in constant use.

'Please, what is the meaning?' I explained cyclonic, understatement, fidgeting, spasm. In spite of the jolting bus and the difficulty of writing down my definitions, every few minutes there would be another word to be defined. Variance, hindsight, protein, dividend. It was like being back at the Military Academy. Mile after mile over the dusty road I remember Sharif's anxious round Turcoman face, his incessant snuff-taking, and the look of that dictionary. Supine, flexible, notation, ultramarine.

But that first morning in Tokat we walked to the *otogar* behind the main street. Hidden away amidst the debris of shops selling spare parts for cars was a mosque of a beauty that would make you gasp and a line of old houses with carved wooden balconies. We crossed the public park which contained tombstones. Sharif translated an inscription. 'When a person's heart is full of love he does not have to go to Mecca.'

We booked for an evening ride to Diyarbakir, the largest and most important town in south-east Turkey. Later, over glasses of tea I learnt more about my new friend. Born in 1940, Sharif came from a middle-class Turcoman family living in Kabul. He had spent three years in the Commerical School, entering as a boy of twelve while I was attempting to teach at the Military Academy. Perhaps we had passed each other in a Kabuli alley-way in those far-off days when the Soviets had been no threat. I remembered taciturn Soviet diplomats and their plain fat wives. Those were the days when for most Afghans everything American was good.

Thirty years later Sharif, his family and two donkeys escaped from Kabul into Pakistan by way of the Logar valley. The Turks had taken in the family as part of their Turcoman quota. Torn by inflation, with little work for her own citizens and generally poor living conditions, Turkey's acceptance of millions of refugees is remarkable.

We drove away from Sivas at nine. In the bus were rows of young conscripts yawning and lying back in their seats, whose shaven bullet heads brought back memories of Kabul. Similar scraped military headstyles had faced me each morning in the Military Academy. And the Afghan cadets had worn khaki uniforms and heavy black boots just like these young Turks. 'Good morning, sire,' they used to shout, jumping up behind their overcrowded desks. I remembered the trumpet sounding outside in the square and wondered once again how many of those I had taught had survived revolution and war.

Beside me Sharif took snuff. 'Excuse me, please, this is dirty habit.' He offered me a few specks. The small brass cuspidor carefully balanced on his knee was used as much as the dictionary. *Narwah* is swallowed rather than sniffed and all night he spat and ferreted out strange words by torchlight that needed explaining. Occasionally we stopped at a teahouse for a few minutes and everyone got out to drink glasses of sticky brown tea, and eat almond cakes and bowls of glutinous rice. At four o'clock I saw the first blaze of dawn behind the hills that were long sloping grey waves. Sharif woke and unrolled his prayer rug from its plastic cover. Standing and kneeling in the small aisle between the seats, avoiding heads, arms, bodies and legs, he prayed as we bumped out way towards Diyarbakir.

At nine o'clock we arrived battered and bruised in a town where the sun already burnt down into hot airless streets. Diyarbakir was a dense closed box filled with minarets and crumbling ancient churches. The wall that enclosed the town was ancient and famous and dated back to 297 BC – Romans, Byzantines and Seljuks had strengthened and rebuilt it.

Sharif had a wash before praying in the large mosque.

'I am not a religious man.'

After he prayed we walked round part of the Black Wall that overlooked the muddy Tigris before seeking refuge from the sun in one of the covered bazaars. We squatted on stools as men in baggy trousers haggled over deadly-looking food, pink and purple meat swarming with flies. There were smells that reminded me of Afghanistan, charcoal, and the sweet decay that came from the rubbery piles of fresh fruit and vegetables. Donkeys, wheelbarrows, L-shaped men staggering under enormous sacks; the occasional low-flying jet from the nearby American base screaming over the rooftops. Soldiers; recent newspaper reports mentioned insurgent Kurds attacking army convoys, and much of the surrounding area resembled an armed camp.

We took another bus to Van, and had another temporary acquaintance with a new group of passengers. Hour after hour we exchanged glances with the pretty girl dressed in the most mournful black who kept smiling at me, the man with the face of a rabbit with protruding teeth and corkscrew grin, the old soldier cleaning his gun. We drove past groups of nomads on their long migration into the hills, burnt faces, black tents, streams of sheep. Higher up the rocky slopes were lines of beehives stacked together to give them the appearance of miniature cities where the whole countryside vibrated to the hum of bees.

We drove through Bitlis at the end of a deep narrow gorge. From the windows of the bus it had a peculiarly tumbledown appearance, its houses sagging over a river in the last stages of decay. Groups of men dressed like bank clerks splattered through the muddy streets. Then on to Tatvan at the edge of the lake which showed itself for a few fleeting moments before the fiery sunset was extinguished. A curve of high snow-covered mountains on the far western side was reflected in the sombre waters that stretched out of sight. It was desolate and splendid. The Armenians used to say, before they were evicted or massacred, Van in this world, Paradise in the next.

After the desolation of the hills Van was a brash modern town where the avenues that led nowhere were lined with carpet shops spruced up for the new tourists. We looked for a hotel down a backstreet near the market where a heap of discarded fruit and vegetable peelings made the narrow pathway as slippery as if it was coated with ice. Generally the further east you travel in Turkey (perhaps in the world) the worse hotels become; my guide book suggested a cockroach rating. This one was very bad; what had attracted me to it were the stuffed creatures in the window, some moth-eaten ducks, a pelican and the carcase of a wolf spreadeagled against a bowl of plastic flowers. Many of the soldiers who had been with us on the bus were now ahead of us, and astoundingly the place was full.

At last we found something better, cleaner, and able to give us a room which had a washbasin and a shower. In the bar groups of men slouched in leather seats watched the latest instalment of a melancholy series about the second world war, always a favourite choice of programme among Turks. Laurence Olivier was dubbed by a voice of deep sadness and drama. Like so many buildings in Van this hotel had sprung up overnight and was unfinished. Rolls of carpet lay scattered around the concrete floor, most of the doors didn't fit and when Sharif pulled the light switch there was a muted explosion.

Next morning I was woken by the sound of Sharif saying his prayers. The sun was streaming in through the bedroom windows and outside I could see unfinished concrete tower blocks breaking the skyline. At their feet were two little cottages and a stream where a woman was washing clothes. The light was very clear and sharp; beyond the new houseblocks I glimpsed poplars stretching out of sight.

In the hotel hallway a busload of haggard Germans had just arrived after a long night's journey; behind them was a mountain of their baggage. Germans come in their thousands to view the homeland of their guest workers. In the dining room, as the waiters stood transfixed, lines of middle-aged men and women, arms clasped behind each other's back, faces white with fatigue, were singing a hearty chorus before tucking into the goat's cheese, olives, bread, cucumber, yoghurt and salad that made up their breakfast.

During the morning Sharif made enquiries in Van and discovered that Rahman Qul and his tribe had been settled in the village of Kara Kunduz and then been moved north to the region of Ercis. Exactly where he could not make out – a trip to Ercis was now necessary. We set off along the empty shores of Van, empty of fishing boats, since fish are few, of tourist hotels – but there will soon be more tourists than fish; a blue haze, a reflection of mountains and far ahead the rounded summit of Suphan Dag like a white pudding.

The journey took about an hour and a half over a very bumpy road where in places the thin coating of tarmac had washed away in the long winter months of ice and snow. We sat squeezed together as the driver tried to avoid the worst bumps, passing through yet another towering lonely stretch of Turkey, over which hovered the odd bird of prey, not a soul in sight apart from the occasional shepherds from crazy little villages hidden away under screes of rock.

By contrast, it was market day at Ercis where we were dropped in a shaded lane full of bewhiskered Kurds and sheep which were cascading into the town from all sides. Their raucous bleating filled the sky. We sat on wooden stools under a large walnut tree drinking glasses of tea as they went slowly by in a long shuffling anxious procession driven by men with enormous moustaches – from behind they stuck out like forks. Bells clanged, women in long coloured dresses strode past majestically; behind a mud wall a soldier urinated against another walnut tree.

We had been sitting there for an hour when in the teahouse opposite, Sharif spotted a young Kirghiz boy with a bland Mongolian face dressed in jeans and tattered leather jacket. Squatting beside him was an older woman, possibly his mother, who wore a bright red dress and knee-length leather boots. From her head flowed the distinctive Kirghiz veil made out of a material that looked like chiffon which is called a *jorluk*. It was white, which meant that she was married; a *jorluk* for an unmarried woman would be red. In the crowd of Kurdish shepherds and farmers drinking their tea she appeared like a grand lady who had stepped out of the *Canterbury Tales*. A hundred years ago Thomas Holdich observed in a book called *Indian Borderlands* how 'all the men and women wear large Russian boots and the head-dresses of the Kirghiz women are distinctive, which by some eccentricity of fashion in medieval times was temporarily accepted in Europe'.

We joined them in the little teahouse with its mud floor; outside a river of sheep passed by. Yes, they were now living in a new village some miles away up in the mountains which had been specially built for them. They had called it after their homeland Ulu Pamir. Yes, the tribe which had come here as refugees were with their Khan. Yes, he was Rahman Qul. The old woman smiled when Sharif told her that I had met Rahman Qul and her people in Pakistan. A lorry was leaving in the direction of their village. Already when we climbed in it was fairly full – sheep, mixed up with some more Kirghiz women, half a dozen Kurdish farmers dressed in their best, baggy trousers, waistcoats and voluminous turbans wrapped round their heads, oval frames for the moustaches.

Beyond Ercis a rough dirt road led away from the lake into the mountains. We passed a Kurdish village built of stone and mud, its harshness relieved a little by a cluster of poplars. Half-naked children were kicking a football around some extraordinary ornate pyramids made out of cow pats. The Kurds, proud people denied their independence, even their language, were considered less a part of the Turkish nation than these imported Kirghiz who spoke an old-fashioned Turkic dialect that could be understood by contemporary Turkish speakers. No doubt it was the equivalent of Chaucerian, like the *jorluk*.

Every time the lorry, trailing thick golden dust, turned a corner sheep and humans were thrown about in confusion. Instead of the deep waters of the lake which stretched to the horizon and far beyond, we were among snow-covered mountains and a landscape that was a fair replica of the old Kirghiz homeland. Here there was nothing but bleak mountains rising one behind the other into the distance. Ahead was a turbulent ice-blue river and beyond it at the far end of a valley a group of buildings shaped like double white cubes with corrugated metal roofs shining in the sun.

Here was Ulu Pamir, the new home of Rahman Qul's tribe of Kirghiz. I was told later the design was unique, that it was a one-off. There was nothing like it in Turkey or indeed the rest of the world. Compared to the wretched traditional Kurdish villages we had passed it seemed like Utopia. Or a trailer camp. Or Célesteville.

The closer we came the stranger it seemed. We left the lorry and walked across a wooden bridge up to the village. Groups of women, in the same long flowing dresses and medieval coifs worn by the old lady we had met in Ercis, were bringing buckets of water up from the river. A white horse with a man astride its back was grazing in a field of buttercups.

Ulu Pamir had only been completed the year before and still wore the half-finished look of any new township. There were no trees or grass, no vegetable plots and the lines of semi-detached houses stood out starkly from the muddy lanes that ran between them. There were two hundred and ninety-eight houses for seventeen hundred Kirghiz and each one had its own bathroom and kitchen (but no running water), its own living room and bedroom. Compared with the refugees' tents, or indeed with their own beautiful inconvenient yurts in the Wakhan, they must have been very comfortable. The houses were built in the alpine fashion with the lower half used as stables. Two families lived in each building with its own separate steps and entrances at either end. On the outside walls a grubby brown line six or eight feet from the ground marked the limit of the winter snow that piled up for seven months in the year.

We were surrounded by Kirghiz. Who was I and why had I come here? My name please? Country? Some said they remembered me, but others whom I had met in Gilgit had died.

Then began the rounds of visiting, being welcomed at different houses, pressed with tea and flat bread served with goat's cheese and yoghurt. We exchanged questions, Sharif translating. Does anyone wish to return home? Perhaps some of the older men will return to the Wakhan. *Inshallah*. No one but God would know what might happen. If the Soviets left, if the government fell, if their corner had survived the hatred and destruction of the past ten years. I wondered if any would return to being nomads. One old man had owned a thousand sheep, six horses and forty yak; he counted them slowly on his fingers.

I was brought around by Salih Sarayburer, a young man who had learnt a little English by working in tourist hotels in Ismir on the other side of Turkey. Unlike his elders in long coats and calf-length leather boots he wore jeans and runners and a denim jacket; he spoke English with an American accent.

Followed by the crowd, I was shown the school and met the newly appointed director who was Turkish. Helped by six other teachers he taught in Turkish two hundred and forty children dressed in black smocks and white collars. All those under ten had been born outside the Wakhan. Here were no yurts nor yak nor two-humped camels; the view from the classrooms was of uniform white houses like a trailer camp and, beyond, the Turkish mountains, far less formidable than the abode of gods which the Kirghiz used to share.

As I paused with the crowd to watch a volleyball game two of Rahman Qul's eight sons came up, handsome boys with dark almond-shaped eyes, thick black hair and a painfully shy manner. While I had been walking around the village their father had arrived and wanted to welcome me.

Rahman Qul said he remembered me, but so much had happened since that I wondered if this was true. He told me that he was sixty-five, but I thought him much older; in the life of a nomadic tribesman experience garnered from hardship and danger was more important than the actual tally of years. He was tall and imperious with a presence and dignity that was unmistakable, and a way of expressing himself that suggested not only complete authority, but also a touching regard for other people's opinions that had been brought about by hard circumstances. He had a large oval head, high cheekbones that curved like the edge of butterfly wings, and a fine white beard. What made his presence particularly striking was the fact that he was completely bald. His massive bronze head glistened in the light.

At one time there had been more than a million nomadic Kirghiz tribesmen; they were first mentioned as a Turkish group in second-century Chinese annuals. Their language belonged to the north-western group of Turkic languages; today anyone who knows Turkish can make himself understood by more than fifty million people along the old silk route, as far as Chinese Turkestan.

Rahman Qul had been born when Central Asia was still secure in very old traditions. Now he was the last of the Khans.

Much of his life could be explained by a Kirghiz proverb: If your father was a Russian, carry an axe with you. Like other Turcomen the Kirghiz had wandered with their flocks of sheep and yak over a boundless territory which latterly fell into becoming distant outposts of the Soviet and Chinese Empires. During the nineteenth century much of the Kirghiz land was under the political sovereignty of the Ferghana Uzbegs, and although there were endless faction fights and little wars, their freedom was never curtailed. Then the Russians took over much of the region during their expansion eastwards. By the time the young Nathaniel Curzon toured Central Asia he considered these people under the general suzerainty of the Russians 'on the grounds that they were subject to the annexed Khanate of Khohand'.

At first the nomads were able to wander freely all over the new political spheres of Russian and Chinese influence. Rahman Qul's father worked for the new Czarist colonial administration. But the relationship, always uneasy, foundered into rebellion; in 1916, when the Russians had other worries, the Kirghiz led an unsuccessful uprising in which it is said that more than a million died in Turkestan. Rahman Qul's father (described as 'particularly knowledgeable, wealthy and powerful') retreated with his people and resettled his tribe among the Pamirs in the Wakhan corridor. Even here there were demarcation lines; the mountains had been carved up between Russia, China, Afghanistan and Great Britain in 1895.

Although they were protected by some of the highest mountains in the world, the tribe, which was far larger than it is today, soon came into conflict with their new neighbours. Hardly a year passed without some armed incursion; on one occasion Rahman Qul and his brother were held prisoner for six months. After the Soviet revolution the restrictions increased, although the nomadic life in one of the bleakest snow wildernesses in the world continued through the nineteen-twenties and thirties. In the thirties Rahman Qul met Eric Shipton when he was British Consul in Kashgar.

In 1946, after he succeeded his father as Khan, he fled to China with almost two thousand Kirghiz. Three years later China's Communist revolution forced them back into Afghanistan. By now their grazing lands had shrunk to the narrow strip of the Afghan Wakhan. Up until the thirties the Russians had allowed the tribe to pay a 'pasturage fee' for the privilege of herding their animals on their traditional pastures. But in due course this land was cut off by a fence and watchtowers. This meant that the tribe lost control of its section of the silk route which once passed their way from China. There was no more profit to be had from furs and pelts (fox, tiger, wolf), spices, pistachio nuts and Chinese silk.

Later Rahman Qul would sign his letters to me H. Rahmanqul Qirghhiz. The H stood for Hadji, a man who had fulfilled the Moslem Hadj to Mecca. As Khan of the Afghan Kirghiz he inherited traditional power and an illustrious lineage. The Victorian explorer John Woods wrote of his visit to the Pamirs, where he met Rahman Qul's great grandfather. 'The Chief of the Wakhan traces his ancestry to Alexander the Great, a descent whether fabulous or true of which he was not a little vain. Mohammed Rahim considered his illustrious lineage a fact which none could dispute.'

Right up until the nineteen-seventies, although the Wakhan was by that time incorporated into Afghanistan, Rahman Qul's authority was supreme. He had the title Pasani Pamir, Safe Keeper of the Pamirs. He undertook many functions that established the legitmacy of his rule, acting as judge in land disputes, regulating trade with outsiders. Above all he was a religious leader and responsible for the Islamic code practised by the Kirghiz. Not only did he control the major flocks of sheep, goats and yak in the area, but he devised what was called the Amanant system where poor Kirghiz who did not possess a flock could lease animals and so remain within the tribal framework.

The nomadic lifestyle survived because of isolation. In the Wakhan there were few roads or social services. Foreigners were kept out, as I knew to my cost; because of the area's proximity to the Soviet Union and China the area was politically sensitive. Outsiders had to visit with the approval of the Afghan king. In 1950 an American couple trekking along the silk route encountered Rahman Qul who treated them graciously. In their subsequent article for the *National Geographic* they described the horrified reaction of the Mayor of Chitral to this meeting:

'"For many years this Rahman Gul (sic) murder and rob people," the Mayor insisted. "Very bad man. Why he no murder you?"'

'I remembered the night we talked with Rahman Qul in his smokey yurt high up on the Great Pamirs.

'"We put our lives entirely in your hands," I had said. And his answer:

'"I accept your trust."

'"Why he no murder you?"

'I looked at the Mayor and shook my head.

'"I don't know." I looked at Jean. I could see that she agreed with me. We didn't know. Probably we would never know. But to us Rahman Qul would always be the man who had saved our lives."'

Almost twenty years later the Afghan anthropologist, Nazif Sharani from neighbouring Badakshan, visited the Afghan Kirghiz in the Wakhan. Even in the nineteen-seventies travelling with Rahman Qul was 'like a royal procession . . . in the company of the Khan and a caravan of thirteen Bactrian camels, nearly thirty horses and almost as many people . . . on our arrival at the Khan's camp Kirghiz from all over the Little Pamir, rich, poor, old and young came to visit the Khan and pay their respects, to receive small gifts of sweets, tea and cloth and so on and to hear the news from Kabul.'

Only a few years later this ancient lifestyle was shattered with the Soviet-inspired coup in Kabul. In 1951 the Refugee Convention defined a refugee 'as one who has a well-defined fear of persecution; i.e. who is a potential victim of persecution, because of race, religion and nationality, a person without a homeland.' This would describe the position of Rahman Qul and his nomads. In June 1978 he sent one of his sons for news of the coup in Kabul; by August, with the agreement of the Kirghiz elders, he made the supremely difficult decision to leave the Wakhan. 'They were motivated,' Shashrani wrote, 'by what they perceived as a direct threat from across the border rather than as a serious threat from Afghanistan,' but precisely what the circumstances were that triggered this vast decision is now difficult to ascertain. Not only was their departure the culmination of all the wrongs they had received over the years from the Russians, but also the end of their ancient nomadic life. It happened at a time when the Russian invasion of Afghanistan had not yet taken place.

We sat among piles of cushions in Rahman Qul's small living

room listening to his description of the journey. After almost ten years it still had an epic quality, the patriarch leading his tribe across one of the most desolate and forbidding landscapes in the world. Already in August many of the passes leading down to Pakistan were snowbound. The Kirghiz moved with most of the animals that they possessed, one thousand yak, thirty thousand sheep, three hundred horses and some of the Bactrian camels. The journey to Gilgit took ten days and no one was lost.

Rahman Qul sat on his cushions smoking his favourite Marlboro cigarette while the other Kirghiz crowded around. Supper was served by two of his sons who brought in plates of food from the kitchen and laid them on a cloth spread over the carpet. Once again I was offered traditional dishes of pilau and its accompaniments. Then everyone was smoking and drinking tea; occasionally the door opened and a startled woman's face peered in.

I showed them photographs I had taken in Gilgit four years before. Many faces were missing. The heat, and typhoid and other diseases had killed one hundred and fifteen Kirghiz.

The dishes were swept away and mattresses were laid on the floor. In the darkness I listened to the occasional roll of thunder while lightning illuminated the room and the embroidered picture of the Kabba would be lit up for a moment, together with the picture of Ataturk, grim as ever.

I thought of yurts with their thick felt cover and trellis of willow that came from distant Kashgar. Francis Younghusband had noted how: 'Round the tents were piles of clothes and bedding for winter – good stout felts and warm quilts; and rows of boxes to contain the household goods and treasures. A small portion of the tent was always partitioned off – there were kept all the supplies of milk, cream and curds which are the stable food of the Kirghiz.' Rahman Qul and his tribe had used such tents ten years ago.

I thought of Afghanistan, of memories of Kabul and efforts to reach the Pamirs; seeing for the first time the dusty Oxus plain and high above it the crested line of ice and snow.

At six o'clock next morning Rahman Qul joined us for breakfast and more cigarettes. The sons brought in yoghurt which they called ayram; there was bread and sharp cheese that tasted like the contents of vitamin pills. Outside I could hear the roar of the river as another day dawned slowly. The first shimmer of light hit the edges of the mountains and crept down the hills. Now I heard the voices of Kirghiz girls driving sheep wearing bells up to the pastures above the village. A man was singing. Was the song traditional, nostalgic, love, a celebration of nature or the glory of being alive? I remembered how often Afghans would burst into song, high notes that wavered and carried on. A Pathan would take the rose out of his mouth and sing of love; or an old countryman, riding in a bus carrying a feathery-grey cock or partridge, its bright red beak peering out of its cage, would sing about flowers in the forest and the music of mountain streams.

Next day Sharif went home. We parted at the mosque in Van where he had gone to pray before catching the bus. We shook hands with great formality while the early morning traffic roared around us. We exchanged addresses; later that year, he told me, he hoped to visit his brother in America and improve his English.

'Please send me a dictionary.'

After he left I sat in one of the numerous tea gardens scattered around Van. Sun shone through the trees onto the gravelled path and the little tables. Beside us a fountain cascaded, stopped and started up again, while a succession of beggars and hawkers passed around like a ballet. A boy sold leather belts and ties neatly folded across his arm, another carried a wooden box full of perfumes in ornate little glass bottles which, for a very small fee, he would inject with a syringe on the back of a client's hand. Then a man passed with weighing scales, and another with a pump and a black rubber belt who offered to take blood pressure. All the time an old man with white mid-week stubble, topped by a luxuriant white moustache, squatted on the ground briskly polishing shoes. For the enterprising and ambitious, the use of the decorated brass box containing the polish and brushes is a step towards more lucrative activities. It is usually the young who are stuck with making leather shine. But this old man had evidently polished footwear all his life, and he brought to his work the skill and dignity of a craftsman. I watched him examine each shoe, scrape it clean, apply the polish with a rag as if he was painting a picture, place the shoe on a small rubber knee-pad and brush away until the leather glowed and sparkled and glittered. The few lira he received for each job were put away carefully in a box. All the shoes passing me shone like mirrors; he averted his eyes when he saw my disgraceful runners.

Three students spotted me sitting under the trees by the fountain.

'Excuse me, sir, I may sit down?'

'You are English?'

'Excuse me, how long are you in Van?'

'What is your hotel, please?'

'It is all right that I practise English?'

'Do you wish carpets?'

The conversation followed fairly predictable lines. Most of the talking was done by Mustafer Acer, a handsome Kurd looking like the young Omar Sharif, who during the summer season worked part-time in a carpet shop. Meanwhile he attended the university. Every day he and his friends toured Van looking for English-speaking victims. His own English was good enough to describe his background, the poor family in Mardin where he had five brothers to support.

When he was a boy he had been so poor that sometimes he couldn't go to school. Like the occasion when he lost his pen, and had to pretend that he was sick for the shame of it.

And the teacher had asked, 'Why were you not at school?'

'I was sick.'

'But I saw you playing around.'

Only because his family had scraped up enough money to buy another pen had he been able to return to his class. It could not have been long after this that he got married. He had been twelve years old.

'Twelve? Are you sure?'

'I am sure.' He held up ten fingers and then two. 'I am married many years.' He waved his hands twice and held up the two fingers again. Now he was twenty-two. He hoped to become a teacher next year. His salary would be three thousand lire a month, just enough for him and his wife to live on.

How difficult was it to obtain work?

'If you want to obtain work, you will find it.'

I wandered around the flats and offices so depressingly similar

to recent developments in every noble and ancient town in
Turkey. Beyond the concrete was the citadel of Van Kalesi and
the bumpy plain which used to be the ancient city which people
try to forget. They have painstakingly flattened the shameful
weed-covered rubble of Armenian Van.

When Captain Fred Burnaby, an Irishman, whose languid
portrait by Tissot hangs in the National Portrait Gallery, rode
through Van in 1876 the population – almost entirely Armenian
– was estimated at around twenty thousand, although he thought
it less. The town was an unhealthy place and many rich merchants built their houses outside the walls to avoid typhus and
the malaria rising out of the lakeside swamp.

The Armenians were under the usual pressure because their
bazaar had just been burnt down. Armenian newspapers 'probably instigated by Russian agents' accused Turkish troops of
being responsible. However, the commissioner sent by Constanti-
nople to investigate insisted that the fire was accidental. 'Several
Armenians kept petroleum and lucifer matches in their warehouses; his idea was that the fire originated either by spontaneous
combustion, or through someone accidentally dropping a lighted
match.' The story was a warm-up for similar excuses to explain
the post-first-world-war massacre and devastation of Van. Once
again the Russians were the villains, provoking the disloyal
Armenians into rebellion that had to be unmercifully crushed.

The barn-like wooden church full of tawdry pictures of saints
derided by Burnaby was destroyed with everything else. The
devastation is shocking and so widespread it brings Hiroshima
to mind. I walked for hours on the plain beyond the new concrete
town tracing the outlines of streets and vanished houses. Here
and there on the uneven broken plain were herdsmen and their
animals throwing up clouds of golden dust. Within living memory
this lumpy stretch of ground had been a city surrounded by
towering Ottoman walls, a bustling place, the pride of Anatolia;
even the Turks had a saying that everyone must see the glories
of Van once in their lifetime. Today a giant metal profile of
Ataturk looks down from the ancient Uratian citadel on the side
of the city which he helped to destroy.

The sun dipped behind the mountains and lake in a smoulder-
ing golden ball and the Refet Umel docked with its cargo of
railway carriages bound for Iran. I watched the Captain in his

smart blue uniform and white naval cap saunter down the long wooden pier, a string of amber beads dangling from his hand. In Van I studied the new tourist image of the town and eastern Turkey which was being promoted with coloured posters of carpets, derelict Armenian churches and cuddly white Van cats with different-coloured eyes who catch fish from the waters of the lake. Groups of Germans slowly circled the beggars squatting on the pavements, many of them children, who in the evening emerged from shadows outside the tourist hotels to count their meagre takings before vanishing into the night. I wondered how the Kirghiz would adapt here. Through Sharif I had discussed with Rahman Qul the problems facing his people and how every winter more of the young men wandered off into the cities in search of jobs. How long would it take them to forget their culture as the old traditions and the memory of nomad life became forgotten?

Next morning I met Malik and Akbar Kutlu, two of Rahman Qul's eight sons, men in their thirties with a shy donnish manner. They were now working as artists at the University of Van. They had always dreamed of being artists, not the easiest ambition for young nomads; as children in the Wakhan they had been constantly frustrated when they tried to draw and sculpt.

'We used to make figures out of mud,' Malik told me, 'and if we found a picture in a newspaper we copied it. The only paper we could draw on came from packets of cigarettes.' Once they had seen a photograph of Michaelangelo's *David* and this greatly impressed them. Before they left the Wakhan, among the trickle of outsiders who visited the Pamirs had been an Afghan professor from Kabul who gave them words of encouragement. And when they came to Turkey and ceased to be refugees, they had been able to fulfil a dream. It was an ill wind.

In the lavish studio they had been given on top of the old university, Malik was the painter and his brother sculpted mainly from wood. Scattered around the large room were paintings and carvings illustrating the traditional Kirghiz life that they remembered when they were boys. Here were men playing *buzkashi*; here were Marco Polo sheep with horns like Michelin tyres. Delicate careful pictures showed nomadic life around felt yurts, scenes of goats and sheep being milked, women weaving and carding wool.

A range of paintings and drawings illustrated the Kirghiz'
flight from the Wakhan. A group of women wept, their hands in
front of their faces, a file of men on horseback and two-humped
camels set out through the snow, a woman and child were caught
in a storm. There was a drawing of the black tents clustered in
the river valley in Gilgit. And finally the arrival by plane at
Adana in southern Turkey.

Yet another group of Malik's paintings were of yak. Yak were
being milked, or clipped for their wool, a procession of yak was
crossing a lonely pass, yak were making up part of the escape
caravan.

'We could not keep our animals. The yak did not live well in
Gilgit which was too low.'

I knew that it was difficult to accustom Himalayan yak to
conditions below ten thousand feet – their huge lungs are adapted
to high altitudes. But I was also aware that yak have been
brought to Europe.

Malik showed me a painting of a wild-eyed bushy-tailed
creature pawing the snow; on its back was a virile young hunts-
man dressed in leather and fur, carrying a gun. In the background
was a wild snowy landscape and glowering sky. This particular
yak looked as fine and fierce and noble as King William's white
horse – and very different from the surly cantankerous creature
that I had ridden with great discomfort a few years back in
Nepal. This was yak made into an icon – a yak depicted in the
romantic tradition.

Malik showed me more pictures. Yak outnumbered people.

'They were important in Kirghiz culture?'

'Very important.'

We looked at another yak caravan. 'If you had yak here in
Turkey – say in Ulu Pamir, would they survive?'

'I think they would live here very well.'

We had a meal together and I began to imagine Ulu Pamir as
a setting for more of Malik's paintings of Himalayan herbivores. I
could see a line of yak being loaded up among the sheep and
goats. I recalled the smell of very dirty dogs that emanated from
their thick matted musty coats; I remembered the groaning and
breathing that gave them the Latin name of *bos grunniens*, grunting
ox.

In the Wakhan three yak could carry a complete yurt and all

its domestic appurtenances from camp to camp. Yak had enabled the Kirghiz to move from one pasture to the next enjoying their nomadic freedom. Would it be possible for this sort of tradition to continue for a little longer among the Turkish hills?

Stuffed aubergines, kidneys in garlic sauce, tripe soup, flakey pastry and honey and countless varieties of kebab were being fetched and carried around the small overcrowded room. Akbar ordered a caramel cream covered in thick gooey chocolate sauce from the demented waiter. I thought about ways of bringing yak to the Kirghiz.

Malik said, 'It would be good if yak came to Ulu Pamir.'

A few days later I went back to Ulu Pamir to say goodbye. In my absence a last group of Kirghiz refugees had arrived from Malatya in eastern Turkey and were being looked after by the Turkish Red Crescent. Rahman Qul had just heard news of the impending Soviet withdrawal from Afghanistan and how America would help any Afghans who wished to return home. But it was not so easy. Ten long years had passed since the tribe departed, and a new generation of Kirghiz occupied the old territory. The Russians were still nearby. In all the decade there had been no news whatsoever about the Wakhan. The country was at war, the place was distant, post was erratic, perhaps non-existent. Besides, very few of the Kirghiz who had decided to stay behind could write.

In the evening I walked down to the river with Rahman Qul and sat on the thick meadow grass. Above the roar of the water I could hear a bird singing; the sun shone from a cloudless sky and in the air were the pungent smells of early summer. We could be in Afghanistan, near Feyzabad or Jurm or some rocky river bank near the Panjshir river. We thought that for both of us the old days would never return and life had gone full circle.

About sixty miles from where we sat a Soviet soldier was gazing out from his watchtower on the borders of Soviet Armenia. Six months later his country would be devastated by earthquake. Today he could see across the wild borderlands the tents of Kurdish nomads pitched on the bleak snow-covered slopes of Mount Ararat. Above them the peak was hidden in its usual cap of grey mist. At neighbouring Dogubeyazit the silly season had begun with the arrival of an American climbing team bearing a prefabricated ark which they hoped to assemble on top of the holy mountain. Only those who had obtained Turkish government approval could climb Ararat; Noah would need a licence to moor the original ark of gopher wood.

I thought of the animals spilling out two by two onto the slopes of Mount Ararat. Every beast, every creeping thing, and every fowl, and whatsoever creepeth upon the earth, after their kinds, went forth out of the ark. If they went alphabetically the yak would be at the rear, zebra behind them. Perhaps I could imitate Noah and bring two yak to eastern Turkey.

17

THE Turkish Embassy in Dublin possesses a file entitled 'YAK – PETER SOMERVILLE-LARGE' which must be almost as bulky as the file dealing with trade between Ireland and Turkey. I owe the diplomatic staff my apologies and thanks.

I brought back to Ireland two paintings which Malik gave me before I left Van. One showed a line of animals – including yak – making their way over the snow into exile. The other was of a Kirghiz warrior, booted and spurred, riding a bad-tempered-looking yak.

Observers have noted that the yak is built like a tank, is evil-smelling, cantankerous and sure-footed, The dictionary definition is: 'long-haired humped grunting wild or domesticated ox of Tibet (from Tibetan *gyag*)'. Its air of working with unconquerable reluctance, its way of broadcasting its digestive processes with loud internal rumblings, at the same time grunting and grinding its teeth, its glowering half-closed eyes, and its permanent sense of grievance, are characteristics that detract from the heroic attributes suggested by Malik's paintings.

'Great hairy, tame, slow, abstemious and agreeable beast of burden of Tibet,' was how Fosco Mariani saw the yak. 'Great ponderous, slow-moving beasts, proof against cold and wind, carrying dependent from their underparts a great sagging mass of tangled woolly hair . . . head and horns carried low, tail vast and bushy, the wool of which would have been enough to stuff three pillows . . . a mass of disgruntled depression:' an anonymous officer writing in *Blackwoods* was perhaps nearer the truth than Paul Theroux's 'lovely long-haired animal like a cow on its way to the opera'.

I hung Malik's painting on the wall and sought inspiration. I wrote to Rahman Qul for an official letter giving his authority and blessing to the enterprise – a sort of firman. There was a long silence. The painted yak and its rider gazed down at me reprovingly and my family sighed with relief.

Two months past before I received two letters in the same envelope.

Dear Mr Peter,

How are you? I hope everything is going fine with you. I received your letters and made me glad. Since the translation of an English letter is very difficult for me due to non English speak in Van. As I could not respond you in time.

But about the yoks. As I have explained to you the climate for training yoks is very faver in Ergis Van Province, but as I have hear recently it costs very expensive. The price of one yok may be estimately for Rs.3000.

The other information about yok is as following:

1. We can train six yok. (Mail 3, Femail 3).

2. Color. The blue color yok is the best it can be find in Pakistan. If blue is not found, the yellow or black is better.

3. Age: The youngest yok is better, so a three or four years old yok is better than the elder one.

I should you some information and I pray to your successful. If you find any falt or short in the letter please pardon me. I am obliged and thanking you, and hoping to be excused for the trouble.

Thank you again,

Yours faithfully H. Rahmanqul.

What could be meant by a blue or yellow yak? The Dalai Lama used to ride a sacred snow-white yak through the streets of Lhasa. I remembered my first sight of Tibetan yak, their horns curved and sharp, decked out with red plumes and bells, as they moved against a pale blue sky ploughing a stony field. Their hair, glossy as bearskin, had been of a colour near to electric blue.

To the Esteemed High ranks Government of Republic of Ireland.

Dear Sirs,

I, Haji Rahmanqul the leader of the Afghan Qirghiz tribe (300 family 1615 persons) are dwelling in Ercis as Afghan refugees. Quirghiz tribe in Pamir (Afghanistan) was shepherds our bussiness was training the sheeps, cows and particuly yoks which is unfortunately not find in Turkey at all. Yoks find only in Afghanistan and Pakistan but we cannot get it because it is expensive.

Hereby I turn your esteemed Government attention to our difficulties and hope your assistance. Kindly help us by donating six yoks
(Three mails and three femails) and make us thankful and oblige.

We pray to your successful, thank you.

Yours obediently.

H. Rahmanqul Qiirghiz.

Of the Himalayan yak those from Chitral, similar in breed to
those from the Pamirs, seemed to offer most promise for the
enterprise. As far as shipping the animals was concerned, East
Pakistan was as near as yak could get to Turkey. Freedom-loving
yak, that was – could there be a case for trying to get some out
of Afghanistan itself after the Russian withdrawal?

I wrote to Mr Yuqut Khan, the Minister of Foreign Affairs in
Pakistan, using an introduction from a mutual friend. The letter
was long, explaining my desire to obtain (and pay for – I had
yet to find sponsors) healthy Chitrali yak for the Kirghiz people.
I got no reply. Perhaps this was as well, since I then discovered
that the import-export of animals from the Himalayas presented
difficulties that were just about insurmountable. The problem
was health – a bovine from the east must be presumed to be
riddled with disease which it would introduce into healthy Turkish stock. Quarantine would be insufficient to pass them as fit,
and correct certification would be almost impossible to obtain.
That seemed to bring an end to my idea. Then I went to London
and had a conversation with Peter Pearce, a friend whose job
involved animal research. He suggested that, since moving bovines from Asia was so difficult, I could try Europe.

'Europe?'

'Zoos. Plenty of zoos have yak. Berlin. Whipsnade has a herd.
I'll take you along to see them.'

Before setting out for Whipsnade, I went to the Royal College
of Physicians in Lincoln's Inn Fields to look at the Yak of
Tartary. This yak came from Bhutan and had been the first yak
in Europe. When Samuel Turner went on his mission to Bhutan
in 1783 he acquired two yak for his patron, Warren Hastings: 'I
had the satisfaction to send two of this species to Mr Hastings
after he left India and to hear that one reached England alive.
This, which was a bull, remained for some time after he landed
in a torpid languid state, till his constitution had in some degree

assimilated with the climate, when he recovered at once both his health and vigour. He afterwards became the father of many calves, which all died without reproducing, except one, a cow, which bore a calf by connection with an Indian bull.

'Though naturally not intractable in temper, yet soured by the impatient and injudicious treatment of his attendants during a long voyage, it soon became dangerous to suffer this bull to range at liberty abroad. He had at all times been observed to bear a marked hostility towards horses. He happened to gore a valuable coach-horse belonging to Mr Hastings, which had the range of the same pasture with him and, lacerating the entrails, occasioned his death. After this, to prevent further accidents, he was kept alone within a secure enclosure.'

This surly animal, which was very likely soured long before his impatient and injudicious treatment, was painted twice by George Stubbs; the version in the College of Physicians was commissioned by the famous anatomist and surgeon John Hunter. Here is the Yak of Tartary against a background painted by William Davis, who accompanied the 1783 mission, of mountains and the Dzong at Punakha which I had tried to visit when I was young. He is standing with his shaggy head in that typical downward position which the Kirghiz say is looking for its long lost brother. He appears to be gazing at a vegetable which may be the species of Bhutanese turnip which Warren Hastings much admired and wanted to introduce into England like the yak itself.

The Yak of Tartary had become accustomed to low altitudes like the yak of Whipsnade. I went down to have a look at them in the shed that they shared with some Bactrian camels – back in the Pamirs yak and camels are herded together. There were about thirty, huge animals, a lot bigger, and with bigger horns than any yak I had seen in Tibet and Nepal. We moved among them very cautiously.

'Just stay calm,' Peter Pearce said reassuringly. Peter presented the phlegmatic image of the bearded unflappable Englishman whom nothing could shake. He had taken a doctorate and produduced learned papers; already he had sent me one entitled 'Pulmonary haemodynamics of the yak, cattle and crossbreeds at high altitudes'. The opening paragraph began: 'the evolutionary advantage of the pulmonary vasoconstrictor response to hypoxia lies probably in the reduction of the blood supply to unventilated regions of the lung, thus ensuring an equal distribution of ventilation perfusion ratio and the panafacure of the arterial P_2 . . .'

In their shed the yak were giving a fine display of rolling their eyes and tossing their horns. The camels were just as dangerous. 'Last month a camel killed a yak – a male,' Richard Kock said. Richard was the Whipsnade chief veterinary officer. Later he took us to his office, a room full of bottled animal embryos, calcinated bones, charts, spinal columns, and impaled insects; there was a tray of frogspawn near the window.

'We believe these yak came from wild stock, and some domestic blood has been introduced over the years.'

'Don't you know?'

'Actually we don't.' The coming of the yak to Whipsnade became a mystery after a disastrous fire destroyed all records about them. Their size certainly suggested an origin in the wild. The survival of the truly wild yak has become a matter for conjecture. Eighty years ago wild yak were fairly plentiful. Sven Hedin took a photograph of a vast bull he shot, while Colonel Bailey described a wild herd as 'the finest and most impressive sight in my life . . . as soon as they smelled a man, the whole herd lifted their heads, waved their bushy tails over their backs, and as though drilled, galloped off'. But throughout the Himalayas wild yak have been slaughtered, and although there is still the occasional awesome report of a sighting, in general wild yak have become as elusive as the yeti.

The most domesticated of yak remains about as trustworthy as a Rottweiler. Any dealing with yak suggests that one is working with an animal that has not yet been bred or tamed into domestic submission, and still carries many of the fierce genes of its wild ancestor. These Whipsnade yak had given a very good imitation of being wild, which did not promise well for transporting them to Turkey.

The Zoo was offering three yak for free – animals that had the incalculable advantages of being acclimatised to sea level altitudes and being disease-free. Settling yak in Turkey would be another stage in Whipsnade's admirable programme of restoration. Recently the zoo had done much to save the Arabian oryx from extinction; the yak, two females and a male, would be

the first time that Whipsnade would donate animals for – hope-
fully – a domestic purpose.

Peter Pearce said, 'Who knows, perhaps I could get permission
to come out with you when you take them. You might want
someone to anaesthetise them if they give trouble on the way
out.'

I had the yak, and began to make plans. I drew up possible
schedules, wrote to Rahman Qul, and informed the bemused
Turkish embassy of the advance in my plans, inviting them to
cooperate.

I thought that it would be easy enough to obtain funding for
my project. If mountain climbers, balloonists, yachtsmen and
explorers could find sponsors for their daydreams, surely the
man bringing yak to the Kirghiz in Turkey could attract support
from big business. I thought that banks would be approachable,
and so would dairies and cooperatives – anything to do with
bovines. This brought me to include on my list a dog-meat
manufacturer and an outfit in the west of Ireland which exported
meat specially slaughtered for Moslems.

'Further to your request for support I regret to advise you that
your activities do not come within the normal parameters of
sponsorship used by our company, and accordingly I am not in
a position to give you any financial aid.' 'Because of our 21st
anniversary commitment, we have sponsorship requests since
1987 for allocation in 1989.' 'Your venture I find very interesting
and admirable and I would like to think there is some way we
can help you.' 'Requests such as yours are handled personally
by Mr Duffy, and as he receives many such appeals of this
nature, he works on a strict budget Unfortunately, his current
budget is completely utilised.' A good many firms did not reply
at all. I had no idea then of the huge volume of begging letters
they receive every day.

'God speed on a fascinating venture . . . nowadays our contri-
butions activity is largely focused on alleviating the effects of
unemployment at home.' 'I have been unable to stimulate
interest in the provision of a seed group for the revival of the yak
population among Kirghiz refugees in Eastern Turkey . . . while
the project is obviously a very praiseworthy one, I fear it does
not have the appeal which would produce financial assistance
from our members . . .'

After two months of letter writing, I had raised thirty-five pounds. Twenty-five came as a personal contribution from the chief executive of a creamery and ten as a gift from a lady, God bless her, who read about the project in the Irishman's Diary of the *Irish Times*. 'Please forward the enclosed £10 to the appropriate body. May the yaks flourish and multiply in their new home.'

Then a letter came from a wonderful outfit called Northern Foods, based in Yorkshire. The chairman wrote, 'If you can fully fund the exercise from various sources then we would be prepared to let you have £2000. I think we would try to relate the expedition to our subsidiary company, Bachelors in Dublin, whom I understand have a couple of celebrities in their advertising – Barnie and Beanie. Would it not be appropriate for two of the yak to be named after these great Dublin characters? To confirm therefore . . . that if you can raise the wherewithall for the total exercise, we would be prepared to go to £2000. I think I have lost all sense of proportion, but that is what happens at a certain stage in one's life.'

It was the turning point. Costs were whittled down to £2500 for air freight and £500 for the construction of the container. 'The weight of the yaks will be one male at 120 kilos, and two females at 100 kilos. The container will be approximately 55 x 79 internally and in view of the fact that these animals are so small, this container should be adequate for the road journey from Istanbul to Van if necessary.'

Meanwhile I was writing diplomatic letters. The Turkish Embassy in Dublin had begun to accumulate its huge correspondence concerning yak.

Your Excellency,

I am seeking your help and that of the Turkish authorities to implement a scheme for which I hope to obtain widespread sponsorship . . .

Your Excellency,

In my letter to you of the 1st August, I gave you details of my plans. At that time I was hoping to bring the animals from Pakistan to Turkey. However, recently I have been over to the Whipsnade Park Zoo near London, a zoo which is world famous for its rare animals and its programme for resettling endangered or unusual species in their right environment . . .

Your Excellency,

   With regard to my proposed plan to send yak to the Kirghiz near Ercis, I have received good news which I feel I should let you know at once. I enclose a letter from Mr Manton, the Curator of the zoological society. As you can see, we have been promised two female and one male yak. Now I am endeavouring to arrange transport . . .

The strain of dealing with a cargo which I suspected no one really wanted began to tell. There was a mention of something called a donation certificate to avoid paying importation taxes when the animals arrived in Turkey. This would include a statement that they were being given to the council of Ulu Pamir village, another that the animals had been inspected and were healthy, and a valuation.

Nineteen eighty-eight faded into 1989 with new problems. I had managed to locate an airline which agreed to take the crate of animals together with Peter Pearce and myself. Then I received a terse letter from the shipper. 'I regret to inform you that since our last telephone conversation reference the transport of three yak to Istanbul I have been informed by the Air Transport that they have ceased operations.'

Whipsnade provided the Donation Certificate.

To Whom it May Concern:

   The Zoological Society of London has donated three yaks from their herd at Whipsnade Wild Animal Park, England, to the Kirghiz people of Ulu Pamir village. We believe these animals to be from a wild herd originally with some domestic yak blood introduced over the years. We would put a nominal value of £400 on each of these animals.

This was turned down. No one could understand why it was not good enough. After a good deal of agitation a new formula was worked out and the new certificate stated that the yak were being given to the local government in Van.

While the shipper was trying to find an airline that would carry the yak, the Turkish Embassy put me in touch with an organisation called the Anatolian Development Foundation which had transported Swiss goats from Switzerland to Van.

These goats had crossed Europe in one vehicle without any change. We hoped that the Foundation would be able to arrange transport for the yak from Istanbul across Turkey to Van more than a thousand miles away. When this was done we could set a departure date. We fixed it for the end of April.

We would travel on a normal Lufthansa passenger flight to Frankfurt where we would spend the night before going on to Istanbul. Peter Pearce would accompany me, and at Istanbul we would meet up with David Shaw-Smith, a film-maker and photographer, his wife Sally, and ten-year-old son Daniel. David had hoped to be commissioned for a film, but we had been unable to interest any TV company in the subject of yak for the Kirghiz.

I worried about handling the animals on the journey. Fresh air . . . food . . . suppose they were too hot? Could their thick coats of hair be clipped like old English sheep dogs?

The telephone rang.

'One of the yaks has died.'

'For God's sake . . .'

'From inhalation pneumentis . . .'

'What's that?'

'Nothing you could do anything about. Technically it means inhaling the regurgitated fluids following sedation.'

'I suppose it's lucky this did not happen on the journey.'

Whipsnade promised to replace the dead animal, but now it appeared that there were problems with the Health Certificates. In normal circumstances any animal coming from Whipsnade would have a clean bill of health. First it would be put into quarantine, then tested, then given its health certificate. Now the Turks wanted the yak injected against foot-and-mouth and rinderpest before they left England. But this was not possible because of health regulations in England. After weeks of blocked communications and language difficulties between the British Ministry of Health, the health authorities in Ankara, the Turkish Embassies in London and Dublin, and Whipsnade, it was agreed that the animals should be injected when they got to Turkey.

A week before our departure the second male yak failed its health test by a marginal amount. This meant that it had to remain in quarantine for another month.

'What happens if it doesn't pass next time?'

'That's most unlikely.'

The flight to Istanbul was postponed until the onslaught of the hot weather which we had been doing our best to avoid.

A month later the male yak failed its second test.

Was there a point in sending two lonely spinster yak to the Kirghiz? It was no way to build up a herd. What about artificial insemination? When I enquired I was given a graphic description of the difficulties of transporting and inserting frozen straws of yak semen into tranquillised cows and waiting to see the results. It would be easier and more practical to send another male.

How? When?

We decided to make a start anyway and embark on taking the females. If they were successfully delivered another male would be forthcoming, either from Whipsnade, or, better still, since the Whipsnade yak were in danger of becoming inbred, from another zoo in Europe which had a stock of yak of a different strain.

It was June, and the earliest flight we could arrange was not until the end of the month. We would be travelling with animals whose genes had fitted them for snow and ice rather than for blazing summer heat. I wrote a letter to Rahman Qul telling him of our imminent arrival, warned the Turkish authorities, borrowed money and got out of Ireland. It had been a year since I had thought of the idea of bringing yak to the Kirghiz.

18

THE sun was blazing over London on the hottest day in thirteen years, Tuesday, 20 June 1989. Peter Pearce and I travelled down the motorway discussing the list of supplies we had to buy for the yak to take on their journey to eastern Turkey. They included a rubber bucket, two bags of nails and a hammer, and a large piece of rope to be used if the animals broke out of their crate.

Peter had been to see them the day before.

'One looks a big scraggy and is beginning to lose its coat. But if the present temperature continues, that's not a bad thing.'

'What about their general condition?'

'They both look a bit stressed.'

'Is that a serious worry?'

'I hope not.'

At Whipsnade we were met by Richard Kock wearing a green dungaree boiler suit marked 'WHIPSNADE'. He had almost as much reason for stress as the yak; the day before he had taken delivery of some Burmese elephants and found that two had died on the way.

The yak were waiting for us with showy indifference to their fate. They were black and, since they were not yet fully grown, seemed comparatively small. They did not have much hair; the smaller animal was moulting and had lost patchy pieces of felt off its back leaving a new growth that resembled the growth on a hairy human chest. Their faces were long and shoe-shaped; in spite of their spiked horns, which were fearsome weapons, they had an endearing funny look like Disney versions of cows. Their black eyes shone wickedly.

Richard said, 'The larger one is about three years old. There is a possibility that she might be pregnant.'

Inquisitive, restless black eyes watched us. Horns were tossed in the air.

Richard said, 'I was worried that the crate mightn't be strong enough and I've had it strengthened.'

'We brought a hammer and nails.'

'Good idea.'

We were shown the crate, a wooden cage with a trapdoor into which we would be shoving food and water.

'Do you really think it will hold them?'

Richard said, 'It should be strong enough.' I wondered why those elephants had died.

Before we left I was given a final account marked 'Zoo Operations Ltd'.

Transportation of yaks to Turkey:
Veterinary costs including VAT – £73.89
Charges re: Health Certificate – £42.00
Transport costs to Heathrow including VAT – £50.00

We were provided with some bales of hay and a large bag of dairy nuts which looked like pieces of compressed muesli. These were the yak's daily requirements:

Concentrate (cattle feed, 30% dry matter) – 2 Kilos of pellets.
Three kilos of hay (ad lib.)
Water – ten litres minimum.

Peter said, 'We'll be lucky if they eat anything.'

Richard said, 'Have a good trip. Hope they arrive safely. Don't let people gaze at them too long or they will get unsettled.' He had other preoccupations.

Next afternoon we arrived at Heathrow with the rope, hammer, nails and plastic bucket. At the Lufthansa cargo terminal building the scene was frantic, telephones ringing, men waving sheafs of paper, and there was a general feeling of panic. In the heatwave London was convulsed with a transport strike and all routes out to the airport were choked. Lufthansa seemed to be having particular problems with some flamingoes and pelicans and had heard nothing about yak.

'They are supposed to have left Whipsnade three hours ago.'

'Brenda may know.'

'Nothing we can do.'

I felt a wave of resigned despair. There had been so many

delays and disappointments that it seemed very likely the yak
were stuck on the M25 and would miss the plane. But Brenda
appeared waving a dossier.

'Are you the gentlemen travelling with the yaks? They arrived
about an hour ago and everything is under control.'

Blessing the lorry driver, who had managed to ease his way
here from Whipsnade, we were led to a large hangar full of
cardboard packages. Two dark shapes were pressed against
woodwork looking out.

'Should we feed them?'

'No, they have their hay.'

We brought them some water in the new black plastic bucket
and shoved it through the trap door. At the best of times yak are
nervy and difficult, prone to sudden bursts of emotion, and
they are not to be comforted by stroking or gentle patting.
I remembered how Nepali yak-herders kept up a continuous
soothing whistle as they coaxed their animals along.

In the Lufthansa building we met the carrier who had organised the travel arrangements. For months he and I had talked
over the phone between Dublin and his base, about changing
plans, rearranging tickets and organising new schedules.

More than once he said, 'Don't mention my name to anyone.
I'm afraid of the animal rights people.' He transported animals
all over the world, and the previous night he had returned from
Amsterdam with a load of pigs.

'Passengers don't know the half of what's below them in
the cargo hold.' His recent shipments had included camels for
Taiwan, tigers, elephants, and numerous polo ponies from the
Argentine. There was nothing difficult about shipping yak.

'You won't have to do anything about them when they are on
the plane.'

'Suppose they escape?' This had long been a nightmare
thought – rampaging yak causing a plane crash and unusual
noises on the black box. 'Don't worry, they won't.' He had
our health certificates in English and Turkish, our donation
certificate and other papers. The cost of the flight for the two
yak came to exactly £2000, while the crate was another £500.
Most generously, Northern Food had footed the entire bill. All
we had to pay for was our own tickets.

I had envisaged a cargo plane with an evil-smelling and

uncomfortable interior covered in straw. Instead the yak were to fly in the hold of a Lufthansa DC10 on a scheduled passenger flight to Frankfurt. From the glass windows of the transit lounge we watched them being loaded. A lorry bearing the crate (which was now covered with sackcloth) pulled up beside the plane, a forklift truck tossed it up and a couple of men pushed it quickly inside with rollers. The other passengers sitting with their duty-free bags, waiting for the flight to be called, noticed nothing.

Later we lay back in our seats and were served smoked salmon, prawns, fruit and champagne. Far below the English coast vanished in a white-edged scrawl and we were handed chocolates with our coffee.

The stewardess said, 'Are you gentlemen with the yaks?'

'Yes.'

'The captain wishes to know whether they prefer hot or cold air.'

'Cold air, please.'

The captain sent a message ahead warning of the yak's arrival and then we had more champagne.

At Frankfurt airport among the gift shops and blue movies we met an official who told us where to go next. 'Please after you go through customs take Bus 77 to the cargo department.'

The cargo complex, surrounded by trees, was as large as a town. There was a high embankment wall down one side, huge runways on the other, and everywhere the shapes of warehouses where work never ceased. Planes stood in lines, loading or discharging, Flying Tigers, Cathay Pacific, Garuda, and a lone Aer Lingus shamrock displaying its three leaves under the arc-lights.

We rang the bell of the animal sanctuary. 'Have you two yak staying here?'

'Wait, I see.' The girl in wellies, leather gloves and pinafore reappeared in a few minutes.

'Please come.'

The place had a zoo smell, a medley of disinfectant, pee and straw. A bored tawny cat sat in a cage labelled Zürich. Past a line of stables we found our familiar crate with its notice 'ANIMALS WITH CARE', and inside two mournful shaggy heads tightly pressed down. We fed and watered them and left them for the night.

We slept in a concrete cell with a washstand but no beds – among animal handlers sleeping bags on the floor were in order. We reminded ourselves of the fortune we were saving by not staying at the Sheraton as we lay awake listening to the banshee scream of arriving and departing jets rattling and shaking our windows, sometimes sounding so close it seemed inevitable that we would be hit.

By six o'clock the new shift of cargo handlers was at work under the glaring arclights, stacking pyramids of cardboard boxes, a good many of them small dark men in peaked caps with the swarthy moustachioed faces that indicated they were guest-workers. The jets' scream rang in our ears as we walked over to inspect the yak whose crate had been moved during the night out from the little room where they had been originally consigned into a passage.

'I hate the pet trade,' Peter said as we looked in at the boxes of battered parrots that had replaced the yak, yellow bills and scaly legs clawing at the wire mesh that held them in. Next door were penguins, then crates of monkeys and beyond in the stables a sleek line of polo ponies and a girl with a mane of cornflower hair who lay asleep on a bale of straw.

Once again Peter measured out a handful of nuts which the yak refused and gave them a bucket of water which they spilled. On the second day of captivity they sulked in their wooden crate in a way that worried us. Even here in a setting filled with exotic animals the two shaggy beasts aroused a ripple of interest.

'Please, what are these?'

'Mein Gott!'

We spent the morning drinking endless cups of coffee and wondering what our reception would be in Istanbul. The nightmare of arriving there with the animals and finding no one to meet us had haunted all our discussions. It had been very hard to get total confirmation, and there had been an air of vagueness about the repeated reassurances that a reception would be waiting for us. A year's problems and delays had left me pessimistic, and the idea of a pair of homeless yak on the sweltering tarmac of Istanbul airport was daunting; worse was the prospect of trying to organise ways of transporting them a thousand weary miles between Istanbul and Van on the perimeter of Eastern Turkey.

The flight to Istanbul was a last carefree exercise in eating and drinking, while the yak were down below, out of sight but never for a moment out of mind, directly below the galley. Four hours later the silhouettes of Istanbul passed under our wing, domes, minarets and lines of small fishing boats bobbing up and down in the polluted Bosphorus, and then we were coming in to land.

Peter held the file containing the health certificate and sheafs of other essential papers. The engines had stopped and the line of tourists was struggling out of their seats. Beyond the transit boarding ramp was a mob of people, loud music, voices and uniformed officials and police.

'Mr Somerville . . .'

A small man was kissing my cheek, another had taken away my bag, and we were whirled past the other passengers, past customs, and passport control into the main lobby. Everything happened so quickly that there was no opportunity to ask about the yak. Attempts to show our documents were politely brushed aside. No one seemed to care about the precious health certificate that had taken so many months to obtain. From the babble of the group surrounding us I picked out a few English words. We had been met by a Director of the Turkish Red Crescent who had come down from Ankara to meet us. He was accompanied by an official from the Agricultural Institute.

Where were the yak? It seemed impossible to find out. And where was the Shaw-Smith family, who had arranged to meet us here? We found them at last, outside sitting in a car, and at least David knew what had become of the animals. He had received permission to photograph their arrival, and together with a number of Turkish TV cameramen had watched the crate being unloaded and put into a lorry.

Dusk was coming on and the Istanbul traffic was at its worst as for more than an hour we followed the lorry bearing the crate through congested streets, to the Agricultural Institute in the suburbs. They would spend the night here, but we would go elsewhere. Having seen them bedded down, we were taken away and driven back into the centre of Istanbul. Somewhere near Taksim Square in the heart of the old city a gate was opened and we were escorted into a lavish guesthouse set in a large garden overlooking the Bosphorus where we stayed the night as guests of the government. Overlooking the Golden Horn we ate a lavish meal washed down with lager as a moon hung over the sea and the floodlit domes and minarets of the Blue Mosque rose behind us. Here in this garden in the heart of the city, traffic sound was changed to a muted whisper, as we looked out over one of the world's great views.

Friday, 20 June dawned, another bright warm day. After our night in Frankfurt where our sleep was destroyed by the scream of jets, Peter and I slept well and over breakfast of olives, bread, cheese and honey, we made plans for the long day ahead. We had been provided with a lorry and two drivers by the Red Crescent who would take the yak across Turkey. When we returned to the Agricultural Institute, and found them still standing marooned in their crate on top of the lorry we went through the routine of feeding and watering the pair of increasingly miserable and angry animals; stiletto horns angrily butted the wood. I gave a thought to the Yak of Tartary and considered the long journey the poor beast must have made in his crate down through the foothills of Bhutan to India, and then on board a three-master round the Cape of Good Hope. No wonder his temper was soured by the time he reached the park and the enclosure at Purley Hall.

Our idea was to leave as soon as possible in the direction of Ankara but there was another delay.

'They must have injection.' The official read out a formula. 'Sap A 10 Tip . . . Virus Fouris Aphosa' was the foot-and-mouth vaccine which they had been unable to receive in England. The vet arrived, a dapper white-haired man carrying a large glass bottle filled with pinkish fluid. A crowd collected as he climbed up to the crate and made repeated efforts to plunge his hypodermic through the slats into the animals who woke into fury. The contest between the yak's horns and the needle was an impromptu *corrida*. Early attempts were ineffectual; it took ten minutes and a burst of courage and determination before the brave man succeeded. 'Okay. All done.' He climbed down to a ripple of applause.

Originally I had planned to travel with Peter and the Turkish drivers, but there was only room for three in the cab. Because he knew a lot more about animals than I did, Peter agreed to go in the lorry, while I joined the Shaw-Smiths.

When David drove his rented car through the excesses of

Istanbul traffic, we lost the lorry and its crown of yak almost at once, and did not see it again that day. Slowly we made our way eastwards through the infernal surrounding suburbs, through a waste of smoking factory chimneys and half-built tower blocks. After Ismit the industrial fumes got less and the landscape gradually changed to a wilderness of rolling forest-covered hills. We drove for eight hours across the vastness of Turkey, crossing the four hundred miles between Istanbul and Ankara without a sight of the lorry with the poor animals on top exposed to the full ferocity of summer heat.

At Ankara we drove along the wide avenue which sweeps grandly through congested shanty villages into the heart of the modern city and its parks and modern palaces. We were tired and hungry and we still had to find the village where we had a rendezvous with the yak. Or we thought we did – once again we were handicapped by language difficulties, and our instructions had not been altogether clear. Another hour's driving brought us to a black hill sprinkled with lights where we found the café specified by the Turkish drivers. There was no sign of the lorry.

For so long I had been beset by every sort of worry, but not that we should actually lose the yak. We sat down under a goldfish tank filled with empty Coca Cola bottles surrounded by groups of unshaven men absorbed in backgammon. We had kebabs and raki, and then more raki. At about midnight Daniel spied our lorry.

'There they go!'

For a moment it looked as if they had driven on past us and disappeared altogether. However they came to a stop further up the street and Peter's worried face peered out of the cab.

'The yak seem okay.'

He had not had an easy journey. First there had been the usual difficulty of finding the way. The drivers came from Van, and had not known much more about Istanbul than we did; they, too, were almost defeated by the terrible suburbs. All the time he could not understand what was being said or make them understand what he said. And the yak were not eating.

We were all yawning with lack of sleep, but after the drivers finished their meal, they insisted that we must all start off again at once.

We tried to argue, but they had been given their instructions, and were determined to keep on driving. We must complete our current delivery and go on with our load of fretful exhausted animals.

We continued all night, taking turns driving over a route that offered a ribbon of headlights and an outline of mountains. Dawn came up ahead of us, and about seven we reached Darende, our first real Anatolian village. Already the place was alive; the older women draped in veils, children playing in the dust; the women were doing all the work while the men swaggered up and down in groups spitting out sunflower seeds. Flies shot out like sparks from the hole that was the public lavatory. The curious among the villagers came over to examine the crate on the top of the lorry, and at the spectacle of two such strange creatures every face broke into a spontaneous grin.

But the yak continued to be a cause for concern, uninterested in provisions.

'Could they just die?' I asked Peter.

'Oh no, that's not likely. But I am a bit worried about stress.' We were exposing them to captive myopathy, the veterinarian term for the potential result of the pressures we were putting on them.

Stress or not, it was time for the animals to move once again. How quickly the countryside changed. One moment we were surrounded by brown desert and screes of barren rock, the next the scene was transformed, lush and green and spotted with trees and wild flowers, purple vetches, stalky white euphorbia, lobelia, white daisies, yellow daisies and flowers found in English summer gardens, and scarlet poppies scattered through the lot. Birds sang, a milky white river rushed through the hills, as we stopped for a swim, a moment to forget our tiredness and the long road ahead. For a few minutes the icy water performed the miracle of awakening us from our torpor.

All day we took turns driving. First we passed near Malatya and the famous carved heads, then rushed by Seljuk and Hittite monuments, and Byzantine fortresses. If you kick a stone in Turkey, the chances are that it will have an acanthus leaf or suchlike carved on it. No time to stop. Before we had embarked with the yak we had even made tentative and impossible plans to see some of these wonders – we had a vision of parking the animals under a shady grove of trees and taking time off to explore the odd spot – the caves at Cappadoc, Nemrut Dag or the Palace of the Pontic Kings.

We sped by towns and villages which seemed deserted, dwarfed by their austere surroundings. The only people we passed were shepherds in long tattered fleecy coats, or nomads outside their black tents. We came to Elazig, a dreary grid of wide straight roads, and a grim municipal square. A few miles beyond, we stopped at a café beside the lake which results from the damming of the Euphrates by the Keban Dam. Here we were given beer and ate some of the carp that still collect in huge shoals before the dam twenty-five years after their way upstream was blocked. Right below where we sat was our lorry, and I could see the two imprisoned hairy beasts in their crate. It was very hot.

'Perhaps they will survive,' Peter said after they had obliged us by drinking a little water. 'How far is it to Van?'

'Four hundred kilometres.'

More tawny hills; a small village full of bullock carts and bushy excesses of storks' nests hanging down from telephone posts along the main street like so many burst cushions; a horrible Kurdish refugee camp guarded by soldiers; Bingol, a Kurdish town in the mountains battered by earthquakes; a break-down . . . the lorry's fanbelt had to be replaced. Another stop when David caught sight of a dead roller and plucked out its brilliant feathers for making fishing flies at home. Another when we skidded to a halt before a tortoise crouched in the middle of the road and Daniel retrieved it from its dangerous position.

All day we drove through rolling mountainous country until late in the evening we reached the port of Tatvan beside the turquoise lake that is another Dead Sea. From Tatvan, whose shops and cafés reaching down to the shores have a seedy Balkan charm, the ferry boat regularly swallows up an entire train and takes it across the blue waters to the town of Van.

We stopped and ate a final meal, stupefied, oblivious to almost anything except the wish to lie down and sleep. But it was a significant moment for all of us; against the odds we had just about arrived. There were only the final miles to go, twisting and turning in the darkness around the curve of the lake. (And another journey which we did not yet think about, out beyond Van up in the mountains to Ulu Pamir.)

When we reached Van it was deserted and silent. A policeman wandered down an empty street, and neon lights glittered above the closed carpet shops.

'Let's find a good hotel.' We left the lorry in the darkness with the forlorn yak dead or alive roped on top.

Next morning they were still there, with their usual downcast expressions, indifferent to the crowd which had tumbled out of the nearby teahouse. They looked smaller, less newsworthy, less aggressive and they had moulted a lot more – great uneven patches had been ripped off leaving hairy acres of skin like a dark girl's arms. Only a day before they would have reacted angrily with a sharp butt of a horn to those who climbed up to peer inside; now they stood and made no movement. They looked old and stuffed. After a week they were standing on an evil-smelling mess of putrefying nuts and dung and spilled water.

There was no one to meet them. No one standing around could communicate. Then I remembered from the year before the tourist office where Mr Orphan could speak a little English. I went in search of him and was very grateful to see his friendly face once more. He left his office and came along.

In my absence a blue Mercedes had driven up with a chauffeur and an elegant young man.

'He is city manager,' Mr Orphan said, and suddenly we were important people. Our lives changed instantly and dramatically. We were escorted to the luxury of the Uratu Hotel where the friendly staff were waiting to greet us and escort us to rooms with private bathrooms. We were given a special car and driver for our personal use for our entire stay in Van. I felt I had a major role in an old film starring Danny Kaye.

But the yak? What about the yak?

'When do you wish to travel to Ulu Pamir?'

'Right away.'

So we set out in a convoy. First came two police cars striped like zebras, then a detachment of soldiers in full battle array with a saturnine commander who went by the name of Genghiz, who were there to protect us from Kurds and bandits, then the manager of Van in his curtained Mercedes, then the rented car containing the Shaw-Smiths and the two Peters; bringing up the rear was the lorry and its precious cargo.

The road was familiar, the sharp silhouette of the citadel, Van rock, the brilliant blue lake stretching out of sight and the looming dark shape of the mountains. Even now in June Suphan Dag, straight ahead of us, had lumps and bits of tassels of snow on its rounded summit.

From Van to Ercis, a distance of over a hundred kilometres, we followed the desolate coastline. A few small villages were hidden away from the main road between wheat and barley among dry dust and rocks. At Karagelleri the little procession stopped near the post office and waited for the lorry to catch up. Families were picnicking under walnut trees, the scent of kebabs mixing with smoke from the wood fires. On the salty lake a few men were bathing, arms outstretched, effortlessly buoyed up by the saline water.

Ercis was a short distance away in a grove of poplars and fruit trees reaching down to the empty lake where a flight of pelicans struggled to keep a V-formation as they flapped along with swishing wings. Our convoy stopped near a small conical *turbe* or tomb that resembled precisely a Kirghiz yurt in stone. We learnt that this tomb, built in 1458, was associated with the so-called 'Black Sheep Turcomans' and in that year the mother of a Turcoman emir had been buried here. It seemed an omen, an encouraging link with the Turcomen of the Wakhan.

The soldiers leapt down from the jeep and dressed ranks to salute the large solemn man who now joined us. We all shook hands, and discovered that this impressive personage whose deportment and girth resembled a Indian maharajah was the chief of police of Ercis province.

In front of us a large tawny Egyptian vulture settled in the middle of the road before slowly taking off and flying away. We left the smooth tongue of tarmac behind and turned into the mountains along the familiar pitted track where I had been driven in early May more than a year ago. The corn was green then and the mountains still covered with snow. Now the corn awaited harvest. In the small mud Kurdish villages, camouflaged in the landscape, women in long brightly patterned dresses were washing clothes in streams or carefully stacking up pyramids of dung. At the last village before Ulu Pamir a soldier snapped to attention outside the archway and the police chief nodded briefly in his direction. Far away at the end of the valley the bright metal roof tops of the new Kirghiz settlement glistened in the sun.

At the bridge leading across the river to the village the convoy stopped, David took photographs and we all shook hands once again with the police chief. It was a little after midday and the village basked in heat. Nothing moved except the river; the only sound disturbing the silence was the ripple of water falling over rocks and stones. There were no Kirghiz to be seen.

After a few uncertain minutes, we moved on again, the police cars, the jeep, the blue Mercedes, the hired car and, lumbering behind us, the lorry with the yak.

My first deep-felt reaction was that no one was here, either among the empty lines of houses or in the deserted squares. The village seemed entirely deserted, a ghost town, a town abandoned because of plague. We drove up to the first two lines of houses and turned down the dusty laneway between them. Then round another corner.

Here suddenly we came upon the whole tribe waiting for us. Lines of men with Mongol faces wearing their best suits stood with their women behind them dressed in bright red dresses, and a big scattering of children. At the sight of the lorry topped by the wooden crate they began clapping and cheering, and many of the older people were in tears.

Standing in front of them before a table covered with a festive red cloth was the unmistakable figure of Rahman Qul flanked by Kirghiz dignitaries. The next minutes passed dazedly as we were greeted by a mob trying to shake our hands. While the perspiring police chief was taking a gaudy handkerchief out of his pocket, I was led to a place of honour beside Rahman Qul and another old man and handed a glass of mare's milk which tasted like very old, very sweet butter. The disadvantage of my privileged position was that I could not see what was going on behind my back where the lorry and its cargo had quickly become the centre of attention. Rahman Qul, his old friends and the police chief, made a studied attempt to ignore what was happening as a dense mass of gesticulating young men and boys were trying to get a better view of the animals. I hoped to God they were not dead.

'They're dangerous!' Peter Pearce kept shouting, but no one was prepared to interpret.

It was years since most of these young people had seen a yak and most of them had little more idea about them than what they gained from Malik's pictures. Up at the official table where I sat as chief guest the idea of a formal reception where speeches would be made and the yak officially received was being rapidly abandoned. For a moment or two longer I sat and sipped my mare's milk, smiling at the old man, until a sudden explosion of cheering made me leave my seat. I could see that a couple of men had managed to climb on top of the crate and were trying to lasso the horns of the larger yak. In the confusion someone had prised open the back of the crate. Amid shouting and chaos there was more work with the ropes, but the yak would have none of that. Far from being moribund they sprang to life.

Four days of mobile captivity had done nothing to subdue their spirits. As they came bounding out, a Kirghiz who got into the way of the older yak was tossed in the air. For about twenty minutes the village became like Pamplona. In the conflict between the Kirghiz and the yak even the women joined in.

Rahman Qul continued to turn his back on the scene, since it was beneath his dignity and that of the elders of the tribe to do anything but ignore the disturbance behind them. So they sat drinking tea, Rahman Qul smoking a Marlboro, while the pandemonium continued.

Half a dozen men, all hauling together at the end of a rope which was entwined around her horns, managed to drag the bucking and protesting elder yak to an enclosure further up the hill. The younger, skipping, prancing and kicking, decided to give up the struggle and go along too. Watched by the entire tribe they were safely tied up at last.

After we left Ulu Pamir and drove back to Van, we were unable to return for three days. First there was ceremony. When we had reached Van once again our first duty was to meet the Governor and thank him. The people with us were very nervous that we should make the correct gestures when we came face to face with him. He had to be given flowers and chocolates like a debutante. We drove to the main government building which next year

would be replaced by a sumptuous new office block. The governor, Mr Adnan Darnerli, sitting behind his desk adorned
with Ataturk and Turkish flag, spoke some English so that
speeches could be smoothly exchanged as the health certificate
and all the other papers in the dossier we had found no previous
use for were formally handed over. Then we were wined and
dined for two long hours at the Uratu Hotel, eating innumerable
spicy dishes, drinking the first-rate Turkish wine that the Turks
didn't drink themselves, making and listening to speeches.

We found that nothing was too much trouble for the authorities.

'Please make an itinerary of what you wish to see,' we were
told by Feyzi, a young carpet dealer who now acted as our official
interpreter. Every day we were offered a different programme –
first a visit to Catak, a paradisical mountain town threatened,
we were told, by PKK guerillas, members of the Marxist Kurdish
Workers' Party. Then down to Hakkari, once a focus of exploration for Freya Stark, now an uneasy ugly place of half-finished
office blocks and general dilapidation crowded with armed
guards and soldiers and a huge number of policemen. We
watched an army helicopter land near the town and soldiers in
battledress emerge from a cluster of trees. We visited ruinous
Armenian holy places, a tottering monastery right in the heart
of an army camp, a church choked with wild flowers, turned into
a bakery, with small incised crosses above the ovens.

Then we were taken on a special expedition to Capanik Island
which faces Suphan Dag on the far eastern shore. Although the
island had not yet been opened up to tourism, the success of
Akdamar and its regular hordes of visitors was changing atti-
tudes. But Capanik was still inaccessible to the ordinary visitor,
and our outing was privileged. We chugged across the calm
glassy lake on a blazing day, when the caustic colour of the water
hurt the eyes, to a white pinnacle of rock and below it yet
another ruined abandoned church with golden walls and delicate
carvings. While the crew spent their time trying to catch the
speckled rabbits that had taken over the island, we approached
through a graveyard choked with giant thistles and white holly-
hocks where headstones had toppled over into the thick grass.
Inside we stumbled over pieces of broken rubble to the altar near
which a pair of doves nestled in a carved niche. Later we bathed

in the oily, soapy blue water which will not let a swimmer sink.

Off the deserted shores of Van we bathed a number of times, like other tourists, setting a new example to the Turks and Kurds. For centuries bathing had been a game for small boys, not a pastime for adults, and Van was still empty, unsullied by resorts But now the delights of floating aimlessly on the saltwater upholstery of Van were being discovered, at least by the men. There was a casualness about bathing, an air of the Twenties and Thirties, a feeling of discovery as they wallowed among the herds of water buffalo, their horns like trophies, their thick curly hair plastered over their heads like Edwardian beaux.

Sightseeing as guests of the town, bathing and tripping through ruins and relics were fine diversions. So was our invitation to a Kurdish wedding, a festival where the swaying guests offered a wholesome innocence that reminded me of De Valera's ideal men and maidens. Only the bride, money pinned all over her, looked sad. But we had strayed from the purpose of our journey, and all the time we were sightseeing we were preoccupied with the fate of the yak. So we were glad enough when we finally returned to Ulu Pamir.

Peter Pearce was full of worries. The Kirghiz had no idea of dealing with wild animals – he had not been able to convey that these yak were indeed wild, and totally different from the tame stock they had herded in the Wakhan. The lack of proper interpreting meant that he had been unable to give any instructions. He listed a variety of ailments that could afflict the animals if they got the wrong treatment. He talked of flatulence, flies, heat and the likelihood that if by any chance the larger animal happened to be pregnant, by now it would certainly have about lost.

We had left the yak behaving as if they were stars in a rodeo. When we returned to see them we found that they had been tamed. The remembered skills of the Kirghiz herdsmen had subdued them.

We walked down to the river where we spotted the two animals enjoying the pleasures of the riverbank apparently without a care in the world. Already they followed a routine; every morning they were led down to the river, and in the evening they returned placidly to their stable and corral. That evening we watched them being herded across the river by Abdul Halim Vatan, who ran the small telephone exchange for the village, but now was pleased to have an additional job. A small tousle-headed man, who a decade ago had run a considerable number of animals in the Wakhan, he found no difficulty in reverting to his old role as yak-herdsman once more.

Last time we had seen the animals the elder had a knot of orange rope twined round her horns; this had now been replaced with a halter.

'We think that the older cow is pregnant,' Abdul Halim Vatan informed us. This confirmed Whipsnade's speculation and allayed one of Peter Pearce's fears.

'I just can't believe it,' he said as we watched them grazing contentedly, two dark shapes half hidden in the long grass. On the far bank women were washing clothes and carpets.

In the evening the yak walked through the mud-caked streets of Ulu Pamir, heads pushed down, dark eyes glowering and thin elegant legs supporting a turgid weight of shaggy, moulting black wool. They seemed as content as any yak ever looks. I remembered a description of Pamir yak by Nazif Sharani in his *Kirghiz and Wakhi of Afghanistan*: 'Generally short tempered and passively stubborn, but not considered dangerous to people. Kirghiz view them as animals of low intelligence and not easy to train.'

After that we returned regularly to Ulu Pamir to witness how the yak settled into their new home and became part of the community. If this part of the plan succeeded, it seemed likely that if we could provide a further male yak a small herd could be built up.

Since my first visit the year before there had been some evidence of progress and improvement in the village. Groves of spindly poplars now surrounded some of the houses where small enclosures with vegetables had been planted, and more import- antly each family had been provided with a small herd which included twenty sheep for each household. In time it was hoped that together with a small allowance from the Turkish govern- ment to their new citizens, they would provide a means of livelihood. For the present the yak would be ornament.

In the village the day began at dawn, five o'clock in the summer, when sheep and goats were being assembled and milked before being turned out on the surrounding hills. Dressed in all her finery, each woman squeezed milk into a pail or went running after her sheep in her high boots and high red or white head-dress, the brilliant colours of her dress and sparkle of her jewellery catching the first glow of the sun. Half an hour later the village resounded to the bellowing bleating animals waiting to be released for another long day.

In a traditional division of labour, women ran the household, fed and milked the animals and washed the carpets and clothes, while the men worked as shepherds or in the fields. One of our first sights in Ulu Pamir was a large section of the ablebodied male population of the village scything the thick meadow grass on either side of the river. Lines of men wearing their stiff embroidered pillbox hats moved over the meadows to the swish of a hundred scythe blades and the scent of grass withering under the sun.

Down by the river where the yak grazed, women washed and stretched the garish carpets woven in the new carpet school where the young girls sat under the looms. The Turkish teacher only knew Turkish designs, and that was what they were being taught while the old beautiful traditional Kirghiz patterns were being forgotten.

We inspected the school attended by two hundred and forty children in black smocks who were taught in Turkish. In this model town a mosque had been provided, the largest and most impressive building in Ulu Pamir with a double row of windows and carpets covering the floor. Midday prayers were attended by five old weatherbeaten men with wrinkled Auden faces in long coats, and leather boots, their small sunken eyes just visible from beneath fur caps. The mullah read verses from the Koran and they prayed, while the young men in their blue suits and blue jeans stayed outside without the need of the daily comfort of Islam after a life torn by tragedy and change.

On a bare mountainside above the village we discovered an ancient obsidian working scattered with shining black arrowheads and scrapers. Thousands of years ago this place had been inhabited by neolithic men surrounded by rolling mountain-tops and wild flowers. They had been herders and farmers like the scythers and shepherds returning at the close of day to their new homes. The bleating animals, each with its long evening shadow beside it, trotted down the hills until they merged into a river of sheep and once again the village echoed to calling and bleating.

Once home, the shepherds dispersed while the women grabbed the animals that they recognised at once as their own. After evening milking the village seemed to go to sleep.

'The winters are long,' Rahman Qul said. 'The streets of the village are blocked with snow.'

'What do you do then?'

'Make children.'

Three weeks after we had delivered the yak it was time for us to depart. We hoped we would return next year with a bull; meanwhile these females must live through the snow and silence of the mountain winter just as the huge yak herds of the Wakhan had endured the ice and snow of the Pamirs. Our gift was a gesture, little more than a souvenir of the past; I knew in my heart that for the most of these young men there would be no real return to the old traditional way. No doubt the best future for many would lie in a smattering of English and a job in a hotel in Van. And yet, to hear the sheep and goats return to the village after the day was over was to hope that something of the past had been preserved – and perhaps the Whipsnade yak, grazing down by the river beside the women washing carpets, had a place here in Ulu Pamir.

On our last evening we went on our round of farewells. The last house we visited was the home of Abdul Halim Vatan, telephonist and herder, who had particular charge of the yak. We said goodbye to him and his wife, Nishahan, a graceful woman in her early twenties. We admired her baby wrapped up in swaddling clothes rocked in his traditional cradle, her TV with its constant programmes of second world war films, her new electric sewing machine and the wonderful bands of Kirghiz embroidery that floated round the room like a rainbow. Would Nishahan ever wish to return to the harsh nomadic life in the Pamirs, to the regular erecting and dismantling of the wickerwork and felt walls of the family yurt?

Outside the house we were caught in the middle of a violent dust storm. One moment the sky had been a hazy blue with only a black cloud on the hill to indicate what was to come. Then a choking gritty wind brought the dust which closed round us in a whirling yellow fog. As we followed each other like a line of blind men, groping our way back to the safety of Rahman Qul's house, I remembered how in the old homeland there had been a similar wind that the Kirghiz called Bad-i-Wakhan which blew down from the Pamirs creating terrible, violent storms.

Inside the house the electricity had gone and in the darkened rooms we listened to the howl of the wind and the rattle of grit against the small window panes as the village was enveloped in a whirling pool of dust.

The storm lasted less than an hour, blowing out before dusk fell, and leaving some damage – the roofs of two houses and the school had peeled back like banana skins. Next morning Ulu Pamir was bathed in sunlight once again. Hens scuffled in the dust, and as usual the morning scene resounded with the bleat of sheep, unhurt by the dust storm.

Rahman Qul, who was going to Van to visit a son sick in hospital, offered me a seat in the village *dolmus*. By six o'clock the vehicle was packed with Kirghiz men and women anxious to experience the delights of life in the big city. In deference to his position Rahman Qul was given a seat behind the driver, while I squeezed down beside him.

We started by rolling down the hill without engines or brakes until the driver suddenly put the *dolmus* into gear, there was an enormous backfire and we were away. I tried to savour those last moments: a line of girls carrying cans of water up from the river; the mountains all around; and the clear, clear light. Rahman Qul sat beside me with half-closed eyes drawing on his Marlboro while behind us the village was reduced to thin white lines on the hillside shining in the sun. Before the *dolmus* turned the corner down by the river I caught sight of two dark shapes with drooping heads and curving horns, half-hidden in the meadow grass, now a familiar part of the Turkish scene.

EPILOGUE

I RETURNED to Ulu Pamir in October 1990 with two male yak.
There had been unusual problems in bringing them to eastern
Turkey. In July, two days before we were about to leave England, the Turkish government banned the animals because they
feared they might bring mad cow disease. Then there was the
start of the Gulf crisis; when we were finally given permission to
go, one of our sponsors had spectacular and very public financial
difficulties. But in due course the journey went ahead and the
animals were safely delivered.

The two anxious female yak, (the elder had not been pregnant
after all), had grown huge and dominated their diminutive
husbands. But the group now formed the basis for a herd.

What saddened me was to discover that Rahman Qul had
died two months previously. Without the presence of the tall
benign patriarch who had led his people to safety and prosperity,
the atmosphere of the village had changed. Only a few old men
remain. I met Barahan, who gave his age as a hundred and ten,
but according to other Kirghiz had been born in 1885. He sat in
the sun wrapped in a thick coat and patiently answered my
questions, a spry old man with a spindly white beard, a single
tooth and a gleaming smile. He would like to marry again. I
remember that Shuba, the old man whom I met in Hunza.

Barahan had stories of hunting the giant *ovis poli* sheep, summer camps in the high Pamirs, and the harsh winters which
killed children. Yes, he had often ridden by horseback to Kashgar
when the silk route went through his country. The journey would
take about ten days. He had visited Hunza at the time when
European explorers like Younghusband were first beginning to
discover the Pamirs, and the Kirghiz themselves were feared as
raiders. Younghusband considered 'the Kirghiz are not a race
with many good qualities; they are avaricious, grasping and
fickle'. But when Wilfrid Thesiger saw them years later he

thought very differently of the 'quilted Mongolian figures on yaks, who had come down from the passes of the north and embodied for me everything that I imagined to lie beyond that forbidden frontier of Inner Asia'.

When Rahman Qul was born Barahan was already an uncle. During his long life he had seen the gradual destruction of the old nomadic life. When he was a boy of ten he saw Colonel Durand whose boundary commission created the Wakhan as a barrier between the two empires of Russia and Imperial India.

I was taken to Rahman Qul's grave just outside the village which was surrounded by concrete bricks; next to him was buried his six-year-old grandson.